How Political Parties
Mobilize Religion

HOW POLITICAL PARTIES
MOBILIZE RELIGION

Lessons from Mexico and Turkey

LUIS FELIPE MANTILLA

TEMPLE UNIVERSITY PRESS
Philadelphia • Rome • Tokyo

TEMPLE UNIVERSITY PRESS
Philadelphia, Pennsylvania 19122
tupress.temple.edu

Library of Congress Cataloging-in-Publication Data

Names: Mantilla, Luis Felipe, 1981– author.
Title: How political parties mobilize religion : lessons from Mexico and Turkey /
   Luis Felipe Mantilla.
Other titles: Religious engagement in democratic politics.
Description: Philadelphia : Temple University Press, 2021. | Series: Religious engagement in
   democratic politics | Includes bibliographical references and index. | Summary: "Analyzes
   and compares the contentious evolution of religious political parties in Mexico and
   Turkey, two rising regional powers with deeply rooted secularist traditions"—Provided
   by publisher.
Identifiers: LCCN 2020032176 (print) | LCCN 2020032177 (ebook) |
   ISBN 9781439920152 (cloth) | ISBN 9781439920169 (paperback) |
   ISBN 9781439920176 (pdf)
Subjects: LCSH: Religion and politics—Case studies. | Religion and politics—Mexico. |
   Religion and politics—Turkey. | Catholics—Political activity—Mexico. | Christianity
   and politics—Mexico. | Islam and politics—Turkey. | Mexico—Politics and
   government—20th century. | Turkey—Politics and government—20th century.
Classification: LCC BL65.P7 M34555 2021 (print) | LCC BL65.P7 (ebook) |
   DDC 322/.1—dc23
LC record available at https://lccn.loc.gov/2020032176
LC ebook record available at https://lccn.loc.gov/2020032177

Printed in the United States of America

9 8 7 6 5 4 3 2 1

Contents

Acknowledgments

This book has been over a decade in the making, and I have accumulated many debts of gratitude during that time.

The collegial and interdisciplinary community of the former Department of History and Politics at the University of South Florida St. Petersburg fostered an ideal environment for writing this book. Ray Arsenault and Michael Francis contributed a great deal to sustaining that unique setting, for which I am enormously grateful. I am particularly indebted to Thomas Smith and Adrian O'Connor, who provided crucial suggestions for turning my manuscript into an actual book. A generous internal research grant allowed me to work with a group of outstanding undergraduates who assisted me in gathering cross-national data and testing the reliability of my findings.

I embarked on this project at Georgetown University, where Thomas Banchoff provided invaluable guidance as I found my way through the complex intersections of religion and politics. José Casanova and Marc Howard provided key insights and helped me develop the theoretical framework that still underpins this work. Lessons learned from Andrew Bennett, Dan Brumberg, Steve Heydemann, and Arturo Valenzuela, among other faculty, can be found throughout the text. Georgetown's Berkley Center for Religion, Peace, and World Affairs provided a matchless set of resources for learning about faith and politics and came to feel like a true intellectual home.

My editors at Temple University Press, Paul Djupe and Aaron Javsicas, were truly exemplary in their responsiveness and encouragement. This book would not be what it is without their help. I am also enormously grateful to them for finding two outstanding anonymous reviewers, whose thoughtful comments and suggestions were critical to the final stages of writing and revision.

Fieldwork in Mexico was made possible by the Rafael Preciado Hernández Foundation and the CEDISPAN archives. In Turkey, I enjoyed the hospitality of the SETA Foundation for Political, Economic, and Social Research and the Turkish Statistical Institute. Scholars and practitioners in both countries were consistently willing to share their ideas, resources, and connections, and they made my time in both countries a highlight of my academic career.

Other friends and colleagues have shaped this book in more idiosyncratic ways. Michael Burch generously read the entire manuscript, and his encouragement made its completion possible. David Buckley kept me focused on the project when my curiosity and impatience threatened to lead me astray. Krzysztof Pelc served as a model of intellectual virtuosity and a font of delightful conversation. Paul Beccio exemplified the work-life balance that I continue to strive for. Leah Gilbert, Payam Mohseni, Enrique Bravo, Lorena Buzón, and Hamutal Bernstein got me through graduate school.

Finally, I thank my family: my parents and grandparents, who have provided more support and inspiration than anyone deserves; my wife, Tracey, whose love and patience made this book possible; and my daughters, Olivia and Nora, to whom it is dedicated.

How Political Parties
Mobilize Religion

Introduction

On the morning of December 1, 2000, Vicente Fox arrived at the Basílica de Guadalupe in Mexico City and was promptly surrounded by a crowd of cheering supporters. He prayed for several minutes before the iconic figure of the Virgin of Tepeyac, received communion from the rector of the basilica, and spent a few private moments in the sacristy with a group of priests. The rector spoke to the gathered faithful and declared Fox "the first *guadalupano* head of state who comes to the feet and the heart of the mother of all Mexicans, to place his hands and heart at the service of the country and to ask that all may be well."[1] Two hours later, he was sworn into office as president. In Mexico, where revolutionaries had embedded anticlericalism at the heart of the constitution and heads of state studiously avoided displays of personal piety, the victory of Vicente Fox, a man whose faith was prominently featured during the campaign, and with him the victory of the Partido Acción Nacional (PAN; National Action Party), a party with historic ties to Catholic activism, provoked uncertainty and concern among defenders of the secular state.

In Turkey, the 2002 national elections produced a shocking result: The country that Atatürk had molded into a paragon of strict secularism had elected the Adalet ve Kalkınma Partisi (AKP; Justice and Development Party), a party rooted in political Islam, to lead its government. The head of the AKP, Recep Tayyip Erdoğan, was barred from holding public office because of a prior conviction for inciting religious hatred. The charge stemmed from his declarations at an electoral rally in 1999, where he had read a poem that included the lines "The mosques are our barracks, / the domes our helmets, / the minarets our bayonets / and the faithful our soldiers."[2] Following the election, which equipped the AKP with a supermajority in parliament, the rule was modified to allow him to stand for office in a by-election. Victorious, he entered the parliament and assumed the role of prime minister.

The events in Mexico and Turkey are not isolated exceptions. The irruption of religious politics into secular states has produced some of the most striking political scenes of the last half century, as resurgent religions have transformed the global political landscape. From Islamic revolutionaries in Iran to Evangelical conservatives in the United States, religious leaders and activists have dramatically altered popular and scholarly perceptions of the role that faith can play in the political arena. Religious politics has come front and center in places as different as Algeria, Israel, India, and Poland. Religious political engagement has taken place in democracies and authoritarian regimes, developed and developing nations, countries with strict religion-state separation and ones with firm ties to specific traditions, religiously heterogeneous and homogeneous societies, and virtually every part of the world.

These episodes, however, have varied substantially in their impact on elections and political parties. The growing salience of religion coincided with the global expansion of electoral politics during the final decades of the twentieth century. Yet the ways in which these trends have intersected are quite diverse. In some cases, religious activists and politicians have collaborated to form assertive religious parties that make open appeals to voters' sectarian identity, maintain strong alliances with religious groups, and foreground religious doctrine in their policy platforms. In others, activists have joined mainstream parties that rely on religion as one element among many and bring devout voters into broader coalitions. And in yet other cases, religious political activism has remained largely outside the electoral arena, in the hands of groups that eschew partisan identification and prefer to negotiate independently with government representatives.

Scholars have long noted that differences in the salience and intensity of religious politics appear correlated to faith traditions.[3] Among contemporary global religions, Islam is often singled out as being uniquely conducive to the emergence of assertive religious parties.[4] In contrast, Catholicism is often seen as having become particularly resistant to explicit partisan mobilization.[5] However, these observations are seldom made on the basis of systematic comparison or subjected to empirical assessment. One of the aims of this book is to describe and compare patterns of religious political mobilization associated with Roman Catholicism and Sunni Islam in an encompassing and even-handed manner. In doing so, it confirms that religious mobilization tends to take different forms in contemporary Catholic- and Sunni-majority countries while challenging the notion that religious political parties are largely absent in the first and nearly ubiquitous in the second.

Mexico and Turkey are emblematic of the distinct trajectories taken by parties linked to Catholicism and Islam during the late twentieth and early twenty-first centuries. As Mexican elections became more competitive from the 1970s to the 1990s, the PAN increasingly focused on expanding its secular sources of support and moved away from explicitly sectarian appeals. Its doctrinal statements remained indebted to Catholic social thought, and many of its leaders and candidates had ties to Catholic organizations, but these features were increasingly sidelined in its campaign efforts. In contrast, the predecessors of the AKP, the Millî Selâmet Partisi (MSP; National Salvation Party) and Refah Partisi (RP; Welfare Party), spent those decades developing assertive approaches to religious mobilization as they navigated a complex political environment punctuated by military interventions. Their platforms were infused with references to religious doctrine, and candidates openly relied on their devout reputations to differentiate themselves from the secular establishment and cultivated ties to religious associations in civil society as a means of reaching out to voters. The AKP abandoned much of the explicitly doctrinal rhetoric but retained the reputation and grassroots networks built by its predecessors. When the PAN and AKP came to power in the opening years of the twenty-first century, both parties included some religiously oriented elements in their agendas and faced resistance from the secular establishment and progressive elements in civil society. However, the PAN adopted a defensive, supporting role in debates about religion and public policy and failed to implement much of its agenda. In contrast, the AKP spearheaded efforts to expand the role of religion in public life and succeeded in gradually implementing important elements of its religiously inspired vision.

Religious politics did not vanish from Mexican politics: Catholic bishops and activists continue to advocate and mobilize in favor of policies that reflect their distinctive faith commitments, ranging from abortion and same-sex marriage to education policy and indigenous rights. This activity frequently extends to the political arena, where the PAN has often provided them with reliable partisan allies. Turkey, in turn, did not become anything like an Islamic state: the AKP's reforms in this area, such as loosening restrictions on the headscarf or expanding religious schools, have been shocking to a Turkish public used to assertive secularism but remain more akin to those promoted by conservative parties in Europe and North America than to those that characterize Iran or Saudi Arabia.

The consequences of religious mobilization for democracy have been notably uneven. In both countries, the electoral success of religious mobilizers was initially a boon for democracy. In Mexico, the victory of the PAN brought an end to single-party dominance by producing the first partisan alternation of executive power in seven decades. In Turkey, the AKP government initially pursued liberalizing reforms and stopped a long history of military intervention in political affairs. Since then, however, the picture has been far less rosy. Mexico experienced growing popular discontent with a democracy marred by political mismanagement, persistent corruption, and escalating violence. In Turkey, democracy was profoundly eroded as the AKP leadership became increasingly autocratic, concentrating power in very few hands and rolling back basic rights, such as freedom of the press.

Why did political parties in these countries adopt distinctive patterns of religious mobilization? What role did religious mobilization play in the evolution of electoral politics and democratic institutions? To what extent do their trajectories reflect broader trends in political Catholicism and Islam? What can a structured comparison of two critical cases tell us about the varieties of religious politics in the world today?

This book argues that different paths followed by religious parties in Mexico and Turkey are not due to essential doctrinal differences between Roman Catholicism and Sunni Islam or to the idiosyncratic preferences of individual party leaders. Instead, they are the result of changes taking place in religious communities and the political institutions that govern religious political engagement. The growing capacity and coordination of the Catholic hierarchy in Mexico, combined with political institutions that rewarded compromise and negotiation with the secular regime, raised the costs of assertive religious mobilization. In contrast, the fractured and contested quality of religious authority in Turkey, aided by political institutions designed to facilitate state intervention in religious affairs, increased the rewards for effective religious mobilization. Many of these features are broadly present across Catholic- and Sunni-majority countries and have thus played a prominent role in the broader evolution of political Catholicism and Islam in the last half century.

To explain these dynamics, the following chapters develop an original analytical framework that can be applied to a broad set of Catholic- and Sunni-majority countries. The balance of this Introduction presents the key ideas, arguments, and methods that give shape to the analysis. First, it sets out the puzzle of Catholic and Sunni divergence and surveys recent developments in the existing literature on religious parties. Then it explains the novel approach used in this book to describe and explain variation among religious parties and briefly describes the methodology and case selection. It concludes by providing a brief overview of the rest of the book.

Religious Parties in Roman Catholicism and Sunni Islam

Sunni Muslims and Roman Catholics jointly account for almost a third of the global population, and approximately the same proportion of the world's countries have either Catholic or Sunni majorities. The impact of these two traditions has long been a point of interest for scholars and has been proposed as a critical factor explaining patterns of global political and economic development.[6] More recently, a substantial number of studies have emerged to explore the political impact of Catholicism on democratization and Islam on violence.[7] This normatively charged distinction between a prodemocratic Catholicism and an antidemocratic Islam reflects in no small part the perceived depoliticization of the former and hyperpoliticization of the latter.

Religious parties in Catholic- and Sunni-majority states have undergone a far-reaching transformation over the last six decades. The shift has been so dramatic that it can be easy to forget what conditions were like in the 1950s. At that time, Catholic-inspired Christian Democracy was the dominant political force in much of Western Europe and a rising contender in Latin America. The intellectual ferment leading up to the momentous Second Vatican Council (1962–1965) initially appeared to reinforce this trend, with key documents calling on Catholics, from bishops to lay activists, to become more involved in the social, economic, and political debates of the time. However, over the course of the next four decades, political parties in Catholic-majority countries in Western Europe and Latin America increasingly seemed to eschew assertive religious mobilization. Even as prodemocracy movements empowered by the church proved strong enough to sweep military dictators from power, parties often drifted away from sectarian appeals, failed to maintain links with religious associations, and avoided framing their policy positions in terms of religious doctrine. Catholic political mobilization seemingly faded from the electoral arena, so religious parties gradually became less distinctive, less effective, or both.

Religious mobilization in Sunni-majority countries took a clearly different path during the same period. The 1950s were a low point for religious mobilization in many Sunni-majority countries across the Middle East, North Africa, and South and Southeast Asia. The most influential leaders of the period, such as Egypt's Gamal Abdel Nasser, promoted secular doctrines such as socialism and pan-Arabism. To most observers these secular projects seemed likely to remain dominant in the political arena. As late as 1969 one of the most insightful scholars of Egypt's Muslim Brotherhood described the object of his study as a movement whose moment of historical relevance had passed.[8] Yet by the 1980s religious mobilization had become one of the most widely noted features of political contention in Sunni-majority countries. Appeals to religious identity became a staple of electoral competition, and even Nasser's successor in Egypt, Anwar Sadat, fashioned himself as the "believer president."[9] Incumbent and opposition leaders formed and deepened ties to Islamic movements and associations originally aimed at nonpolitical ends such as provision of social services or the revival of religious mores. These ties provided them with a steady supply of cadres and voters. Candidates became adept at framing their policy proposals in explicitly Islamic terms—for example, by pointing to the importance of *shura* (consultation) for democratic reforms or by developing economic frameworks that could accommodate the religious ban on *riba* (interest-bearing loans). Assertive religious mobilization thus became a regular feature in electoral contests across an array of the Sunni-majority countries.

Few scholars have systematically explored these contrasting trends in a comparative perspective.[10] The scarcity of empirical work comparing Catholic and Sunni political parties over time enables essentialist arguments about the inherent and inflexible differences between the two traditions. By recognizing that both Sunni and Catholic parties exhibit a great deal of variation among themselves and over time, historically and contextually sensitive comparisons can generate more convincing and robust causal arguments about the conditions that favor religious political mobilization. Critically, such an approach belies the notion that current patterns of religious political engagement are a product of essential qualities of the religions themselves.

A growing number of studies cast doubt on the notion that Islam is inherently political and that modern Catholicism is thoroughly depoliticized. Empirical case studies reveal substantial within-tradition diversity of policy proposals, mobilization styles, and framing efforts. Among Christian Democratic organizations, for example, some have strong roots in Catholic associations and social thought, while others are personality driven and lack distinctive doctrines.[11] Similarly, Islamic parties range from loose coalitions of traditional authorities to highly centralized organizations led by urban professionals, and they vary dramatically in their religious policy preferences.[12]

Yet these case studies lack a critical comparative dimension, as they are almost always formulated and evaluated within a single tradition. Thus, they rarely compare the behavior of parties linked to different faiths. When comparisons are presented, they tend to ignore the internal and historical dynamics of other religious communities, instead treating them as static comparison categories. The most robust comparative empirical work is usually restricted to a small number of cases, often separated by large spans of time.[13] These comparisons provide important insights regarding broader patterns of religious political engagement but have difficulty isolating the conditions that lead to its emergence or shape its evolution.

As attractive as the prospects of comparing across traditions may be, there are significant conceptual and empirical lacunae that need to be addressed if a coherent and sustainable research program on religious parties is to emerge. There is a general scarcity of work comparing religious parties across traditions and over time. With some recent and notable exceptions,[14] cross-country comparative studies tend to restrict themselves to cases within the same religious contexts. This can result in important misconceptions about the likely causes of religious phenomena. For example, scholars of Islamic politics often view it as uniquely salient, with little consideration given to similarities with Catholic activism earlier in the century.[15]

This lack of comparative work is matched by the scarcity of research examining religions' "differential appeal, persuasiveness, and political salience over time."[16] For example, while scholars of theology and the sociology of religion have spent substantial time examining the dramatic change associated with Catholicism's *aggiornamento*, the contentious process by which the church sought to bring itself up to date during the 1960s, political scientists have generally been hesitant to hypothesize about its impact.[17] One reason is that changes in religious doctrines such as those associated with Vatican II are often assumed to apply evenly and immediately across a transnational religious community, while changes in political-religious behavior, such as shifts in willingness to engage in democratic advocacy, are rarely, if ever, observed to occur uniformly.[18] But clearly the first assumption is flawed; there are numerous local dynamics and conditions that interact with doctrinal change to produce different effects. Equally important is the temporal dimension of doctrinal reform, which, even in the case of apparently bounded events such as Vatican II, unfolds over extended periods of time that can vary substantially across cases. For social scientists focused on short-term causation, the slow-moving character of religious change can disguise its significant causal impact.[19]

Existing scholarship is thus moving in a constructive direction. However, to further advance the comparative study of religious political parties, some new conceptual foundations remain necessary.

Describing Religious Parties

A comparative analysis of religious parties requires a definition that identifies what makes these organizations distinctive and facilitates comparison across regions, regimes, and traditions. The definition must be flexible enough to encompass a broad range of organizations, note their differences, and articulate clear conceptual boundaries that distinguish between religious and nonreligious parties. To meet these requirements, this book takes as its starting point the classic, minimalist definition of political parties as organizations that field candidates to compete in elections.[20] All political parties must therefore, at a minimum, be able to recruit candidates and appeal to voters for support. Religious parties are those that rely on religion to perform these basic tasks of electoral competition.[21] I refer to the processes of recruitment and appeal as religious mobilization because they entail more than a passive inclusion of religion: relying on religion to compete in elections is an inevitably contested process that can profoundly alter religious communities.

Religious mobilization in the electoral arena can take place along multiple dimensions, reflecting the various ways in which party organizations can recruit candidates, voters, and supporters. The typology of religious mobilization developed in this book distinguishes between three dimensions: appeals to religious identity, cooperation with religious associations in civil society, and inclusion of religious doctrine in platforms and manifestos. The next chapter describes the three dimensions of religious mobilization in more detail, but they can be briefly delineated here.

The first dimension includes a range of appeals to religious identity, from the explicit, such as Egyptian Muslim Brotherhood's "Islam is the Solution," to the more subtle, such as the RP's revalidation of Turkey's Ottoman-Islamic heritage.[22] In a Catholic context, use of labels such as "Christian Democracy" and symbols such as the cross or ichthys can also constitute such an appeal. In both traditions, regular reliance on recognizably religious rhetoric or candidates' consistent displays of personal piety can play an important role in these efforts. The second dimension of mobilization consists of ties to religious associations in civil society. These can help secure crucial resources for political actors and endow them with a capacity to penetrate society greater than that of all but the most robust mass parties. In Mexico, links to Catholic Action allowed the PAN to appeal to activists and voters despite suffering acute financial shortages during its first four decades.[23] Sunni opposition parties managed to become powerful contenders in very challenging political circumstances partly as a result of their links with local mosques, Islamic charities, and religious brotherhoods.[24] The third dimension—incorporation of religious doctrine into party manifestos and policy proposals—is present when parties claim that their positions are derived from the teachings of a particular tradition. A party that relies on Catholic doctrines regarding the sanctity of life from conception to articulate an antiabortion stance is mobilizing religion in its platform. An Islamic party that calls for financial-sector reform by invoking religious prohibitions on usury is doing the same. Each dimension of religious mobilization may play a more or less salient role in a party's overall electoral strategy. The three can be mutually reinforcing but can also be used separately; that is, parties may use one, two, or all three to compete in elections.

Using this framework, scholars or analysts interested in classifying parties can set different thresholds for considering political parties religious. At a high threshold, one may require substantial religious mobilization along all three dimensions before a party is considered religious. This results in a clearly defined set of parties that are unambiguously reliant on religion to participate in elections. However, it substantially narrows the range of parties considered religious and excludes many organizations that local voters, activists, and analysts recognize as religious. Alternatively, at a low threshold, one can consider any party organization that relies on religious mobilization along any dimension to be religious. In that case, two parties may be classified as religious without sharing a specific attribute: a party that mobilizes voters primarily by highlighting its denominational identity but eschews elaborate doctrine counts as religious, as does one that draws on doctrinal principles but makes appeals across denominational boundaries. This means that, at a low threshold, religious parties may bear only a "family resemblance" to each other;[25] that is, they may share some of a cluster of traits rather than a single defining characteristic.

As the next chapter shows, scholars and analysts are already making these kinds of judgments. However, they are often made implicitly, complicating efforts to compare findings across countries, regions, and traditions. The approach developed in this book allows scholars to make these kinds of classificatory decisions explicitly and thus to avoid talking past each other. Chapter 1 demonstrates how significant these decisions can be: setting different thresholds for considering parties religious results in very different accounts of the factors that contribute to the presence and success of these organizations.

Beyond issues of classification, an important advantage of this approach is that it retains clear conceptual boundaries while providing enough flexibility to cover a diverse range of cases. Mobilization through religious identity, association, and doctrine can be observed across faiths and regime types. All three dimensions can be pursued by parties linked to any religious tradition, insofar as its members possess a shared sense of identity, a recognized corpus of doctrines, and some associational structure. All three can also be pursued wherever elections are held, even when these are far from free and fair. This enables comparisons across the spectrum of electoral regimes, from highly constrained authoritarian ones to established liberal democracies.

In addition, the framework is especially useful in describing how parties evolve over time. Chapters 3, 4, and 5 analyze shifting patterns of religious mobilization in Mexico and Turkey, examining how shifting opportunities and constraints led parties to adopt different styles of religious mobilization. The analysis therefore avoids getting bogged down in debates about whether particular parties are (or were) religious and instead examines the different ways in which these organizations have mobilized religion and how the importance of appeals to identity, doctrinal platforms, and associational linkages has varied in response to particular factors.

Explaining Religious Parties

This book argues that much of the divergence between Catholic and Sunni parties during the last half century can be explained by two factors: the structure of religious communities and the institutions governing political competition. The divergent evolution of community structures and political institutions in Catholic and Sunni contexts has generated very different constraints and incentives for religious mobilization in their electoral arenas. Analyzing the impact of religious community structures and political institutions allows this book to address critical questions about religion and politics without relying on static and essentialist notions of faith traditions or delving into the extensive debates about democratic compatibility that have shaped much of the scholarship on this subject. The analytical framework sketched here and developed in more detail in Chapter 1 centers on how religious community structures and political institutions affect the ability and willingness of partisan actors to mobilize religion as well as the forms that this mobilization is likely to take.

The term "religious community structure" refers to the patterns of relations among followers of a religion, particularly those that deal with authority and representation. Who has the ability to speak for the religious community? How is formal religious authority organized, and what are its limits in practice? What are the intracommunal constraints on autonomous religious activism? Religious communities may be more or less centralized and hierarchical in practice. They may possess more or less specialized leadership. Members of the broader community may have more or less ability to shape the salience of particular issues and make their voice heard in doctrinal debates.

The structure of religious communities can either limit or facilitate religious political mobilization. I argue that, in addition to the overall mobilizing capacity of religious communities, which largely depends on the material resources available to them, the ease with which they can be mobilized depends to a great extent on the relative strength of professional clerics and lay activists. Well-organized clerical leaders can act as gatekeepers and contest the legitimacy of partisan religious claims in order to safeguard their authority.[26] In contrast, communities led by lay activists are more disposed to cooperating with and joining political organizations. The ability of political entrepreneurs to mobilize religion, therefore, depends on the relative capacity of the clergy in relation to the laity.[27] Crucially, I argue that the relative degree of coordination exhibited by clerical and lay actors is not determined by the canons and doctrines of a particular tradition. Although a strict theological perspective presents a sharp contrast between a hierarchical Roman Catholicism and an egalitarian Sunni Islam, this disguises a much more dynamic distinction between clergy and laity in each tradition. Clerical authorities can be found in both Catholicism and Sunni Islam and include bishops and ulema, papal representatives and Sufi leaders.[28] As the case studies of Mexico and Turkey demonstrate, the relative power of clerical and lay groups in both traditions has varied substantially over time and must therefore be understood historically and contextually.

The second factor in the analytical framework is the institutional arrangement that governs religious participation in elections. The political strategies available to religious parties, as organizations that straddle the world of faith and politics, are regulated by two clusters of institutions: those that govern the public activities of religious actors and those that set the rules of electoral competition for political parties. The former include regulations that directly impinge on religious partisan activity, such as bans on religious political parties, and those that indirectly alter incentives for mobilization, such as reliance on state funding for religious activities. More restrictions on religion and more reliance on state support can increase the risks faced by those who seek to mobilize religion in politics but also raise the stakes of political contests and increase potential rewards. This book finds that the presence of interventionist institutions tends to encourage assertive religious political engagement. Notably, this is true whether or not the institutional arrangements are designed to support or undermine religious communities.

Electoral institutions, such as the magnitude of electoral districts and vote thresholds, play a critical role in determining how feasible it is for religious parties to gain representation in national legislatures. The role of these rules in shaping political parties is well-known and has long constituted one of the most fertile areas for comparative institutional scholarship on parties and party systems.[29] However, analyses of electoral institutions are often absent from comparative discussions of religious politics, which tend to limit their focus to the distinction between authoritarianism and democracy even though authoritarian rulers increasingly rely on electoral rules to manipulate religious oppositions.[30] In broad terms, restrictive electoral rules encourage religious mobilization through large, mainstream parties and discourage the emergence of small, niche-oriented competitors. Less restrictive electoral environments make it feasible for religious activists to pursue niche-party strategies by establishing strong links with smaller, more devout constituencies. However, as the case studies in this book demonstrate, electoral rules can interact in complex ways with other institutions and community structures to generate complex webs of incentives and constraints for religious political engagement.

The case studies of Mexico and Turkey demonstrate how religious community structures and political institutions interact with each other and with other factors that affect the strategic calculations of key actors in the electoral arena. In addition, the case studies demonstrate that these factors have a powerful independent influence on actors' choices and operate in similar ways across varied traditions and regimes, making them a cornerstone for a research program on religious parties.

Methods and Cases

Describing and analyzing the development of religious parties across faith traditions pose a number of empirical challenges. In response, this book adopts a two-pronged approach. First, it presents a cross-national statistical analysis of religious mobilization across a range of Catholic- and Sunni-majority countries. This provides a bird's-eye view of patterns of religious mobilization and allows a preliminary assessment of competing causal arguments. Second, the bulk of the book develops a comparative historical analysis of religious parties in Mexico and Turkey that examines the causal mechanisms that link structures and institutions to religious political mobilization and provides an opportunity to observe how Catholic and Sunni parties have evolved over a longer span of time.

The statistical analysis, developed in Chapter 1, relies on an original data set of religious mobilization that covers every election held in twenty-two Catholic-majority and eighteen Sunni-majority countries between 1990 and 2012.[31] The data set draws on a variety of primary and secondary sources to describe the extent to which political parties in these countries mobilize religion along each of the three dimensions, the overall salience of their religious mobilization, and the degree of electoral success they achieve. The countries represent a majority of Catholic- and Sunni-majority countries, drawn from around the world and with a wide range of outcomes in regard to religious political mobilization. Regression analyses based on this panel data set allow a more precise measurement of patterns of religious mobilization in Catholic- and Sunni-majority countries than has been previously available.

Given the many differences that exist between Catholic- and Sunni-majority environments, the comparative historical analysis takes advantage of important parallels between the Mexican and Turkish experiences to trace the effects of shifting community structures and political institutions on patterns of religious mobilization by Catholic and Sunni political parties. In that way, the study leverages the unique advantages of paired comparison,[32] a technique that allows for the kind of sustained attention to specific cases that is usually beyond the scope of all but the most expansive multicountry studies.[33] It thus enables the systematic evaluation of contextual differences and similarities and explicitly addresses concerns about the validity of findings.

Mexico and Turkey are a uniquely useful pair of cases with which to conduct context-sensitive comparative research on religious political parties. There are, of course, very many differences between them, which the case-study format allows me to take into account. However, the countries also share useful similarities. Mexico and Turkey have populations of comparable size and similar levels of economic development and religious diversity.[34] Both are located on the edges of major centers of economic and political power with which they have well-established but complex relationships that have often spilled into the political and religious arenas. Yet the most notable similarity between the two cases lies in their parallel historical trajectories. Until the early nineteenth century, both were led by monarchies with deep ties to their dominant religious tradition. They then experienced large-scale, contentious attempts to implement liberalizing reforms during the mid-nineteenth century, many of which were aimed at asserting the dominance of the state apparatus over the religious establishment. These efforts laid the grounds for modernizing dictatorships late in the nineteenth century and for revolutionary struggles during the beginning of the twentieth. These devastating conflicts, each of which cost millions of lives, ended with the imposition of single-party regimes committed to assertive secular policies. During this period, a variety of laws endowed political authorities with the power to regulate public worship and other expressions of faith while prohibiting political activism by religious groups and individuals. These laws aimed to secure state autonomy from the influence of established religious groups, to promote the emergence of an enlightened and privatized religious faith, and to encourage the spread of secular worldviews. Anticlerical and secularist reforms triggered violent and unsuccessful reactions in the 1920s, exemplified by the Sheikh Said Rebellion in Turkey and the Cristero War in Mexico. The violent suppression of these movements established the supremacy of the secular state but also demonstrated the high cost of insisting on the effective application of secularist projects. This realization paved the way for political liberalization and increased religious tolerance in the 1940s and 1950s, although religious tolerance often took the form of informal shifts in policy enforcement rather than full-fledged reform. The 1980s witnessed further liberalization, most notably in the economic realm, where it strengthened often conservative business sectors but also had implications for long-fought battles over the role of religion in education.

Key differences between these similar cases make the comparison particularly fruitful. Critically, there have been significant differences between Mexico and Turkey in regard to their political institutions and religious community structures. In regard to institutions, Mexico, despite an avowed commitment to multiparty competition, long combined a profoundly uneven playing field with a highly disproportionate electoral system, ensuring overwhelming majorities for the ruling party for several decades. Changes to the institutional status quo were always gradual and tentative, and only by the 1990s could these adjustments be construed as a real step toward democratization. In regard to religious institutions, an informal pact between the secular regime and the Catholic Church denied any formal recognition of the church until the 1990s but ensured that the anticlerical provisions of the constitutions remained effectively in abeyance. In effect, it left few channels open by which the state could directly influence the religious community and thus made room for the consolidation of autonomous clerical authority.

Political reforms in Turkey were both more dramatic and less consistent. The introduction of multiparty elections in the late 1940s quickly led to the defeat of the secularist establishment at the hands of a conservative opposition party, and elections remained extremely competitive. However, the secularist elite remained entrenched in the core institutions of the state:

the military, judiciary, and bureaucracy. Over the next four decades, these groups regularly intervened to constrain the power of elected officials, most dramatically through recurrent military coups. The Turkish state remained profoundly involved in regulating religion, most notably through the powerful Directorate of Religious Affairs. For decades, this body, along with the courts and the military, has guided and constrained a broad range of religious activities, not least those potentially associated with political activism.

There were also important differences in religious community structure. In Mexico, as in much of the Catholic world, the Second Vatican Council encouraged the emergence of myriad lay Catholic groups and discourses, resulting in an often vibrant but structurally fragmented and doctrinally diverse lay associational sphere. At the same time, Vatican II also encouraged the reorganization and expansion of clerical institutions. After decades of leading a skeletal existence, the Mexican Episcopal Conference gained a new vitality, setting the stage for much more assertive and coherent stances by bishops regarding the pressing social and political questions that shaped Mexican politics from the 1970s onward. Even as political openings created new opportunities for religious political mobilization, bishops were usually cautious and wary of explicit partisan alliances.

While religious communities in Turkey experienced no event of equivalent magnitude, the religious sphere ultimately underwent a no-less-striking transformation. Religious associations began to expand rapidly in the 1940s. Although initially restricted to local associations, there were several larger beneficiaries from this process, perhaps most notably the communities led by Said Nursi and the Nakşibendi Sufi order. The expansion of these groups created a new crop of committed religious activists who, despite generally preferring to work outside the political arena, nevertheless dramatically expanded their communities' capacity for religious political mobilization. The Milli Görüş (MG; National Outlook) movement, led by Necmettin Erbakan, drew on these resources to forge an explicitly political project, but other religious associations also forged more or less explicit alliances with political parties. The increasingly well-coordinated groups were generally unfettered by clerical establishments, which remained beholden to and strictly supervised by the state. Thus, when economic liberalization expanded the resources available to members of these religious networks, these resources reinforced vibrant networks and politically engaged religious associations.

These divergences shaped the strategies adopted by politicians, activists, and candidates and thus go a long way toward explaining the divergent patterns of religious mobilization in Turkish and Mexican elections throughout the second half of the twentieth century. Restrictive electoral institutions in

Mexico led well-organized lay activists to coordinate their efforts around the PAN and prevented the formation of an effective niche competitor until the 1980s, by which time an increasingly well-coordinated clerical organization acted as a substantial impediment to assertive religious mobilization. In Turkey, the initial weakness of lay activists combined with a restrictive electoral system to discourage politicians from aligning themselves with religious causes, resulting in low levels of religious mobilization until the late 1960s, at which time growing lay coordination and a shift to less restrictive electoral rules resulted in the rise of a successful niche party that engaged assertive religious mobilization. The return to restrictive rules after 1980 and the existence of increasingly powerful lay associations led party leaders to transform their organization into a mainstream party, but one that remained capable of robust religious mobilization.

Overview of the Book

This Introduction provides a broad overview of the theoretical foundations, general arguments, methods, and cases used throughout the book. Chapter 1 develops a definition of religious parties that explicitly draws on and synthesizes the existing literature on Catholic and Islamic politics. It goes over the three dimensions of religious mobilization in detail and proposes a strategy for measuring them in practice. Then it elaborates the causal arguments that constitute the core of the book's analytical framework. It presents the data set that describes 220 elections in thirty-eight Catholic- and Sunni-majority countries, explaining the process used to create the data set, with particular emphasis on the coding of qualitative historical data. Then it uses multivariate panel regressions to assess real differences in levels of religious political mobilization in Catholic and Sunni countries, finding that these remain significant even after accounting for causal factors associated with alternative theories.

Chapter 2 frames the historical case studies of Turkey and Mexico by systematically comparing their religious demography, levels of religiosity, economic development, regime type, and geopolitical situation. It then describes the interaction of religion and politics during the century leading up to the formation of religious parties. It pays particular attention to the rise and fall of clerical authority and the emergence of lay sectarian associations, as well as to evolving patterns of religion-state relations that set the stage for later institutional developments. Most important, it shows how comparable religious community structures and political opportunities gave rise to initially similar party organizations and patterns of religious mobilization.

Chapters 3 and 4 discuss the evolution of religious parties in Mexico and Turkey from the 1940s to the 1990s, paying particular attention to how changes in political institutions and religious community structures gradually or suddenly modified the patterns of mobilization adopted by party leaders and other key actors. Each chapter explores particular periods, punctuated by major shifts in religious and institutional contexts. Through a systematic consideration of the incentives and constraints produced by the interplay of institutions and structures, I apply and test the analytical framework to explain prevailing patterns of religious political mobilization.

Chapter 5 compares the development of key parties in both countries after they reached power at the turn of the millennium. It demonstrates how institutional and structural continuities led to the endurance of many prior trends despite the impact of electoral victories at the local and national levels. At the same time, it shows how the very different institutional arrangements governing religion-state relations in each country played a central role in enabling the AKP to pursue meaningful religious politics, while the absence of such arrangements hindered the PAN's ability to manage the expectations of religious constituencies.

The Conclusion presents four broad lessons drawn from the quantitative and qualitative analyses and explores how these can be applied to cases in four countries characterized by different faiths and political institutions: Brazil, India, Iraq, and the United States. These tentative extrapolations demonstrate the usefulness of the framework developed in this book as a tool for enabling broader conversations about religious politics across boundaries of region and tradition.

1

Religious Parties
in Comparative Perspective

What's in a name? The AKP, which has dominated Turkish elections since its formation in 2002, has consistently objected to being called an "Islamist" party, preferring to refer to itself as a "conservative democratic" one.[1] While the term "Islamist" raises particularly thorny semantic and political issues, the AKP also rejects the notion that it is an Islamic or a Muslim Democratic organization. Indeed, while the party has deep roots in religious activism, visible ties to religious movements, and a platform of policies grounded in religious values, it systematically rejects any effort to ascribe to it an explicitly religious identity.

A similar phenomenon can be observed in Mexico, where spokespersons of the PAN dismiss the notion that the party is in any way a Catholic one. For decades, its leadership went as far as to resist efforts to affiliate the party with Christian Democracy because of its sectarian implications, even as it espoused doctrines grounded on Catholic ideals and relied on lay Catholic organizations to recruit cadres and mobilize voters.[2] While acknowledging the influence of the social teachings of the Catholic Church on its principles and the prominent role played by Catholic activists in its ranks, the PAN has consistently presented itself as a strictly nonsectarian organization.

Both the AKP and the PAN have pragmatic reasons for rejecting religious classification: religious parties have long been formally banned in Turkey and Mexico, which makes acknowledging religious ties a provocative legal proposition. However, there is more to their arguments than strategic dissimulation. Representatives of both parties correctly emphasize the diversity of their supporters and the absence of explicit sectarian elements in their party platforms. Neither the AKP nor the PAN calls for the establishment of a religious state or for discrimination against members of other faiths. Like many contemporary parties that mobilize religion in the electoral arena, they do not fit the stereotypes often associated with religious parties. Yet any attempt to understand them that does not recognize and incorporate the role of religion in their development would be substantively incomplete.

Links between religions and political parties are often contentious and difficult to assess. Religion can play a salient role in parties in many ways, and these can be quite discreet even when they are highly influential.[3] The challenge of assessing parties' ties to religion becomes particularly acute when comparing organizations associated with different traditions, such as Roman Catholicism and Sunni Islam. Precisely for this reason, a robust definition of religious parties must be a cornerstone for any systematic comparative analysis of religious parties across different countries, regions, and traditions.

Defining Religious Parties

There is no generally accepted definition of a religious party. Policy makers, analysts, and reporters focusing on a particular country or tradition often adopt an I-know-it-when-I-see-it approach that treats the category as a self-evident one: Tunisia's Ennahda, for example, was repeatedly described as a religious party even after it proclaimed the end of its religious activities and supported a women's rights advocate who did not wear a hijab as its candidate for mayor of Tunis.[4] While the notion that a party is religious may appear unambiguous to a given observer in a specific political context, the absence of a clear definition inevitably undermines attempts to describe cross-national patterns of religious political engagement or to develop causal arguments about the evolution of religious parties that can be applied across countries and traditions. The diversity of approaches to the study of religious parties can be briefly illustrated by contrasting the strategies used by other scholars to identify parties associated with Catholicism and Sunni Islam. My definition, proposed in the subsequent section, attempts to bridge the distance between them, but first one must appreciate the nature of this gap.

Reflecting the formal verticality and organizational robustness of the modern Catholic Church, most comparative studies of religion and party development in Catholic Europe have emphasized the importance of ties between parties and the Catholic hierarchy. Maurice Duverger's classic study of political parties in Europe, for example, defines Catholic parties as mass organizations made distinctive by their ties to formal confessional associations.[5]

The support of Catholic bishops often serves as a litmus test for ascertaining whether or not a party can be considered Catholic. At the extreme, this approach treats Catholic political parties as agents of the clerical hierarchy rather than as autonomous political actors. This was the view adopted by many nineteenth- and early twentieth-century opponents of early Catholic parties, who argued that these organizations were compromised by ties to an external authority and could not be trusted to be unbiased representatives of the nation.[6] Unsurprisingly, these arguments still produce strong, negative reactions from both party leaders and Catholic authorities. Nevertheless, whenever Catholic authorities declare that there are no Catholic religious parties because the Catholic Church does not support any party in particular, they implicitly rely on that definition.

The importance of ties between the hierarchy and partisan organizations remains central to more recent studies of Catholic political parties, albeit in more complex and subtle ways. In his seminal work on the origins of Christian Democracy in Europe, Stathis Kalyvas focuses on how the mobilizing strategies of the church inadvertently produced confessional parties by providing the organizational infrastructure that lay activists used to construct partisan organizations, even as the formation of these parties is revealed as a suboptimal outcome for the Catholic hierarchy.[7] In another influential study of Catholic politics, Carolyn Warner focuses on the conditions under which members of the Catholic hierarchy will either favor the formation of religious parties or opt to act as an independent interest group.[8] By this account, Catholic parties are those that act as vehicles for the political projects of the bishops. Anna Grzymala-Busse's study of different avenues for Catholic political action examines the influence of church-sponsored parties—that is, those that secure explicit and sustained support from clergy—and finds that they are virtually always an inferior alternative to direct and discreet ties between religious and state leaders.[9] In these studies, the beliefs held by party leaders and activists are less important for classifying a party as religious than the links between the party organization and the Catholic Church.

The approach used by most scholars to identify Sunni Islamic parties is very different. Rather than focus on ties to formal religious authorities, most studies of Sunni religious politics associate Islamic parties with a set of more or less fixed doctrines assumed to shape the worldviews of their leaders and supporters.[10] In that view, shared beliefs are treated as the basis of Islamic identity and, by extension, as the core of what makes parties Islamic.[11] Indeed, the widely used concept of Islam*ist* parties, as its suffix implies, focuses on ideology, and references to Sharia in party platforms are often treated as their defining feature.[12] As it does in the classic view of Catholic parties, a strong reading of this argument implicitly restricts the political agency of Islamic parties as well as their potential commitment to democracy.[13] Most mainstream Islamic actors emphatically contest this implication, even as many of them accept the centrality of belief and doctrinal commitment to the definition of Islamic parties.[14] Recent scholarship has questioned whether the appeal of these parties is based on their reliance on doctrine-infused policies, arguing that they in fact stem from their reputations as political outsiders and social-service providers.[15]

The prevalent emphasis on religious ideology as the core feature of Islamic parties has been reinforced by scholarly interest in the dynamics of moderation, which has become a central theme in the study of Islamic politics.[16] Moderation is typically divided into behavioral and ideological variants, with the former emphasizing adherence to formal democratic institutions and the latter emphasizing changing beliefs and normative acceptance of liberal democratic principles. This distinction, which typically treats behavioral moderation as both shallower and less reliable than ideological moderation, ultimately reinforces the emphasis on belief and doctrine as the key constitutive element of Islamic political parties. Seminal works on moderation in an Islamic context, such as Jillian Schwedler's study of religious parties in Jordan and Yemen,[17] have substantially deepened scholarly understanding of the nature of ideological moderation and the conditions under which it happens while reinforcing the tendency to understand Islamic parties in terms of the beliefs of their members.

As this comparison suggests, applying the criteria used to identify religious parties in one tradition to those in another context is likely to produce striking distortions. Focusing on parties that call for the application of religious laws, for example, can capture an important, though not encompassing, set of contemporary Islamic parties but excludes virtually all Catholic ones. In contrast, relying on ties to organized religious hierarchies can capture some prominent Catholic parties but excludes many Islamic ones. In addition to underestimating the degree of variation that exists among parties associated with particular religious traditions, as evidenced by case studies of both Islamic and Catholic organizations,[18] this kind of conceptual stretching can distort our understanding of religious politics and contribute to the impression that religious parties are the exclusive domain of a particular tradition.

Recent frameworks that aim to facilitate cross-tradition analysis attempt to strike a balance between these approaches. For example, Manfred Brocker and Mirjam Künkler define religious parties as organizations that "hold an ideology or a worldview based on religion . . . and mobilize support on the basis of the citizens' religious identity,"[19] thus highlighting but softening the emphasis on ideology and noting the importance of identity-based appeals to religious voters. Luca Ozzano goes further, proposing the category of "religiously oriented" parties, understood as organizations that reference religious values in their platforms while also "explicitly appealing to religious constituencies, and/or including significant religious factions."[20] This definition casts a substantially wider net, as the role of ideology is further weakened while the notion of "religious factions" raises the possibility that only a subset of the party need be committed to religious principles. In an innovative reformulation, Kalyvas proposes the notion of "unsecular" parties, understood as organizations that use religious rhetoric to critique liberal institutions, reconstruct religious identities, rely on selective incentives, have cross-class appeal, and form ties to established religious institutions.[21] This definition covers a narrower set of organizations by requiring the use of transformative mobilization and explicitly antiliberal rhetoric while also pointing to the importance of nonreligious factors in the electoral strategies of these organizations.

The definition proposed in this book is informed by these recent contributions and by the specific challenges raised by the comparative study of religious parties in Catholicism and Sunni Islam. It thus aims to provide a robust theoretical foundation for the comparative empirical analysis of religious parties across faith traditions.

A New Definition

Religious parties are organizations that mobilize religion for the purpose of competing in elections. In this view, religious mobilization is a strategy willfully pursued by political parties, a manifestation of parties' political agency rather than an unavoidable consequence of religious doctrines or a natural result of party members' identity. Consequently, there can be a great deal of variation in religious mobilization among different parties within the same tradition, and its importance can rise and fall over time. Rather than evaluate whether or not a party has an essential religious identity, this study focuses on how and when particular political parties rely on religion to mobilize voters and under what conditions they succeed in doing so.

Religious mobilization is multidimensional. Religion is not only a body of beliefs and doctrines with potential implications for public policy, but it is also a collective identity that provides individuals with a sense of belonging and a set of associations potentially capable of engaging in various forms of autonomous political action. This emphasis on multidimensionality has become a standard feature of scholarship on religion and political behavior,[22] but it is undertheorized in comparative studies of religious political organizations.[23] While religion can and has been understood in a variety of ways, this study proposes that political parties can mobilize religion in the electoral arena along three distinct dimensions: as a collective *identity* articulated by specific symbols and terms, as a body of shared albeit contested *doctrines*, and as a set of formal and informal *associations* with varying degrees of influence over their individual members. Moreover, each of these dimensions of mobilization may feature as a primary or a secondary element of the party's electoral strategy.

Appealing to Religious Identity

Religion is a powerful source of collective identification that often acts as a cornerstone of an imagined community,[24] and its use by political leaders to motivate and justify political action is as old as politics itself.[25] When parties mobilize religion by means of identity, they claim to be parties of, by, and for members of that faith, though these claims may not be articulated explicitly or interpreted exclusively. Appeals to identity need not imply adherence to specific doctrinal positions; nor do they necessarily require endorsement by religious authorities, although both of these can enhance the appeal's credibility. Parties can attempt to mobilize religious identity by adopting denominational labels, such as "Christian" or "Islamic"; by incorporating confessional symbols; or by systematically relying on religious rhetoric and highlighting the devotional practices of their leaders and candidates.

A broad range of labels is available to parties appealing to religious identity, some of which have complex pedigrees. The "Christian Democratic" label, for example, loosely indicates an affinity to a confessional community,[26] a set of values consistent with its norms, and other similar if often vague religiously inspired positions.[27] Notably, these connotations remain legible even though Christian Democratic parties and supporters display an enormous range of policy preferences on economic and social policies.[28] While there is no Sunni equivalent to Christian Democracy,[29] variations on the Arabic words *nahda* (renaissance) and *jama'a* (assembly), among others, have been used in ways that suggest a similar flexibility. Alternatively, the labels that signal religious identification can be local: terms such as "justice" and "popular," for example, may have easily legible religious connotations to domestic audiences because of their historic or ongoing use by other social and political organizations. A similar phenomenon can be observed in terms of religious symbols, with modified crosses and ichthyses recurring regularly in Catholic-majority environments and crescents and outlines of minarets found in Sunni-majority ones.

Beyond these explicit labels and symbols, political parties appeal to religious identity through the sustained use of religiously charged rhetoric and symbolic action. Party statements and slogans that prominently proclaim the need to defend unspecified Christian or Islamic values, link national and religious identities, or proclaim the piety of the party leadership are commonly found among political organizations in both religious traditions. Recurrent displays of faith by party leaders, such as wearing traditional religious garb, attending religious festivals, or delivering speeches at religious events, can also play a role in articulating appeals to religious identity.

Incorporating Religious Doctrines

Religious traditions encompass an enormous range of principles, beliefs, and norms that can be potentially incorporated into party platforms and policy proposals. Some of these, such as rules governing marriage and divorce or restrictions on usury or alcohol consumption, draw on well-developed and explicit religious texts. Alternatively, parties may propose policies that do not directly replicate religious ordinances but articulate concepts such as family and justice in ways that refer to recognized religious ideas and exegetical traditions. Policies derived from these doctrines can range from restrictions on abortion and antipornography statutes to welfare expansion and anticorruption reforms. The benefits of mobilizing religion by incorporating religious doctrine can be substantial. Complex policies can be simplified and made relatable by linking them to religious principles. Moreover, adopting particular doctrinal positions allows political parties to effectively claim religious legitimacy for their policy aims.

Religious doctrines are not monolithic, and political parties rarely adopt them wholesale. Political actors select among a range of potentially salient doctrinal elements, implicitly or explicitly arguing for their preeminence among the broader range of religious principles and beliefs. As Sultan Tepe notes, the ideologies espoused by religious parties vary substantially, even among parties belonging to the same religious tradition.[30] A brief glance at the platforms of religious parties in the Muslim world suggests that parties have substantial flexibility in the degree to which they emphasize particular points of religious law.[31] Moreover, the highly pragmatic behavior of Islamic parties supports the notion that religious doctrines can be applied and contested in numerous ways.[32] Conservative Catholic political parties often place their emphasis on abortion and same-sex marriage, while progressive organizations prefer to highlight themes of social justice and equality often associated with movements such as liberation theology.[33] Across this range of cases, we see that party stances may fit neatly with orthodox interpretations of doctrine advocated by local clerical elites or draw from more heterodox sources and alternative theologies.

Yet the fact that religious traditions are adaptable does not mean that incorporating religious doctrine into party platforms is free of costs and risks. Richard Gunther and Larry Diamond argue that religious ideologies are distinctive because "religious beliefs . . . are determined by a combination of tradition and interpretation by clerics and/or a religious institution outside of the party itself," so, in contrast to other types of parties, a religious party "is not fully in control of its core ideological precepts."[34] While that view may underestimate the internal diversity of traditions and overestimate the ability of religious elites to dictate their interpretation, it is certainly the case that political parties seeking to mobilize religion by leveraging doctrines expose themselves to the possibility of critiques by clerical authorities and religious experts. Even when their opinions are not binding, religious authorities can weigh in on the appropriateness of religious interpretations and evaluate the extent to which the party has adequately lived up to its promises. In addition, failure to implement doctrinally informed campaign promises may no longer be a mere political failure, to be compensated by successes in other policy areas, but rather a failure to live up to religious obligations.

Linking to Religious Associations

Major faith traditions form the basis for an enormous variety of associations, ranging from transnational clerical hierarchies to local charity groups. These organized groups rather than religions as a whole are capable of providing physical resources and mobilizing voters on behalf of political parties. A wide range of scholarship has consistently emphasized the importance of these links in the development and evolution of religious parties.[35] In practice, the functions and purposes of these links vary widely, with religious associations training cadres, reaching out to voters, or vouching for the credibility of politicians, among other electoral activities. Through these actions, religious associations allow parties to build trust, provide selective benefits to supporters, engage in discreet proselytism, and identify and recruit potential candidates.

The set of religious organizations with which parties can maintain links is quite diverse and ranges from official clerical bodies and mass movements to local charitable societies and volunteer groups, among others. In the case of Catholicism, these links can include alliances with hierarchical, organized bodies such as bishops' conferences and transnational groups such as Catholic Action or Opus Dei. Catholic parties have also been linked to less formal movements that advocate for causes as diverse as traditional marriage, indigenous rights, labor unions, and restrictions on abortion. In Sunni contexts, scholarship has often noted ties between parties and broader religious movements, such as the Muslim Brotherhood.[36] However, the range of civil-society organizations to which parties are linked is very diverse, as Janine Clark's study of health clinics, charitable associations, and women's groups demonstrates.[37] Though less prominent than their Catholic counterparts, Islamic clerical organizations, such as Nahdlatul Ulama in Indonesia, have also sponsored prominent religious political parties.

These ties can vary significantly in their impact on the activities and programs of the party, ranging from substantial integration of parties and religious movements, such as in the Muslim Brotherhood and its partisan vehicles, to conditional and discreet cooperation between religious and partisan elites, such as in Catholic hierarchy support for Christian Democratic parties across much of Latin America. Moreover, the relative power of parties and movements can vary, with some parties dependent on the endorsement and support of religious movements, while others dominate subsidiary religious associations.

Each of these dimensions of religious mobilization may be more or less central for a particular party. For the sake of parsimony, I distinguish situations in which a given dimension is a primary element of the overall mobilization efforts by a party from those in which it is a secondary element. The dimensions of mobilization, along with the specific indicators used to assess them, are described in Table 1.1.

Despite being conceptually distinct, the three dimensions of religious mobilization have a tendency to blend in practice. Appeals to identity can be embedded in doctrinal policy frameworks, maintaining links to associations may require adopting doctrinally informed platforms, and visible closeness to religious associations may act as an implicit appeal to identity. However, parties can and do mobilize religion along some dimensions but not others, or some more than others, in varying combinations. Some parties explicitly claim a religious identity and reference religious doctrines even as a rivalry with the religious establishment keeps their ties to religious associations at a minimum. Others rely primarily on allied groups in civil society to mobilize religious voters while engaging in discreet appeals to religious identity and avoiding religious doctrine altogether.

Which Parties Count as Religious?
Thresholds of Religious Mobilization

As noted previously, the salience of religious mobilization varies substantially across parties and over time. Where one sets the boundary demarcating

TABLE 1.1: DIMENSIONS OF RELIGIOUS MOBILIZATION

Dimension	Salience	Indicators
Identity	Primary	• Explicit confessional label • Prominent and regular use of religious symbols on party banners and publications • Consistent displays of piety by candidates and leaders
	Secondary	• Discreet religious label • Limited use of religious symbols • Irregular or individual displays of piety
Doctrine	Primary	• Consistent and specific references to religious beliefs across multiple elements of party platforms • Prominent references to religious principles in party statements of doctrine
	Secondary	• Generic references to religious beliefs in particular parts of party platform • Occasional references to religious principles in statements of doctrine
Association	Primary	• Visible contributions to voter mobilization during elections • Party leaders and candidates predominantly members of religious associations • Provision of substantial share of party resources
	Secondary	• Discreet collaboration between party and religious associations • Links between party and associations through specific individuals only • Minority of party leaders or candidates members of religious associations

substantial religious mobilization can have dramatic consequences for one's assessment of the prevalence and trajectory of religious political parties. Rather than draw a single line that divides religious parties from their secular competitors, this study sets up three thresholds for considering a party religious based on patterns of religious mobilization, as described in Table 1.2. This strategy not only allows us to describe differences in religious mobilization across cases and changes in mobilization over time but also yields a better understanding of how differences in measurement can affect our perceptions of the prevalence of religious parties.

At the first, lowest threshold, a party is treated as religious if there is evidence of religious mobilization along at least one of the dimensions discussed previously. At this lowest standard, political parties that regularly use religious rhetoric or symbols to appeal to a religious community, that include references to religious principles in their manifestos, or that obtain the support of religious leaders or lay associations are considered religious. Relying on

TABLE 1.2: THRESHOLDS OF RELIGIOUS MOBILIZATION

Religious mobilization	Characteristics	Examples
Low (limited, partial)	Secondary religious mobilization along at least one dimension	• True Path Party (Turkey) • Conservative Party (Colombia) • National Liberation Front (Algeria)
Medium (substantial)	Secondary religious mobilization along all dimensions *or* primary religious mobilization along at least one dimension	• Muslim League-Nawaz (Pakistan) • Croatian Democratic Union (Croatia)
High (robust, assertive)	Primary religious mobilization along three dimensions	• Freedom and Justice Party (Egypt) • League of Polish Families (Poland)

this threshold, religious parties share only what Ludwig Wittgenstein called a "family resemblance" rather than a single basic essence or core attribute.[38] These parties can be recognizably religious even if they mobilize religion in different ways. Parties that meet this threshold but no other are described as engaging in *low* or *limited* religious mobilization.

Examples of low-mobilization religious parties are the Conservative Party (PC) in Colombia and the Doğru Yol Partisi (DYP; True Path Party) in Turkey. These organizations explicitly reject a sectarian identity but have appealed to religious voters by promoting key policies that align with their conservative religious preferences and providing discreet references to religion, such as the repeated references to God and Christianity in the PC's doctrines or the DYP's maintenance of discreet ties to religious associations.[39] Some incumbent parties in electoral authoritarian regimes that include appeals to religious identity or make formal references to religious doctrine in an attempt to legitimate their policies but generally rely primarily on patronage and coercion to secure support, such as the National Liberation Front (FLN) in Algeria, are also engaging in limited religious mobilization. By many accounts, these would not be considered religious parties at all, particularly when there are more robust religious mobilizers competing with them. Of course, parties that mobilize religion more assertively would also cross this lowest threshold and be counted as religious.

At the second threshold, secondary religious mobilization must be present along all three dimensions, signaling a broad but shallow reliance on religion, or it must be a primary aspect of mobilization along at least one dimension, signaling a deeper but still incomplete reliance on religion. By this standard, simply having a religious label or cooperating with religious associations is in itself insufficient to consider a party religious. However, if the party exhibits either of these features along with clear references to religious doctrine in manifestos, or if both of them are present and generally reported to be substantial, then the threshold would be crossed. The set of parties that count as religious by this threshold is necessarily less diverse than the set captured by the lowest threshold, but these parties can still exhibit a great deal of differences. Indeed, these may still share only a family resemblance with each other, specifically when they rely on primary mobilization along one dimension rather than secondary mobilization along all three.

Examples of parties that meet this threshold but not the highest one are the Croatian Democratic Union (HDZ), which has explicitly presented itself as a defender of Croat Catholicism as an important component of its nationalist agenda,[40] or the mainstream Muslim League parties in Pakistan, such as the Muslim League-Nawaz, which rely on religious rhetoric and have promoted a wide range of religious reforms.[41] These organizations, while not consistently guided by religious principles or deeply tied to extrapartisan religious movements, nevertheless engage in consistent and widely reported appeals to religious identity and maintain important links to religious associations in civil society. Parties that meet this threshold but not the highest one are described as engaging in *medium* or *substantial* religious mobilization.

For an organization to cross the third threshold, robust religious mobilization must take place along all three dimensions. Local voters widely regard such organizations as religious, the organizations have well-reported ties to religious associations, and religious doctrines play an important part in justifying policies. Even at this highest threshold scholars may disagree about the relative importance of religious mobilization relative to other factors, such as clientelistic mobilization, or about the degree of autonomy possessed by the party leadership in relation to religious movements or clerical hierarchies. Yet, unlike those in the two lower thresholds, this set of parties is defined by a fixed set of shared features. The threshold also captures a substantially smaller set of parties, as the empirical analysis shows.

Examples of parties that have met this highest threshold are the League of Polish Families (LPR) in Poland and the Egyptian Freedom and Justice Party (FJP), both of which have robust ties to religious movements, appeal to voters largely on religious grounds, and incorporate substantial elements of religious doctrine into their manifestos and policy proposals. These parties are described as engaging in *high* or *assertive* religious mobilization.

These thresholds of religious mobilization are not equivalent to indicators of moderation or radicalism. As noted previously, scholars of religious politics have engaged in a fruitful and ongoing debate about the nature and causes of moderation. Nevertheless, by fusing questions of religious influence and democratic commitment, and treating those as mutually exclusive, the notion of moderation risks eliding the complex ways in which religious political engagement can take place in democracies. While it is clearly the case that political parties that appeal exclusively to members of one denomination, embrace inflexible interpretations of religious doctrine, and are subservient to religious movements are likely candidates for radicalism, this is not always or necessarily the case, as illustrated by mainstream religious parties in Indonesia.[42] Moreover, it is also clear that radical parties can be entirely secular, as repeatedly demonstrated by organizations ranging from communists to ultranationalists in Eastern Europe.

Observing Religious Mobilization in Catholicism and Sunni Islam

Religious mobilization, as defined here, is a strategy that party leaders, candidates, and activists actively pursue and debate. It can thus be identified by analyzing their public statements, campaign behavior, and intraparty polemics. Candidate speeches, party manifestos, public endorsements of (and by) religious associations, website content, banners and slogans, and newsletters and communiqués, along with a variety of primary materials associated with electoral campaigns, can provide direct evidence of appeals to identity, associational linkages, and doctrinal references. The data are not consistently available and are typically dispersed across a wide range of primary and secondary sources. Identifying parties that engage in religious mobilization is therefore a time-intensive process of triangulation that requires gathering data from a variety of sources. Although it raises problems of comparability, this diversity also constitutes a useful check on individual observer bias. Multiple independent sources are used when assessing religious mobilization in a particular case, and the set of relevant studies is not limited to works explicitly dedicated to analyzing religious parties. Studies of religious movements frequently describe ties to political parties, and historical descriptions of particular periods often comment on prominent campaigns to mobilize religious constituencies. Complementing political analyses with sources written from different perspectives, such as history and sociology, can aid this process of triangulation. Descriptions of rallies, discussions of party platforms, and summaries of speeches in news coverage of particular elections can also provide useful bits of information when combined with more reliable scholarly sources.

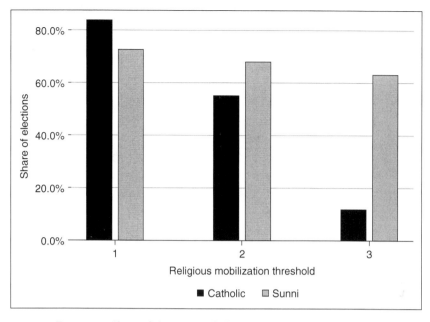

Figure 1.1 Share of elections including Catholic and Sunni parties
by threshold.

By applying this strategy, we can measure the prevalence of religious
parties across Catholic- and Sunni-majority countries. Aided by a team of
research assistants,[43] I examined all elections in thirty-eight Catholic and
Sunni-majority countries between 1990 and 2012 and identified 115 religious
parties that secured at least 1 percent of seats (six of the countries did not have
any parties that met that threshold).[44] These parties are listed by country in
Appendix 1.

This list of parties gives us a sense of their relative abundance across
countries and mobilization thresholds but not necessarily their presence in
elections. Figure 1.1 presents the share of elections in Catholic- and Sunni-
majority countries that include a religious party at each of the three thresholds of mobilization. That is, it describes the presence of religious parties
without taking into account their degree of electoral success beyond the 1
percent threshold necessary to appear in the data set.

This initial view of religious political parties across Catholicism and
Sunni Islam is broadly consistent with what an informed observer might
expect, even as it complicates common narratives about the depoliticization
of Catholicism and the hyperpoliticization of Islam. The vast majority of
elections in both traditions include at least one party that crosses the lowest
threshold of religious mobilization. Elections involving medium levels of

religious mobilization are also common in both traditions though somewhat more so in Sunni-majority environments. Finally, high levels of religious mobilization are frequently observed in Sunni environments but are quite rare in Catholic ones. The slope of the decline as one moves from one threshold to the next is quite sharp in Catholic cases, while it is almost flat in Sunni ones.

It is not the case that Catholicism has entirely extricated itself from the electoral arena; indeed, limited Catholic political mobilization is quite frequent. Mainstream Christian Democratic organizations that reference Catholic teachings in their doctrinal statements or conservative parties that rely on Catholic frames to define their stances on abortion and same-sex marriage, for example, are almost ubiquitous. This kind of limited religious mobilization goes virtually unremarked, except of course by local secularist critics and partisan rivals. However, the prevalence of Catholic parties drops sharply as we apply more exacting thresholds. Parties that engage in substantial mobilization, such as nationalist parties that use religious rhetoric to frame their appeals to national identity and Christian Democratic organizations that maintain effective ties to Catholic associations in civil society, are present in only roughly half of all elections. Finally, by the most exacting standard, which requires primary reliance on religion along all three dimensions of mobilization, only a handful of organizations, such as the League of Polish Families, qualify as religious. In other words, Catholic religious mobilization is broad but shallow: many parties engage in it, but very few rely or specialize in it.

The trend in Sunni-majority countries is clearly different. At the lowest threshold, religious parties are somewhat less abundant in Sunni-majority elections than in their Catholic counterparts, reflecting the absence of religious political mobilization in some electoral authoritarian regimes dominated by secular incumbents, such as Kazakhstan. However, there is virtually no drop-off as one moves across thresholds: approximately two-thirds of elections include religious parties, no matter which threshold one uses to classify parties as religious. What this suggests is that in elections where religious mobilization is feasible, there is virtually always at least one party that mobilizes religion in a highly assertive fashion. Cases such as Algeria, where an incumbent party engages in limited religious mobilization while facing competition from an assertive religious challenger, are quite common.

The picture changes as one shifts from measuring the mere presence of religious parties to considering their electoral success. The broad but shallow quality of religious political mobilization in Catholic-majority contexts remains evident when we examine the share of legislative seats captured by religious parties, as shown in Figure 1.2.[45] However, while low-level Catholic mobilization is common, it is by no means universally successful. Even by

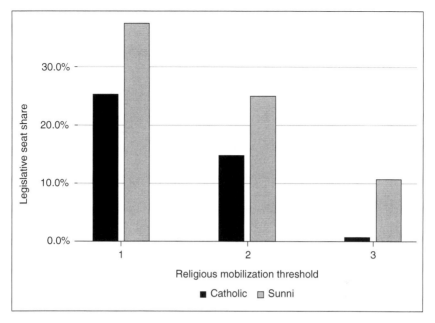

Figure 1.2 Average legislative seat share of religious parties
by threshold.

the lowest threshold, religious parties hold only a quarter of legislative seats
in Catholic-majority countries. The drop-off as one moves to more exacting
thresholds is still precipitous: less than 15 percent of seats are held by parties that engage in substantial religious mobilization, and virtually none are
held by parties that mobilize religion assertively. Assertive religious mobilization does not appear to be a winning proposition in contemporary Catholic-
majority contexts.

An even more notable difference emerges when considering Sunni cases.
In contrast to the flat line that describes the presence of Sunni religious parties, their degree of electoral success does exhibit a substantial decline as one
increases the religious mobilization threshold. By the low threshold, religious
mobilizers have held over a third of seats on average, reflecting in part the
predictable success of limited religious mobilization by incumbent parties in
electoral authoritarian regimes. In contrast, parties that engage in at least substantial religious mobilization have captured only a quarter of legislative seats,
while assertive religious mobilizers, a category that includes most parties considered Islamist, have captured only a tenth of seats. For every election like the
one in Egypt in 2012, where assertive religious mobilizers captured a robust
majority of seats, there are many more where they remained marginal players.

What we see, then, is not the consistent domination of electoral competition by religious parties in Sunni environments and their absence in Catholic ones but rather a different style and intensity of religious mobilization. Broad appeals to Catholic identity, informal collaboration with Catholic social movements and associations, or references to Catholic social doctrine are quite common, even if they are not always electorally successful. However, there are very few Catholic religious parties that even attempt to engage in robust religious mobilization along all three of these dimensions, let alone succeed electorally while doing so.[46] In contrast, religious parties in Sunni environments tend to be far more explicit in their adoption of a sectarian identity and their reliance on doctrinal references and to maintain far more robust ties to religious associations, even though the success of high-level religious mobilizers is far lower than that of their less assertively religious counterparts. What drives these patterns?

Explaining Variation in Religious Mobilization

The extent to which Catholic and Sunni parties participate in elections and achieve electoral success varies dramatically across countries. Why do parties engage in religious mobilization in some countries but not in others? When does this mobilization succeed electorally, and when does it fail? The factors that shape religious parties' electoral performance are clearly complex, and scholars of religious politics have proposed a variety of potential explanations. In broad terms, four theoretical approaches dominate scholarship on religious politics: secularization, civilization, religious pluralism, and state intervention. Each of these is built around a particular set of causal arguments regarding the conditions under which religion is likely to play a major role in political affairs. The causal account that this book proposes, presented in the following section, draws on some aspects of all of these.

Secularization theory points to the level of socioeconomic development as the key factor behind differences in the political salience of religion across states and societies.[47] In the classic perspective, modernization leads to the differentiation of states and markets from religion, relegates religion to the private sphere, and erodes popular religiosity.[48] Religious parties may emerge in an attempt to forestall these trends but will wither away as individuals increasingly reject religious identities, norms, and associations in favor of their secular variants.[49] A diverse body of work has emerged to challenge secularization theory. Prominent scholars of religious politics in the United States have objected to the notion that modernization inevitably displaces religion from the electoral arena.[50] While some dismiss the notion of secularization altogether,[51] others suggest that contentious secularization processes may produce cleavages that parties and activists can seize.[52] A parallel set of studies on the rise of Islamic activism suggests that the impact of economic development may well be reversed, with economic expansion empowering previously marginalized religious communities and granting them greater voice in the political arena.[53]

Civilization-based accounts focus on differences between faith traditions, typically derived from core sets of texts and beliefs, arguing that these have distinctive, stable implications for the political behavior of religious groups.[54] In their strong variant, these accounts are highly deterministic: religious parties should emerge wherever the population adheres to systems of belief that do not embrace the distinction between religious and political authority.[55] Other versions of this argument account for the possibility that the political application of religious traditions may vary substantially across space and time while nonetheless pointing to the role of historically contingent but identifiable sets of core principles that act as meaningful constraints on religious actors.[56]

The religious pluralism approach, also referred to as the religious marketplace approach, draws on economic and rational choice models to propose that religious competition is the driving force behind variation in religious behavior in the political arena.[57] Looking specifically at the interaction between religious communities and political entrepreneurs, Anthony Gill argues that greater religious pluralism facilitates the emergence of religious liberty, as minority denominations eschew direct involvement in political affairs and push politicians to craft neutral rules that will allow them to grow peacefully in civil society rather than clash in the political realm.[58] However, he also notes that the majority is likely to resist these tendencies, potentially leading to greater religious mobilization in the short run. Similarly, Guillermo Trejo finds that Catholic bishops tend to become involved in political and social mobilization when they face competition from growing Protestant denominations.[59]

The fourth approach emphasizes the importance of state involvement in religious affairs, most often, though not exclusively, in its repression of religious communities and political organizations. Taken broadly, this category includes structuralist accounts of party formation that emphasize the critical role of conflict between religion and state,[60] as well as religious marketplace models that emphasize the role of regulation in restricting pluralism.[61] For example, Monica Duffy Toft, Daniel Philpott, and Timothy Shah argue that state-led efforts to restrict religion in the public sphere provoke the rise of extremist movements, which in turn can become the foundations for militant religious parties.[62] Work on the rise of Islamic parties often points to the repression carried out by authoritarian regimes as a factor distorting electoral competition and encouraging the salience of politicized religion.[63] Another variant argues that the combination of state repression and selective endorsement creates a particularly propitious environment for religious political engagement.[64] There is no equivalent literature on authoritarianism and Catholic parties, but organizations directly or indirectly supported by the Catholic Church did a better job of enduring sustained exclusion under authoritarian regimes than many of their competitors and often succeeded in operating in challenging environments such as Latin American military dictatorships or Eastern European communism.[65] Restrictions imposed by authoritarian states may therefore constitute an important explanation for the relative success of religious mobilizers in Catholic contexts as well.

While these approaches are not easily reconciled, each has made important contributions to our understanding of religious political engagement. My argument draws on their key concepts and arguments, adapting them to the specific context of electoral competition.

Religious mobilization does not occur mechanically or automatically. Party leaders, candidates, and activists choose to invest time and energy in crafting appeals to sectarian identity, forming and maintaining alliances between parties and religious associations, and designing doctrinally influenced policy proposals. Mobilizing religion can be a powerful means for attracting and consolidating voter support, but like any political strategy it has costs and risks. Will the use of religious symbols and slogans be perceived as manipulative and illegitimate? Do potential associational partners have the ability to reach a substantial number of voters? Will religious authorities challenge the legitimacy of doctrinal policy prescriptions? Do the benefits of courting a devout constituency compensate for the potential alienation of more secular voters? Will state authorities tolerate religious appeals? The answers to these kinds of questions weigh heavily on the calculations of political actors. In other words, politicians choose to mobilize religion but do so while facing constraints and incentives derived from both religious and secular contexts.

I argue that the most significant factors affecting whether and how politicians mobilize religion in the electoral arena derive from (1) the structure of religious communities and (2) the restrictiveness of political institutions. Each of these can dramatically affect the likelihood of observing religious parties in a given context, the type of religious mobilization parties pursue, and their degree of electoral success.

Religious Community Structure

In broad terms, religious community structure refers to the internal organization and resources available to faith communities. Understood in this way, it shapes religious political mobilization in two basic ways. First, the mobilizing resources available to faith communities at a particular time determine whether they are capable of playing an effective role in a given political contest. Religious communities with more devotees and more abundant human, social, and physical capital provide more fertile ground for the organization and success of religious political parties. Second, the internal organization of religious communities affects the availability of these resources to political entrepreneurs. When religious leadership is effectively concentrated in the hands of well-coordinated clerical authorities, leaders are in a position to potentially defend their preeminence and resist efforts by politicians to mobilize religion. In contrast, when faith communities are fractured, individual leaders are likely to favor political activism and be willing to contribute to electoral mobilization, not least to gain influence within the community, even if it endangers the clerics' collective moral authority.

The first of these effects is reasonably straightforward: when religious communities are larger, more devout, and possess more resources, their ability to participate effectively in politics becomes more substantial. In the long run, the strategies and performances of political parties may positively or negatively affect the mobilizing resources of the religious community.[66] In a historical perspective, causal arrows linking the resources available to religious communities and religious mobilization therefore point both ways. However, at any given time, one may expect a positive correlation between resources and mobilization success. In this way, religious groups are no different from their secular counterparts.

This view has important implications for our understanding of the effects of modernization on religious political activism. On the one hand, there is substantial evidence that economic development tends to erode religious adherence, shrinking the pool of potential activists, cadres, and voters.[67] This suggests a negative relationship between modernization and religious political activism, particularly since the presence of at least a sizable minority of devout voters is plausibly necessary for any form of religious mobilization. In regard to electoral success, assertive religious mobilization in particular should work best in the context of widespread confessional identification, familiarity with and acceptance of doctrinal principles, and well-articulated religious networks and associations.

On the other hand, economic development can simultaneously enhance religious communities' ability to engage in political action: greater rates of literacy, better health, and higher incomes may lower average levels of religious commitment by encouraging the emergence of secular worldviews, but they also provide the remaining religious community with vastly expanded capacities to engage in electoral politics. Charitable societies, independent religious schools, organizations of devout business owners, and many other groups organized around churches and mosques all benefit from the capacities and resources created by expanding economic activity.[68]

Focusing on the divergent effects of modernization on the structure of religious communities—specifically by distinguishing the negative effects of development on the size of religious communities from its positive impact on the economic resources available to religious communities—should help us address some of the persistent ambiguities associated with research on the political effects of economic development on political mobilization. Thus, our first two hypotheses are as follows:

> *H1:* Larger, more devout constituencies increase the likelihood of religious mobilization and enhance the electoral prospects of religious parties.
>
> *H2:* Higher levels of economic resources increase the likelihood of religious mobilization and enhance the electoral prospects of religious parties.

Religious groups vary not only in the absolute level of resources they possess but also in their ability and disposition to engage in coordinated political action. Religious communities should not be treated as preexisting, coherent, and organized actors that are uniformly capable of forming alliances with political operators to pursue defined goals. Members of a religious faith need not consistently act as a voting bloc; nor do they necessarily have a clearly defined collective political identity. The salience of religious rhetoric in the public sphere, the coherence of religious voting blocs, and the political involvement of religious associations cannot be understood without taking into account the behavior of elite religious and political actors.[69] Clerical authorities, religious activists, and political entrepreneurs, among others, actively shape and contest the manner in which religion manifests itself in the electoral arena.

Political parties, by aggregating diffuse interests and articulating policy platforms, are crucial players in organizing religious groups and bringing them into politics. Partisan efforts at religious mobilization can bring about significant changes in religious identities.[70] At the extreme, belonging to a particular denomination and supporting a particular party can become synonymous in the eyes of many voters, altering the scope of the religious community itself. Individuals who do not share the worldview of the party may come to be reimagined as less religious than their partisan brethren, while those who object to party policies may find themselves drifting away from the religious community.[71]

Precisely for this reason, political parties' efforts to bring about assertive religious mobilization can face meaningful resistance from traditional religious leaders. Clerical authorities who enjoy a secure position at the center of religious networks may be wary of sharing their status as representatives of the religious community with lay activists and politicians, particularly when politicians' actions may undermine their moral authority.[72] When they are well organized, religious leaders can present a united front and defend their privileged status as representatives of the community against these potential partisan usurpers. Specifically, they may reject efforts to formally link sectarian and partisan identities, seek to maintain veto power over alliances between religious associations and political parties, and object to efforts by political entrepreneurs to frame policy proposals as the realization of religious doctrines. Each of these tasks may be more or less feasible in a particular national context, but the overall ability of clerical authorities to do any of them is likely to be tied to their overall capacity for engaging in coordinated action.

This does not mean that any religious-partisan cooperation is impossible when clerical authorities are strong, autonomous, and united. When clerics perceive threats to their religious community as emanating primarily from the political arena, they may be willing to tolerate the long-term risks of partisan alliances for the sake of averting the immediate crisis that might result from the victory of an assertive secularist opponent.[73] Yet in general terms strong clerical leaders should prefer to provide tacit support for parties that engage in limited religious mobilization rather than entangle themselves in potentially compromising public alliances with assertive religious mobilizers.[74] This is in part a survival strategy, since having close ties to a particular political party can backfire dramatically when its opponents come to power or if the party is brought down by corruption scandals, exposing religious authorities to state reprisals and public rebuke.

Religious leaders may not always be able to act as an effective constraint on religious political mobilization. When clerical authorities are too fractured to coordinate their responses to important social and political developments, they are less likely to be able to restrain, let alone guide, the political strategies that lay activists adopt.[75] Indeed, they may be less willing to do so: when religious authority is fractured, particular clerical leaders may find it to their individual advantage to secure political influence through partisan alliances, even if that risks imposing a collective cost to the community of clerics by endangering their overall moral authority. This temptation may be particularly acute when religious authorities are co-opted by states and disconnected from their social base, since the potential rewards to individual clerics for supporting a friendly ruling party may be particularly substantial. However, when religious authority is widely seen as being dependent on the state, the effectiveness of clerical leaders' potential interventions is also likely to be significantly reduced.

Religious communities organized around multiple, autonomous, and robust lay associations and networks enable voter coordination and make it easier for religious communities to influence existing parties or sponsor the formation of new ones.[76] Lay activists, whose survival does not typically depend on maintaining an effective monopoly on religious authority, are less likely to object to assertive religious mobilization, particularly when they can influence the way in which doctrine-based policies are formulated. They are therefore more likely to form partnerships with political entrepreneurs, contributing directly to the consolidation of associational linkages, the fusion of partisan and religious identity, and the incorporation of religious doctrines into party platforms. The situation exerts a pull on politicians, as the presence of a well-articulated religious community encourages them to court religious voters in coherent and sustained ways.[77]

The capacity for collective action of clerical authorities and the liveliness of lay associations are not fixed features of religious communities, and the ahistorical treatment of religious community structures can lead to deterministic assumptions about the relative ability of clerical leaders and lay activists to effectively participate in politics.[78] Like the absolute levels of mobilizing resources, the de facto capacity of religious leaders to shape their communities varies over time. The emergence of new religious movements may dramatically increase the internal pluralism of a given religious community. Alternatively, investments in bureaucratic capacity and regular communication among clerical authorities may enhance their effective veto over religious political mobilization. So our third hypothesis can be written in two parts:

H3a: Autonomous and coordinated clerical authorities diminish the likelihood and success of high-level religious mobilization and increase the likelihood and success of low-level mobilization.

H3b: Fractured or state-captured clerical authorities increase the likelihood and success of high-level mobilization.

Political Institutions

Religious parties encounter political institutions on two fronts: as participants in electoral contests and as religious actors. As seat-seeking electoral organizations, religious parties are responsive to the overall quality of democracy as well as to specific electoral rules such as district magnitudes (the number of representatives elected from each district) and vote thresholds. As religious actors, they are subject to state regulations that restrict or enable particular forms of religious activism, speech, and worship, as well as institutional arrangements that favor or disfavor their religious traditions as a whole. Religious parties are not necessarily passive adherents to these rules. Insofar as they are able to gain political influence, they may also seek to alter institutions of both types to enhance their electoral prospects and achieve policy goals.

The effects of overall democratic quality on religious party performance are powerful but ambivalent. On the one hand, free and fair elections create more opportunities for all political parties, including religious ones. Democratic liberties allow parties room to craft religious appeals, form alliances with religious groups in civil society, and articulate religious policy platforms, as they do for secular ones. On the other hand, unfree and unfair competition in electoral authoritarian regimes may provide religious actors with a competitive edge that is lost as democracy becomes consolidated. The depth of religious identification, legitimacy of religious appeals, and resilience of religious networks make religious challengers particularly well equipped to endure the "menu of manipulation" typically deployed by electoral authoritarian regimes.[79] This can give them a comparative advantage over potential secular competitors who lack these means for mobilizing voters and supporters.[80] As the extension of democratic rights and procedures creates more room for political mobilization by nonreligious means, the relative electoral advantage of religious parties may therefore diminish. Another factor that may dampen the positive effects of democracy on average religious party performance is that hegemonic incumbent parties in electoral authoritarian regimes often engage in low-level religious mobilization as a means of legitimizing their rule and buttressing their use of coercion and clientelism. Democratization, insofar as it erodes the electoral success of these hegemonic incumbents, should thus lower the average seat share captured by low-level religious mobilizers. Therefore, insofar as it facilitates all kinds of political activism, democracy should make religious mobilization more likely but not more electorally effective. Thus:

H4: Democracy enhances the likelihood of observing religious parties but does not have a consistent effect on their electoral performance.

As religious actors, religious parties are affected by the myriad institutions that govern state-religion relations. Challenging the long-cherished notion that democracy entails an unproblematic separation of religion and state, recent research suggests that the impact of these institutions is substantial even in democracies. Indeed, strict separation is neither common nor a default position in democracies.[81] The vast majority of states, including democratic states, are deeply engaged in the regulation of religion, and religious communities frequently operate in democratic public spheres.[82] Empirical studies of the variety of state involvement in religion have repeatedly documented a substantial range of institutional arrangements structuring state-religion relations around the world and have shown that many of these are compatible with a range of regime types.[83]

The varieties of state-religion relations have distinctive histories and implications for religious politics. Assertive secularist regimes, in which the state takes on an active role in governing religion, articulate a very different set of constraints on, and opportunities for, religious political activism than do passive secularist regimes rooted in liberal ideals of separation.[84] Religion-friendly regimes can also vary from those with a strong establishment designed to favor one particular tradition, to frameworks designed to accommodate and support multiple religious communities.[85] However, as in democracy itself, the effects of state regulation of religion may be double-edged. Institutional arrangements that provide support for the majority religious community may reassure and appease religious leaders and thus discourage them from challenging the political system,[86] but these arrangements may also create conditions under which religious identities, doctrines, and associations come to be seen as normal features of a political arena and thus legitimate instruments for political contention. Similarly, institutions that impede religious activity can raise the costs of mobilizing religion for electoral purposes but may also incentivize religious mobilization in favor of institutional reform. Many regimes, particularly but not exclusively in Sunni contexts, simultaneously endorse and regulate religion, creating an institutional context that may be particularly suitable for the emergence and persistence, if not necessarily the electoral success, of religious political parties. In sum:

> *H5a:* State support of religion increases the likelihood of observing religious parties but does not have a consistent effect on their electoral performance.
>
> *H5b:* State regulation of the majority religion increases the likelihood of observing religious parties but does not have a consistent effect on their electoral performance.

In contrast to our complex expectations for the effects of democratization and state involvement in religious affairs, the expected effects of electoral rules are straightforward: Permissive rules—that is, those that make it easier for smaller parties to secure seats in the legislature—should increase the likelihood of observing religious parties at all three levels of mobilization. Permissive electoral rules should favor assertive religious mobilization, while restrictive electoral rules should favor limited religious mobilization. When electoral rules are restrictive—that is, when district magnitudes are low or vote thresholds are otherwise kept high—it becomes difficult to secure seats through appeals to dedicated religious constituencies. Only the most committed politicians and motivated activists are likely to pursue assertive religious mobilization strategies if these do not consistently yield seats. Unable to form independent partisan organizations, religious activists have to choose whether to remain outside the electoral arena altogether or form coalitions with secular political actors to more effectively pursue voters.[87] Coalition building entails diminished control over party decision-making and less capacity to pursue religious mobilization. Religious leaders and activists, whose support is crucial to the effective implementation of religious mobilization, may hesitate to join parties whose behavior they are unable to control. Instead, they may favor conditional alliances, encouraging friendly mainstream parties to adopt limited forms of religious mobilization. In contrast, less restrictive electoral institutions make it possible for religious activists to organize parties that can gain legislative seats by engaging in assertive religious mobilization without relying on costly preelectoral alliances with secular partners. In contrast to their equivalents operating in restrictive electoral environments, these organizations can still attract resources from pragmatic supporters and donors who see them as an effective means for reaching office or promoting desired policies. The ensuing flexibility enables parties to pursue assertive religious mobilization as a viable electoral strategy. So:

> *H6a:* Permissive electoral rules increase the likelihood of religious mobilization and increase the seat share of high-level religious mobilizers.

H6b: Restrictive rules increase the seat share of low-level religious mobilizers.

These six hypotheses summarize expectations regarding the presence and performance of religious mobilizers in elections. Political parties are more likely to engage in religious mobilization when devout religious communities possess substantial mobilizing resources (H1, H2), but religious authorities are divided or co-opted by the state (H3). Democratic institutions, state support for religion, and state regulation of religion should all enable religious mobilization but not necessarily enhance its electoral returns (H4, H5). Finally, permissive electoral rules should make religious parties more likely and improve the electoral prospects of assertive mobilization (H6). One key point stands out: the effects of religious community structure and political institutions on the *presence* of religious parties should be more consistent and robust than their effects on the electoral *success* of religious parties, not because these factors do not matter for electoral success but because their effects may vary across contexts in rather complex ways.

Statistical Analysis

The original data set of religious parties (DRP) makes it possible to conduct an exploratory statistical assessment of the six hypotheses. As noted previously, the DRP covers all elections in thirty-eight Catholic- and Sunni-majority countries during the post–Cold War period. These countries are all the Catholic and Sunni cases covered by the World Values Survey (WVS) during the post–Cold War period.[88] One of the benefits of such an analysis is that it makes it possible to estimate the impact of religious tradition after taking into account other factors correlated with tradition, such as levels of religiosity, democracy, economic development, and religious fragmentation.

At this point in the study we are interested in religious mobilization at the national level rather than the fate of any particular party. Consequently, the dependent variables are (1) a dichotomous measure of the presence of any religious party in a given country election and (2) the total share of legislative seats captured by religious parties in a given country election. Applying the three thresholds discussed earlier results in three alternative measures of each: a low threshold that captures a broad set of organizations ranging from those that engage only in limited mobilization to assertive religious mobilizers, a medium threshold that captures those that at least meet the second standard in regard to religious mobilization, and a high threshold that counts only parties in which religion is a central and highly salient element of electoral mobilization along all three dimensions.

The first independent variable (IV) is majority religious tradition. Every country included in this data set has a clear Catholic or Sunni majority, and this dummy variable therefore takes a value of 0 for Catholic-majority countries and 1 for Sunni-majority countries. The regression coefficient on this variable provides an estimate of the average difference in religious mobilization across these traditions once other factors are taken into account. In addition, it serves as a tentative assessment of H3—that is, the role of autonomous and robust clerical authorities—since Catholic countries generally possess these to a higher degree than Sunni Muslim countries during the post–Cold War period. After including controls, I expect that the religious community structures characteristic of contemporary Sunni-majority countries will result in more high-level religious mobilization, but not more low- or medium-level mobilization, than that observed in Catholic-majority countries.

The remaining IVs are linked to each of the five other hypotheses. The second, share of devout voters, is drawn from the WVS and measures the share of the population that belongs to the majority religion and considers religion to be very important in their life. This measure was selected for its comparability across religious traditions, where conventional measures of practice, such as rates of attendance or prayer, may not be strictly comparable. It is linked to the core effect of the secularization hypothesis—that is, the notion that if religious communities shrink and devoutness declines, religious political engagement is also likely to decline. Alternatively, as long as popular religiosity is high, religious parties should remain abundant and effective. If H1 is correct, the coefficient on this variable should be positive for all three levels of religious mobilization and contribute to the electoral performance of high-level mobilizers.

The third key IV is log gross domestic product (GDP) per capita, a standard measure of levels of economic development. GDP per capita is a standard measure for the resources available to the average inhabitant of a country and thus also for religious communities. Following convention, I take the log of GDP per capita to account for its diminishing impact. If H2 is correct, I expect this to have a positive impact on the presence of religious parties after controlling for the size of the devout community.

The fourth IV is democracy, which, following convention, is measured using Polity II. While imperfect, this is a standard measure of regime type and adequately captures the overall openness of the regime to opposition participation. H4 suggests that the coefficient on democracy should be positive, with stronger effects for low- and medium-threshold measures of religious parties.

The fifth and sixth IVs are associated with H5, and each captures a different aspect of state intervention in religious affairs. The fifth is a measure of the overall relationship between religion and state, as measured in Jonathan Fox's Religion and State Database.[89] This variable includes fourteen ordinal categories, ranging from total state hostility toward religion to a mandatory state religion. The sixth measure, also drawn from the same data set, describes the number and intensity of restrictions faced by the dominant religious community. These include restrictions on religious parties, but also on religious civil society organizations, and bans on clergy holding office or engaging in other forms of political activity. There is a three-tier measure of intensity, indicating whether each restriction is largely nominal, partially enforced, or fully enforced. If H5 is correct, one should observe a positive correlation between both measures and the presence of religious parties but not necessarily for their electoral performance.

The seventh IV is the effective number of parliamentary parties (ENPP) with a standard correction to account for the presence of independents, which I use to evaluate H6.[90] I rely on ENPP as a measure of the permissiveness of the electoral system because there is a variety of rules that affects the ease with which smaller parties can capture seats, most strikingly in semidemocratic contexts. A robust body of literature links their effects to the overall level of party system fragmentation,[91] and there is no a priori reason to assume that electoral institutions would affect religious parties differently than it would their secular counterparts. If H6 is correct, the coefficient on this variable should be positive for the presence of religious parties at all thresholds and positive for seat share at high thresholds.

In addition to these independent variables, the full models include controls for the overall level of religious fragmentation as measured by the World Religion Database (WRD) and the number of years elapsed since 1990.[92] Their inclusion is aimed at accounting for alternative theories of religious party performance, such as religious marketplace accounts that emphasize the importance of interdenominational competition and arguments that there has been a general increase in the salience of religion since the end of the Cold War.[93]

These variables, along with the dependent variables of religious party presence and seat share, are summarized in Table 1.3.

Equipped with these measures, we can proceed with the analysis. The nature of the data, which are based on an unequal number of observations of each country corresponding to every election from 1990 to 2012, makes this

TABLE 1.3: DESCRIPTION OF VARIABLES

	Variable	Mean	Std. dev.	Min.	Max.	*N*
Dependent variables	Presence: low	.795	.404	0	1	220
	Presence: medium	.6	.491	0	1	220
	Presence: high	.327	.470	0	1	220
	Seat share: low	.300	.260	0	.943	220
	Seat share: medium	.205	.246	0	.923	220
	Seat share: high	.054	.246	0	.814	220
Religious community structure	Tradition: Sunni	.382	.487	0	1	220
	"Religion very important" share	.449	.268	.038	.958	220
	Log GDP per capita	4.016	.365	2.964	4.981	220
Political institutions	Democracy (Polity II)	7.419	2.773	1.5	10	220
	Overall religion status	7.918	2.719	1	12	220
	Regulation of majority religion	9.809	10.326	0	41	220
	ENPP	3.697	1.921	1	10.87	220
Controls	ENR	1.664	.564	1.02	3.28	220
	Years since 1990	10.791	6.679	0	22	220

an unbalanced panel. Because we are interested in variation across as well as within cases, and because some key IVs, such as tradition, do not vary over time and others, such as the level of democracy, vary inconsistently across countries, I rely on random-effects regression analyses.

The first set of models focuses on the presence of religious political parties without taking into consideration their electoral success. Consequently, the dependent variable is a dichotomous dummy variable, and I use probit regressions.[94] The coefficients, standard errors, and statistical significance are reported in Table 1.4.

The directions of the coefficients are generally consistent with the hypotheses and with the broader argument that religious community structures and political institutions affect the presence of religious parties. The statistical significance of coefficients, in contrast, varies significantly and is sensitive to model specifications. This reflects at least in part the limitations of the data, such as the lack of variation over time for several key variables.

Despite these limitations, the analysis strongly suggests that the relative importance of particular factors varies dramatically depending on the threshold one uses to deem political parties religious. Relying on the low-threshold measure for identifying religious parties, the presence of these organizations is most consistently affected by structural factors, such as the predominant religious tradition, the share of the devout population, and the level of economic development, and by some institutional ones, specifically the overall

TABLE 1.4: RANDOM-EFFECT PROBIT REGRESSIONS ON RELIGIOUS
PARTY PRESENCE

	Variable	Low threshold	Medium threshold	High threshold
Religious community structure	Tradition: Sunni	−4.195*	−1.825	2.489
		2.366	*2.584*	*1.891*
	Religion important	14.305**	3.137	7.696**
		6.260	*5.147*	*3.881*
	Log GDP per capita	6.125*	4.221	3.382*
		3.546	*3.225*	*1.989*
Political institutions	Democracy	.008	−.041**	.006
		.022	*.020*	*.014*
	Religion status	.727**	.589*	.174
		.334	*.354*	*.200*
	Regulation majority	.004	.096	.002
		.115	*.101*	*.070*
	Effective number of parliamentary parties	.513*	−.160	.473**
		.290	*.180*	*.193*
Controls	Effective number of religions	−.463	−.479	2.015*
		1.260	*1.424*	*1.034*
	Years since 1990	−.129*	−.028	−.102**
		.069	*.063*	*.041*

Note: Standard errors are in italics.
*$p < .1$, **$p < .05$

relationship between religion and state and the electoral system, as well as by time elapsed since 1990. Of these, only the relationship between religion and state is significant for parties identified using the medium threshold, which is additionally associated with the level of democracy. In contrast, at the highest threshold, the level of popular religiosity and economic development once again matters, but among institutions only the electoral system appears significant. The years elapsed since 1990 are also statistically significant once again. How one defines what constitutes a religious party clearly affects which factors will be linked with their presence.

The impact of majority religious traditions merits more discussion, since it challenges widely held expectations about the depoliticization of Catholicism and the hyperpoliticization of Sunni Islam. As H3 notes, religious communities led by robust, well-coordinated clerical authorities are likely to favor low-level religious mobilization by political parties and resist high-level religious mobilization. Moreover, Figure 1.1 had already suggested that Sunni parties were only substantially more abundant than Catholic ones when defined on the basis of a high threshold of mobilization. The regressions paint a more striking picture: When relying on the low threshold to identify mobilization and once other factors are included in the models, Catholic countries actually appear significantly more likely than their Sunni counterparts to host religious parties. Only at the high threshold does the emergence of a positive coefficient suggest that Sunni Islam is more conducive to religious political mobilization, and in that context the variable approaches but does not reach statistical significance.

The coefficient on the second structural variable, the share of the population made up of individuals who belong to the majority religion and declare religion to be very important in their lives, is consistently positive and highly significant at the low and high thresholds. This matches the expectations presented in H1 and reinforces the notion that the presence of religious political parties is tied to the overall level of popular religiosity. It is also broadly consistent with secularization theory, which stresses the link between shifting social demand and patterns of religious political engagement. If popular religiosity diminishes, one should expect religious parties to become less abundant.

The coefficient on the third structural variable, log GDP per capita, is also consistently positive and statistically significant for both low- and high-threshold measures of mobilization. The positive sign is consistent with the argument in H2 that economic development expands the resources associated with economic development and can provide the skills and tools necessary to enable religious mobilization in the electoral arena. This is an important check on conventional versions of secularization theory, which assumed a negative impact of development on religious activism. Once the effects of economic modernization on rates of adherence are taken into account, increased resources favor religious mobilization.

In regard to institutions, the effect of democracy on the presence of religious parties represents the clearest deviation from hypothesized expectations, as the variable's coefficient oscillates between positive and negative and is significant only in a negative direction. This does not mean that democracy has no impact on the presence of religious parties but that its effects may be more ambiguous or locally contingent than is often assumed. Given that scholarly attention has often focused on the interaction between religious mobilization and democracy, at the very least this result suggests that some caution may be needed when making general claims about this relationship.

The institutions that govern religion-state relations fare somewhat better. The status of the majority religion is highly significant in the predicted direction at both low and medium thresholds of mobilization, indicating that states in which religion is given a more prominent role appear more likely to host religious parties. In this relationship causality probably flows both ways: countries with friendlier religion-state relations may normalize and facilitate religious political mobilization, and successful religious parties may contribute to the maintenance of friendly religion-state relations. The variable measuring restrictions on the majority religion is also consistently positive but does not attain statistical significance in any model. This suggests that while these restrictions may raise the costs and risks of mobilization, they also likely function as a target and motivation for religious political engagement.

The permissiveness of electoral institutions, measured by the effective number of parliamentary parties, has a positive and significant effect at the low and high thresholds and a negative but insignificant one at the medium threshold. The positive coefficients are consistent with the idea that religious parties, like their secular counterparts, are more likely to secure seats in the legislature when the electoral system is more permissive. The specific institutional design features at work are not detected here, though features such as district magnitude and vote thresholds are likely to play a prominent role.

Finally, in regard to controls, the degree of religious fragmentation is positive and significant for parties that engage in high-level mobilization, but not otherwise, suggesting that these organizations may be particularly sensitive to the risks of interdenominational competition. Interestingly, the consistently negative and often significant coefficient on the last control variable, year since 1990, suggests that religious parties have become less prevalent as time has passed. This may indicate that religious political mobilization increased in the early post–Cold War period and has gradually diminished since then, but the data are inadequate to probe this line of argument much further.

Analyzing the effect of the independent variables on the electoral performance of religious parties paints a somewhat different picture, as summarized in Table 1.5.

The hypotheses presented here are generally less ambitious in regard to electoral success than to the presence of religious parties. The rise and fall of aggregate religious seat shares will necessarily be more sensitive to the particular conditions and idiosyncratic features of national politics. On a more technical note, independent variables that vary little over time, when they do so at all, will necessarily be of limited usefulness when predicting oscillating seat shares. As a result, high standard errors should result in limited statistical significance.

The notable differences in share of seats captured by parties associated with Catholicism and Sunni Islam, described in Figure 1.2, is supported by the consistently positive coefficient on the religious tradition variable. Religious parties are more likely to be successful in Muslim-majority contexts.

TABLE 1.5: RANDOM-EFFECT GENERALIZED LEAST SQUARES
REGRESSIONS ON RELIGIOUS PARTY SEAT SHARE

	Variable	Low threshold	Medium threshold	High threshold
Religious community structure	Tradition	.014 *.115*	.130 *.104*	.067* *.036*
	Religion important	.482** *.217*	.231 *.197*	.251*** *.069*
	Log GDP per capita	.248** *.102*	.176* *.095*	.114*** *.033*
Political institutions	Democracy	.001 *.006*	.014** *.006*	.003 *.003*
	Religion status	.008 *.013*	.011 *.012*	−.003 *.004*
	Regulation majority	−.001 *.002*	−.002 *.003*	−.001 *.001*
	ENPP	−.008 *.007*	−.010 *.006*	.009** *.004*
Controls	ENR	.011 *.035*	.031 *.035*	.027 *.019*
	Years since 1990	−.006*** *.001*	−.004** *.002*	−.002** *.001*

Note: Standard errors are in italics.
*$p < .1$, **$p < .05$, ***$p < .01$

However, this relationship is statistically significant only at the high threshold. This is consistent with the idea that the distinctiveness of Muslim-majority contexts emerges only when one focuses on parties that engage in assertive religious mobilization. For more limited religious mobilizers, it suggests that the effects of tradition may be complex and conditional on other factors.

In contrast, the two structural variables associated with modernization—popular religiosity and levels of economic development—are consistently positive and significant for both the low- and high-threshold measures, though only economic development retains significance at the medium threshold. These observations are consistent with the idea that elections in which a larger share of the population is made up of devout members of the dominant tradition are more likely to result in higher aggregate seat shares for religious parties. More interestingly, higher levels of economic development also contribute to better electoral performance by religious mobilizers, highlighting the importance of material resources in successful religious political mobilization. These effects can contribute to our understanding of the double-edged nature of modernization: economic development may limit the success of religious mobilization insofar as it erodes popular religiosity, but once that is accounted for, its resource-enhancing effect tends to increase the effectiveness of religious political engagement.

In contrast, institutional variables do far less well in these models. None of them have a statistically discernible impact on religious parties identified using the low-threshold measure. Relying on the medium threshold, only the overall level of democracy achieves significance. In that model, democracy has a positive correlation with aggregate religious seat share. This is intriguing, since democracy had no impact on the presence of religious parties. While difficult to interpret, these results suggest that democracy complicates efforts to organize parties but can enhance the electoral performance of parties that do manage to participate. When we apply the high-threshold measure, only the coefficient on the effective number of parliamentary parties is significant. Its positive value is consistent with H6a, which proposes that assertive religious parties benefit from electoral rules that enable parties to appeal to niche constituencies.

Finally, in regard to additional controls, the level of religious pluralism appears to have no effect on the electoral performance of religious parties, but the time elapsed since 1990 is significant and negative across all threshold measures. Combined with its negative effect on the presence of religious parties, this raises questions about claims that religious parties are becoming increasingly powerful players in global politics, at least in the case of Catholic- and Sunni-majority countries.

Jointly, these models paint a complex picture of religious mobilization in Catholic- and Sunni-majority countries in the post–Cold War period. Most of the hypotheses presented in this chapter find some support. The community structure variables associated with H1, H2, and H3 generally behave as expected in their effect on both the presence and success of religious parties. In contrast, the institutional variables proved to be a motley lot. Democracy generally defies the expectations, with negative significance in regard to the presence of medium-threshold religious parties but positive impact on their electoral success (H4) and no impact at other thresholds. Institutions governing religion-state relations yield some results for the presence of religious parties (H5a) but have no discernible impact on performance (H5b), which is in keeping with expectations. Finally, the permissiveness of electoral rules was consistent with pertinent hypotheses in regard to its positive impact on the presence and success of assertive religious parties (H6a) but not for those that engage in limited mobilization (H6b). The findings are not conclusive, which is unsurprising given the limitations of the data and their bounded temporal scope. They are, however, consistent with the argument that both religious community structures and political institutions shape religious political parties.

Summary and Conclusion

This chapter carries out several major conceptual and empirical tasks. First, it provides a new definition of religious parties that emphasizes the importance of religious mobilization along three distinct dimensions: identity, doctrine, and association. It articulates a pragmatic strategy for applying this definition based on three different thresholds by which one can determine what counts as a religious political party. It then applies this measurement strategy to a diverse set of thirty-eight Catholic- and Sunni-majority countries, identifying dozens of religious parties that secured at least 1 percent of the seats in their legislatures in elections between 1992 and 2012 at each of these thresholds.

Building on these descriptive foundations, it develops a theory that can account for variation in the success of religious political parties across countries and religious traditions. Drawing on multiple bodies of scholarship on religious political engagement, it proposes that much of this variation can be explained by observing differences in religious community structures and political institutions. It sets out six hypotheses derived from the theory. Finally, it conducts an exploratory assessment of these hypotheses using data on religious political parties in thirty-eight Catholic- and Sunni-majority countries. The results are broadly consistent with most hypothesized expectations and highlight the extent to which the significance of different explanatory factors is contingent on the threshold one uses to identify religious political parties.

The theory should not be interpreted deterministically. Religious parties are coalitions of individuals and factions, and their members will often disagree over the best course of action to follow at any given time. Actors invested in particular styles of religious mobilization may resist adopting new strategies despite shifting incentives. The effects of community structures and political institutions are consequently mediated by the choices, debates, and struggles taking place within particular countries and party apparatuses. Religious mobilization can be attempted in the face of staunch clerical resistance, and party leaders who have built up religious reputations and invested in relationships with sectarian associations may try to convince supporters to remain committed to assertive mobilization despite the poor payoffs offered by new and unfavorable political institutions. Yet the constraints imposed by community structures and political institutions are real, affecting the success or failure of religious parties operating across various regimes and traditions. Efforts by party leaders to resist changes in party strategy may lead to schisms, intraparty coups by rising activists, persistent electoral failure, and ultimately extinction.

Religious community structures and political institutions necessarily operate in conjunction with other causal factors, many of which act in idiosyncratic ways. Shifting religious demographics, the strategies of secular parties, and the preferences of state elites, to name but a few prominent features, interact with structures and institutions in often surprising ways and alter the religious mobilization strategies favored by party leaders and candidates. Nevertheless, as the rest of this book shows, religious community structures and political institutions are important factors in their own right.

Finally, the data used here have a limited temporal scope and variation. Because they are drawn exclusively from the post–Cold War period while many parties and most of the hypothesized causal factors extend further into the past, there is a real risk of endogeneity. For example, countries with assertive religious mobilizers may opt to regulate religion more aggressively, permissive electoral rules may be crafted to reward small religious parties that have managed to participate in ruling coalitions, and so forth. The quantitative analysis must therefore be supplemented by empirical work that can trace the performance of religious parties over longer periods of time and with more attention to the interaction between causal factors.

Carefully selected, in-depth case studies therefore provide a good means for considering how structure and institutions evolve over time and interact with other causal factors to shape patterns of religious mobilization. The case studies of Mexico and Turkey are developed in the next chapters.

2

Comparing Mexico and Turkey

A paired comparison of religious politics in cases that differ in both faith tradition and world region requires robust justification. Consequently, this chapter provides a framework and background for the case studies of Mexico and Turkey that make up the remainder of the book. In brief, I argue that these countries can be fruitfully treated as a particular type of most-similar cases—one that explicitly takes into account the critical differences associated with religious tradition. This argument for similarity-given-difference, which underpins the subsequent qualitative analysis, has two foundations. The first is a strikingly synchronized pattern of historical development covering the period from 1800 to 1950. The second is a very comparable set of contextual features during the period after 1950 on a wide range of relevant areas, such as religious demography, economic development, and geopolitical situation.

These similarities do not constitute formal controls of the sort found in experimental research designs. Rather, they facilitate the systematic identification of differences between cases, making it feasible to consider these differences explicitly when focusing on the effect of critical variables.[1] This eases the problem of unit heterogeneity that bedevils many cross-tradition comparisons,[2] in which the sheer number of differences between cases makes it virtually impossible to address complex causal interactions and leads to deterministic, decontextualized claims.[3] Manageable background variation thus makes it possible to identify and meaningfully compare recurrent causal relationships and sequences and to consider how they interact with variables associated with alternative causal explanations.[4]

The paired-case-studies approach used in this book relies on two basic methods. The first is congruence testing, which entails a repeated assessment of the correspondence between hypothesized causes and effects,[5] generating multiple observations from each case. In contrast to quantitative observations, those generated by qualitative congruence testing permit a more detailed and less reductionist description of the pertinent factors and their relationship to religious mobilization. The second technique is process tracing—that is, the identification of causal sequences leading from initial conditions to outcomes.[6] Process tracing is a method of within-case analysis, and applying it in a comparative framework requires careful attention to the context in which causal sequences are embedded and their interaction with other potential explanatory factors.[7] It also demands rigorous consideration of temporal dynamics and the way that processes unfold over time.[8] Identifying causal sequences that recur in space and time offers a valuable complement to shallower but more generalizable findings derived from multicountry statistical analysis.

The case studies of Mexico and Turkey rely on these techniques to achieve four specific goals. First, they evaluate the hypothesized effects of religious community structures and political institutions by examining their consistent impact on religious mobilization over time. Second, they aim to identify the particular mechanisms linking these causal factors and observed outcomes. Third, they consider the role played by factors associated with alternative explanations, paying particular attention to their interaction with religious structures and political institutions. Fourth, they examine how changes unfold over time and identify recurring temporal dynamics.

The first goal requires a "structured, focused comparison" of religious mobilization across time and space.[9] Consequently, Chapters 3 and 4 are each divided into clearly defined temporal sections that provide the structure necessary for an evaluation of consistent covariation. For example, Turkey from 1946 to 1960 is characterized by restrictive political institutions and a poorly coordinated religious community structure. According to the hypotheses, this is an unlikely environment for successful religious mobilization. As expected, an examination of the period reveals that the largest conservative party did not substantially mobilize religion along any of its three dimensions and that parties that attempted to do so promptly failed. In 1960 a coup dramatically altered the conditions governing mobilization, resulting in a new situation: Turkey from 1961 to 1980 had permissive political institutions and a moderately coordinated religious community structure. This is a high-likelihood environment for successful religious mobilization, and, indeed, we observe the emergence of a durable party dedicated to mobilizing voters along all hypothesized dimensions. In this manner, the careful sectioning of the case studies allows for the consideration of "recurring empirical regularities" by which similar relationships can be observed in a range of settings within each country.[10]

The second goal is to identify clear causal pathways linking independent variables and outcomes. For each temporally defined section, process tracing reveals the mechanisms through which electoral institutions and community structures shape religious mobilization. Thus, within-case analysis provides a crucial complement for the observed correlations, demonstrating the sequence of events underpinning each correlation and greatly increasing the reliability of observations.[11] To achieve this, each section provides evidence that party leaders, activists, and key supporters were aware of the risks and benefits of pursuing religious mobilization under specific conditions and that the divergent interests of various factions often led to differing preferences with regard to strategy.

Third, comparative case studies are well suited for the systematic consideration of alternative explanations and their interaction with hypothesized causal pathways.[12] Process tracing offers recurrent opportunities to examine how factors such as levels of economic development, which plays a central role in secularization theory, interact with other features of religious community structure and with political institutions to shape patterns of religious political engagement. These examinations yield interesting findings regarding the often contradictory role of economic development in the emergence of new religious associations, which add depth and substance to the correlations identified in Chapter 1. The findings also indicate that the effects of religious community structures and political institutions cannot be treated as spurious consequences of development, civilization, or levels of religious pluralism.

Finally, the case studies examine the temporal dynamics of religious mobilization, particularly issues of tempo and sequence.[13] The qualitative analyses show that religious mobilization strategies used by partisan actors in Mexico and Turkey did not adapt immediately to changes in religious community structure or political institutions. Accounting for the lag between hypothesized and observed outcomes demands paying direct attention to the speed at which political actors responded to shifting incentives and the order in which they adopted religious mobilization strategies. Some adaptations took place over a matter of months, while others took almost a decade to unfold. Moreover, the order in which party leaders adopted different religious mobilization strategies also influenced how mobilization patterns unfolded, with earlier strategies acting as precedents that guided later efforts. For example, the assertive mobilization strategies adopted by one set of party leaders amid restrictive electoral conditions and weak clerical authority in 1940s Mexico continued to influence mobilization long after these conditions had abated in the 1980s.[14] Similarly, experiences with assertive religious mobilization in Turkey during the 1970s shaped the strategies adopted not only by party leaders in the 1980s but also by dissident cadres in the 2000s.[15] In both cases the sequence in which changes to religious community structures and political institutions took place suggests some measure of path dependence, but close examination of the cases is required before the quality and depth of this sequencing effect can be fully understood.

The case studies that constitute the core of this book are designed with these four goals in mind. The result is less a free-flowing historical narrative than a series of carefully organized analyses describing structural and institutional conditions during particular historical periods. This allows us to undertake a detailed examination of the strategic choices and struggles taking place within relevant political parties. This most-similar case design, with its careful focus on how selected differences generate divergent outcomes, depends on the plausibility of the comparison. The remainder of this chapter makes the case for plausibility, presenting the historical background for each of the case studies and the broad contexts in which they unfolded.

Historical Background

Religion and politics intersected often in Mexico and Turkey during the hundred years before the emergence of sustained multiparty elections, and they did so in ways that bear directly on the episodes of religious mobilization examined in the case studies. Given this complex interaction, examining the historical background in Turkey and Mexico serves three important purposes. First, it sets out the historical roots of the religious community structures and political institutions at the center of the analytical framework. The effects of these structures and institutions during the mid-twentieth century can be properly understood only when they are seen in historical perspective. Second, it further clarifies the similarities between the cases, pointing out how parallel historical trajectories created a comparable set of historical legacies in both countries. These legacies go a long way toward explaining the structural similarities between the two countries. Third, these similar historical legacies came to constitute a powerful frame of reference for the strategies and decisions taken by actors in later periods. In this sense, history remains an active element shaping religious mobilization in both countries.

TABLE 2.1: MEXICO AND TURKEY, 1798–1955

Period	Mexico	Turkey
Old regimes	Viceroyalty of New Spain	Ottoman Empire
A time of troubles	Independence War (1810–1822)	Napoleonic and Greek Wars (1798–1832)
Liberal reforms	Juárez and Reforma (1858–1872)	Tanzimât (1839–1876)
Modernizing dictatorships	Porfirio Díaz (1877–1911)	Abdülhamid II (1876–1909)
Revolution and war	Mexican Revolution (1910–1920)	World War I and Independence (1914–1923)
Emergence of secular single-party states	Calles and Cárdenas reforms (1926–1938)	Atatürk reforms (1922–1937)
Secularism and religious reaction	Cristero War (1926–1929)	Said and Ararat Rebellions (1925–1930)
Toward multiparty elections	Ávila Camacho (1940–1946)	CHP and DP Reforms (1946–1955)

This historical account, summarized in Table 2.1, describes the strikingly similar sequences of conflict and accommodation between state and religious authorities in Mexico and Turkey while at the same time pointing out potentially relevant differences. Covering a vast swath of history in a few paragraphs cannot provide a detailed analysis of these historical trajectories and does not seek to do so. Rather than aim to provide an encompassing historical overview, the summary focuses on the emergence of religious community structures and political institutions that remained in place during the period covered by the cases studies and on those events and figures that found an echo in the religious mobilization strategies used by modern party leaders.

Old Regimes (~Pre-1800)

The old regimes in Turkey and Mexico were based on centralized, imperial authority and a close relationship between political and religious power. In the Ottoman Empire, the head of state was also the leader of the largest religious denomination. The Ottoman sultans had claimed the title of caliph since 1517, endowing them with a nominal leadership over the global Sunni community. However, the title was used sparingly until the nineteenth century, and the institutions of the caliphate remained only weakly developed. The lack of emphasis on religious authority reflected at least in part the multiconfessional character of an empire that had numerous Christian subjects, particularly in its strategically and economically important Balkan and Caucasian provinces. Non-Muslims were largely governed by their own communal authorities, which dispensed justice and collected taxes from members of their *millet* (nation).[16] Until the nineteenth century, the sultan's authority over his subjects was nominally absolute, although he frequently delegated the running of the empire to powerful advisers and family members.

The situation in New Spain, as Mexico was known when it formed part of the Spanish colonial empire, was also characterized by the convergence of political and religious authority. The Spanish Crown had effectively claimed the *patronato real*, the right to appoint bishops and to collect and administer the revenues of the Catholic Church across its territories. In exchange, imperial authorities protected and upheld the religious monopoly of the church over its subjects. While the Spanish king, unlike the Ottoman sultan, was not the formal head of the church, he nevertheless possessed substantial effective power over the exercise of religion across the empire. Unlike the Ottoman Empire, New Spain had limited religious diversity. Native American traditions were formally banned, although there were many instances of syncretism, leading to the emergence of distinctive practices and beliefs under the banner of Catholicism. The Catholic Church also acted as a crucial pillar for the colonial administration, handling marriages, burials, and civil registries, among other crucial tasks, and as its largest landowner. The effective power of the monarchy varied over time; for example, in the eighteenth century the Bourbon monarchy set forth a series of reforms aimed at implementing a more effective absolute imperial authority throughout its domains.

A Time of Troubles (~1800–1840)

The status quo of the old regimes came under increasingly severe pressure during the late eighteenth and early nineteenth centuries. For the Ottoman Empire, this was a period of accelerating decline in the face of assertive European powers. A series of wars lost to Russia and the Austrian Empire cost the Ottomans many of their European provinces. The Napoleonic invasion of Egypt (1798–1801) further demonstrated Ottoman weakness and ultimately allowed Egypt's ruler (Muhammad Ali) to secure virtual independence from Ottoman control. In addition, the Ottomans briefly lost control of the holy cities of Mecca and Medina to a rising Saudi state and recovered them only with the aid of Ali's Egyptian forces. The spread of nationalism among the empire's subject populations in Europe was an equally pressing challenge, as unrest threatened some of its richest and most populous parts. The struggle for autonomy by Serbs (1804–1835) and Greeks (1821–1832) threatened to put an end to the empire's long-standing Balkan presence. Domestically, reformist sultan Selim III faced stiff resistance from the traditionalist Janissaries and their allies, who successfully deposed him in 1807. He was replaced by his cousin, Mustafa IV, who was in turn overthrown a year later and replaced by the reformist Mahmud II.

The decline of the old order in Mexico was equally dramatic. Napoleon's invasion of Spain in 1807 provoked a crisis across the Spanish Empire. In New Spain, as elsewhere, this led to largely ad hoc elections to choose members of governing bodies (*cortes*) tasked with resisting the French.[17] Yet the struggles in the metropolis made conservatives into revolutionaries who called for the restoration of the legitimate monarchy while channeling local resentment against the privileges of *peninsulares*, those born in Spain. The Spanish priest Miguel Hidalgo launched the Mexican War of Independence in 1810, but his defeat by Spanish forces the following year and the execution of his successor and fellow Catholic priest José María Morelos in 1815 nearly brought the war to an end. However, when an uprising in Spain forced the recently reinstated Bourbon monarchy to adopt a liberal constitution in 1820, the ambitious general Agustín de Itúrbide joined the insurgents and rapidly secured Mexico's independence. The new governing coalition established a conservative constitutional monarchy and guaranteed the privileges of the Catholic Church; at the same time, and to appease its liberal allies, it also called for a representative congress and equal rights for Mexican-born whites (*criollos*). But the Mexican Empire proved a short-lived polity and never consolidated its institutions. Itúrbide declared himself emperor and did not call for a congress, alienating his liberal supporters. An uprising in 1822 brought an end to his regime, which was replaced by an unstable republic characterized by ongoing struggles between liberals and conservatives.

Liberal Reforms (~1840–1880)

After the failed efforts to reaffirm the old order under Mustafa IV and Itúrbide, the nineteenth century witnessed a series of reforms that fundamentally altered debates about religion and representation in both countries. Sultan Mahmud II initiated what became known as the Tanzimât (reorganization), an attempt to transform the Ottoman Empire while preserving its traditions and the authority of the sultanate.[18] The initial wave of reforms was largely aimed at the military but also sought to reduce the autonomy of religious authorities by controlling their finances and incorporating them into the national bureaucracy. The reforms continued under Mahmud's successor, Abdülmecid I. Among its many changes, the Tanzimât brought an end to the millet system by extending universal rights and guarantees instead of religious community-based ones. Royal decrees such as the Hatt-ı Sharif Gülhane (1839) and the Hatt-ı Hümayun (1856) formalized equality in education and legal rights for all subjects irrespective of faith, opening up administrative posts for minorities and putting an end to the capitulation tax on non-Muslims. The Nationality Law of 1869 went further by establishing a common, secular Ottoman citizenship. Finally, in 1876 the Ottoman Empire obtained its first constitution, which, among other provisions, established an indirectly elected representative body, though this body remained largely under the shadow of the sultan.

During the mid-nineteenth century, Mexico witnessed a period known as the Reforma. In contrast to the top-down quality of the Ottoman reorganization, the Mexican reforms were characterized by violent conflict and civil strife. Although Mexico had been ruled as a republic and held elections since 1824, these were managed by local officials and manipulated by dictators such as Antonio López de Santa Anna.[19] The disastrous failures of this dictatorship led to the Ayutla Revolution in 1855 and the liberal Constitution of 1857. Electoral institutions remained weak during the subsequent period, with highly restricted suffrage and the calamitous interruptions of war. Yet throughout this period, liberals managed to implement a number of legal changes that dramatically altered the Mexican political landscape. The new constitution restricted the rights and influence of the clergy and transferred much of its administrative power to the central state. Moreover, it was buttressed by laws expropriating church lands and limiting the collection of church taxes. The reforms triggered a conservative response and led to a civil war, which was eventually won by liberals under Benito Juárez in 1861, but the costs of the war forced Mexico to renege on its sovereign debt, leading to an international crisis culminating in occupation by French forces and the establishment of a Second Mexican Empire. However, the withdrawal of French forces doomed the regime, and liberals swept back to power in 1867.

Modernizing Dictatorships (~1880–1910)

By the late nineteenth century, the defeat of traditional forces coupled with the ongoing unrest caused by the reform process led to a new form of conservative reaction. The regimes led by Abdülhamid II (1876–1908) and Porfirio Díaz (1876–1911) built from liberal foundations but consolidated their power by reviving their relations with conservative forces and repressing political dissent. Abdülhamid II rose to power vowing to uphold the Ottoman Constitution of 1876, a document that called for an indirectly elected parliament and asserted the equality of Ottoman citizens while preserving the supremacy of the sultan. Yet within two years he had suspended the constitution, closed down the parliament, and moved toward an emphatically autocratic form of government. Abdülhamid II used the growing power of the central state to impose severe restrictions on intellectual freedom and persecute political opponents. He also moved away from the religious pluralism of the Tanzimât era. The loss of much of the empire's European territory in 1878 left it with a substantial Muslim majority for the first time since the fifteenth century. To strengthen his position, Abdülhamid II increasingly emphasized his position as caliph, shifted resources toward the religious establishment, and called for pan-Islamic unity.[20] Although these policies gained him some popular support, by the early twentieth century he faced growing opposition among the emerging domestic intelligentsia and the substantial exile community his persecution had created.

In Mexico, conflicts among members of the liberal camp led to a series of brief civil wars, which culminated with the victory of Porfirio Díaz and his capture of the presidency in 1877. Like many of his predecessors, Díaz retained the formality of elections but manipulated them to ensure his re-election. The Porfiriato, as his decades in power came to be known, was a period of autocratic modernization, with Díaz committed to securing his own power through a combination of repression and rapid economic development.[21] Although clearly influenced by positivist ideology, his government had a highly pragmatic character, co-opting figures from across the political spectrum.[22] Thus, despite his liberal background, Díaz developed a constructive relationship with the Catholic Church, which found in his informal support the stability and security that had eluded it since independence. Jesuits and other orders were welcomed back to the country, and the Catholic Church expanded its influence by building schools, clinics, and other institutions. The Papal encyclical *Rerum Novarum* of 1893 had a direct influence in Mexico, prompting the emergence of new religious associations for students and workers that often pushed for social reforms that did not coincide with the preferences of the government.[23] Indeed, by the early twentieth century, severe repression of political dissent, striking income disparities, and widespread corruption led to mounting popular discontent.

Revolution and War (~1910–1920)

The modernizing dictatorships in both countries were brought to an end by constitutionalist uprisings that sought to place formal limits on autocratic power. Both soon moved in a more revolutionary direction, however, driven in part by stalwart conservative opposition. As early as 1889, domestic opponents to Abdülhamid II had formed an underground opposition called the İttihad ve Terakki Fırkası (İTF; Committee for Union and Progress). Despite continuous persecution, the İTF managed to form links with discontent military officers. In 1908 they staged a military revolt, calling for the restoration of the Constitution of 1876. The sultan conceded, lifting restrictions on political life and calling for parliamentary elections. Religious members in the new parliament organized the İttihad-ı Muhammedi Fırkası (Committee for Muhammedan Unity), a short-lived religious party that supported a counterrevolutionary uprising by theology students and rank-and-file soldiers in 1909. The İTF-led army crushed the revolt, disbanded the religious opposition, and deposed Abdülhamid II, replacing him with a figurehead, Sultan Mehmet V. Over the next decade, the İTF sought to consolidate its power but faced increasingly severe challenges. Two successive Balkan Wars (1912–1913) deprived the Ottoman state of virtually all its European provinces. World War I (1914–1918) proved even more disastrous. Attempts to maintain Arab support by appealing to pan-Islamic sentiments ultimately failed, leading to the loss of the Arab provinces.[24] Indeed, the partition plan forged at the end of the war left the Ottoman state controlling little but the Anatolian heart of the empire and threatened further encroachment by European powers.

Escalating economic crisis in Mexico led to growing popular discontent with Díaz, whose repeated reelections through uncompetitive contests had already alienated a large portion of the political class. Discontent escalated to revolt following the fraudulent elections of 1910, when opposition candidate Francisco I. Madero called on his supporters to seize power. Within a few months revolutionary forces spread across the country, and by 1911 Díaz was forced to resign. The subsequent elections saw Madero ascend to the presidency, and legislative elections in 1912 witnessed the rapid formation of the first party to engage in assertive religious mobilization, the Partido Católico Nacional (PCN; National Catholic Party). The PCN was built as an oppositional coalition of Díaz supporters and Catholic activists and was directly linked to prominent individual members of the Catholic hierarchy.[25] In 1913 a counterrevolutionary coup led by General Victoriano Huerta succeeded in taking over the government and executing Madero. The Huerta regime found support among members of the PCN and much of the Catholic clergy, earning the clergy the lasting enmity of the remaining revolutionary forces. Huerta's defeat in 1914 led to the suppression of the PCN and deepened the anticlerical currents of the revolution.[26] Fighting soon broke out again among revolutionary factions, but by 1917 the new government led by Venustiano Carranza was sufficiently secure to ratify a new constitution. Among its many reforms, the Constitution of 1917 deprived churches of any legal corporate identity, prohibited them from owning lands or properties, and guaranteed a secular public education.

Emergence of Secular Single-Party States (~1920–1930)

The devastation wrought by wars and revolutions paved the way for the emergence of powerful single-party states in both countries. With foreign forces occupying Istanbul and Ottoman authorities ready to concede to their demands, military commanders in Anatolia established a parallel government and mounted a military counteroffensive. The success of this struggle endowed its leader, Mustafa Kemal Atatürk, with enormous popularity and authority over the fledgling Turkish state.[27] Atatürk's government consolidated its power by abolishing first the sultanate (1922) and then the caliphate (1924), thus setting up a secular republic. It moved the capital of the country from Istanbul to Ankara, highlighting the Anatolian orientation of the new country. It granted universal suffrage and rested sovereign power in the legislature, known as the Grand National Assembly, but the country was far from a representative democracy. The assembly selected the president, and Atatürk held this position until his death. His control over the legislature was secured by his leadership of the Cumhuriyet Halk Partisi (CHP; Republican People's Party), which was the only recognized party competing in elections. His popularity and control over the entire governing apparatus allowed Atatürk to pursue a series of dramatic reforms aimed at achieving Turkey's rapid modernization.

Mexico's struggle also continued despite the signing of the Constitution of 1917. Infighting among revolutionary leaders continued until the 1920s, when Álvaro Obregón and Plutarco Elías Calles managed to secure their supremacy by defeating and executing Carranza. Their Sonora faction, known for its fervent anticlericalism, became the dominant force in the emerging revolutionary regime. Elections remained highly controlled affairs, with Obregón securing the presidency in 1920 and passing it over to Calles in 1924. Obregón won the presidency again in 1928 but was killed by a Catholic activist before he could take office. In the aftermath of the assassination, Calles established the Partido Nacional Revolucionario (PNR; National Revolutionary Party) as a means of incorporating the various factions and securing the peaceful transfer of political offices. The PNR also served as an informal means to preserve his authority after he left office since, as a legacy of Díaz's abuses, the constitution prohibited consecutive reelection for any political office. With the aid of the PNR, Calles established what came to be known as the Maximato, a period during which he effectively controlled politics despite not being president.

Secularism and Religious Reaction (~1925–1935)

Among the most notable policies that Turkish and Mexican governments pursued were their respective forms of "assertive secularism,"[28] a process that met with vigorous reaction from religious communities. Atatürk was convinced that modernization could be achieved only by a dramatic overhaul of Turkish society and its reorientation toward the West. Secularism played a key role in this process, becoming one of the pillars of Kemalism, as his ideas came to be known. Under Atatürk, the office of the sheikh al-Islam was abolished, along with all religious schools. The ulema were reorganized as part of a new state bureaucracy and became employees of the Directorate of Religious Affairs, known as the Diyanet.[29] Sharia was replaced by the Swiss civil code, completing the process begun with the legal reforms of the Tanzimât. Sufi orders were abolished and their monasteries shut down. Religious headgear, such as the fez, was banned. The Qur'an was translated into Turkish, and the call to prayer was now made in Turkish. These reforms had a profound effect on Turkey's society and met with various forms of resistance. Members of the Nakşibendi Sufi order led a series of unsuccessful Kurdish revolts in the southeast, notably the Sheikh Said Rebellion in 1925.[30] The government used smaller, local conflicts pitting religious traditionalists against agents of the state, such as the Menemen Incident in 1930 in which a group of religious extremists called for the restoration of Sharia and the caliphate and beheaded a lieutenant before they were stopped with deadly force,[31] as evidence of the need to continue with the secularization campaign.[32] The government also used the threat of religious reaction as an excuse to limit electoral opposition. Two regime-initiated attempts to form loyal opposition parties came to a premature end as a result of their excessive success, and in both cases accusations of fomenting religious reaction were used to close down the organizations.[33]

The evolution of assertive secularism in Mexico took an equally dramatic path. The anticlerical provisions of the Constitution of 1917 had remained largely unimplemented while the country was torn by war. After Calles's ascent to the presidency, he and his supporters committed themselves to breaking the power of the Catholic Church.[34] Anticlerical governors began expropriating church properties and arresting or expelling recalcitrant priests. In 1925 Calles endorsed the formation of a Mexican Apostolic Catholic Church, which would operate independently from Vatican control. In 1926 he passed a law aimed at bringing the anticlerical articles of the constitution into effect. The Calles Law closed down religious schools, expelled foreign priests, limited the number of priests who could operate in a particular territory, and demanded that they obtain a license from local authorities. The response among Catholics was dramatic. Bishops suspended mass on the day when the law took effect, and Catholic associations such as the Asociación Católica de la Juventud Mexicana (ACJM; Catholic Association of Mexican Youth) mobilized to resist its implementation. Thousands of peasants took up arms in the conservative Bajío region of central Mexico, marching under the banner of the Virgin of Guadalupe. The result was a three-year civil war known as the Guerra Cristera, or Cristero War.[35] This concluded only when both sides, weary of the enormous cost of the conflict, agreed to the *arreglos* of 1929, by which the bishops accepted the constitution and the government agreed to limit the implementation of its most anticlerical provisions. These informal arrangements kept the clergy largely out of politics, even as smaller episodes of violence flared during the next decade as enduring conflicts over secular education and other policies pitted the government against its lay Catholic opponents.

Toward Multiparty Elections (~1935–1945)

By the late 1930s, the secular single party regimes in both countries were experiencing significant challenges. In Turkey, the pressure for reform came from both domestic and international sources. Although Turkey managed to remain neutral until the final moments of World War II (1939–1945), the conflict forced the government to adopt highly unpopular restrictions on individual and collective rights and put a severe strain on its economy. Atatürk's successor, President İsmet İnönü, saw limited liberalization as a way to ease domestic discontent and gain favor with the United States, which was rapidly emerging as a crucial strategic partner.[36] What form this liberalization would take, however, was far from clear. Prior attempts to adopt multiparty competition had come to naught when faced with the balancing act of opposing the CHP without threatening the foundations of the Kemalist state. Indeed, the most challenging dimension of the transition to multiparty competition was disentangling the complex state-party knot created by twenty years of single-party rule. Since the beginnings of the Kemalist political project, the CHP had become cojoined with the state apparatus. Thus, İnönü was at the same time permanent chairman of the party, president of the republic, and national leader. Chairmen of provincial party organizations were governors of the provinces, and the six principles of Kemalism, as spelled out in the 1934 CHP congress, were embedded in the Constitution of 1937. Predictably, Turkey in 1946 was caught up by uncertainty regarding the credibility of the electoral process.

In Mexico, the grip of the Maximato was finally broken by President Lázaro Cárdenas, who outmaneuvered Calles and had him arrested and deported in 1936. Cárdenas pursued an ambitious set of policies, including massive agrarian reform and the nationalization of oil companies. In addition, he created workers' and peasants' unions and affiliated them to the governing party, establishing a far more robust social foundation for the renamed Partido de la Revolución Mexicana (PRM; Party of the Mexican Revolution). Cárdenas also continued with efforts at educational reform, proposing a new socialist education system. While his efforts gained him fervent support among many popular sectors, they also provoked intense opposition from landowners and businessmen, who joined recalcitrant Catholics as the main opposition to his government.[37] The economic crisis that gripped the country during his final years in office led many to consider the 1940 elections a unique opportunity to redirect the revolution in a more conservative direction. Cárdenas recognized the dangers this coalition posed and adopted a conciliatory tone, supporting the centrist Manuel Ávila Camacho as his successor. His opponents rallied around the candidacy of Juan Andreu Almazán, a revolutionary general who promised to turn back the perceived excesses of the Cárdenas administration and posed a potentially substantial electoral challenge.[38] The months leading up to the election were characterized by a great deal of uncertainty regarding the extent to which it would be a real competition and pave the way for further multiparty elections.

Summary

This overview of the hundred years preceding the period covered by the case studies provides a striking example of distant countries following remarkably parallel historical trajectories. The contemporaneous character of key events in Mexican and Turkish history resulted in comparable legacies of contentious religion-state interaction and deep secular-religious social cleavages. By the 1940s their secularist establishments were firmly in place, heirs to a reformist legacy stretching through to the early nineteenth century but most directly shaped by violent struggles during the first half of the twentieth. Lay opposition movements had deep roots as well, although they had not yet found a stable organizational form and were recovering from extended periods of conflict and persecution. Clerical authorities, in turn, were severely weakened by persecution and suppression. Despite these historical parallels, changes in electoral institutions and the structure of religious communities would lead to dramatically different patterns of religious mobilization over the next fifty years.

Contemporary Turkey and Mexico

Given these parallel historical trajectories, it is perhaps unsurprising that contemporary Turkey and Mexico share a number of notable contextual similarities in regard to their religious demography, degree of social secularization, level of economic development, and geopolitical situation, all of which are potentially pertinent to the study of religious political mobilization. These similarities, while far from absolute, facilitate constructive engagement with some of the most frequently postulated alternative explanations for patterns of religious mobilization, including religious pluralism, levels of economic development, popular demands for religious politics, and transnational influences. In addition, shared but highly distinctive features of their political environment, most notably the presence of multiparty elections constrained by persistent undemocratic institutions and complex patterns of state secularism, play a major role in the ebb and flow of their religious politics. Through careful preliminary observation we can take into account the impact of these factors when developing the case studies in the following chapters.

Demography and Religious Diversity

A bird's-eye view of Mexico and Turkey's contemporary demographic profiles suggests some similarities. Mexico has a somewhat larger population than Turkey (127 million versus 80 million in 2017), with both countries among the top twenty most populous in the world. They also have very similar literacy rates (94.5 percent and 95.6 percent, respectively) and comparable levels of urbanization (80 percent and 75 percent) and life expectancy (77 and 75). In addition to these contemporaneous similarities, both countries have followed similar trends over the last half century, with their populations, literacy rates, and life expectancies tracking closely during the second half of the twentieth century.[39]

Their patterns of ethnolinguistic fragmentation are somewhat different, but not necessarily in ways that suggest complications for paired comparison. Standard measures describe Mexico as slightly more fragmented than Turkey,[40] even though minorities make up a larger percentage of the Turkish population. The reason is that there are numerous indigenous groups in

Mexico, several of which have more than half a million members. As a whole, speakers of native languages make up slightly less than 10 percent of the population. In contrast, the minority population in Turkey is highly concentrated, with Kurds by far the largest group. Although the number of Kurds in Turkey is disputed, estimates range from ten to twenty million, which makes up roughly between 10 percent and 25 percent of the total population. In both cases, tensions with ethnic minorities—such as the Zapatista insurrection in Mexico and the Kurdistan Workers' Party (PKK) insurgency in Turkey—have figured prominently in national politics, but in neither case do patterns of ethnolinguistic diversity map clearly onto the religious arena.

In terms of religious diversity, both countries are relatively homogeneous. A solid majority of Mexico's population self-identifies as Catholic (~85 percent), despite the recent growth of Pentecostal and Evangelical communities. Some Mexican states, particularly in southern parts of the country, exhibit significantly higher levels of religious pluralism as a result of ongoing Protestant missionary activity. The rise of Protestant competitors is a relatively recent development, and the number of adherents in Mexico has expanded rapidly over the last three decades. For most of the period covered by the case studies, conversions were concentrated among indigenous minorities in the south of the country, long neglected by Catholic authorities and far from the centers of political power. These populations still represent a disproportionate number of alternative Christian denominations compared to their nonindigenous counterparts elsewhere in the country. Areas with high conversion rates have resulted in local conflicts and have encouraged political activism by Catholic leaders.[41] However, during most of the period covered by the case studies the emerging religious communities tended to avoid direct political engagement, a strategy that limited their political influence.

The Turkish population evinces a comparable level of religious pluralism. Although the Ottoman Empire included substantial Christian minorities, these account for less than 1 percent of modern Turkey's population;[42] as a result, the country has an overwhelmingly Muslim majority. However, the Muslim majority is divided between Sunnis, who account for roughly 75 percent to 85 percent of the population, and a significant Shi'a Alevi minority, whose members constitute between 15 percent and 25 percent of the total population.[43] Alevis are present throughout the country, but disproportionately concentrated in east-central Anatolia. Like many other Muslims in Turkey, Alevi Turks have been influenced by Sufi traditions, particularly those associated with the Bektaşi order. Alevis have deep roots in Turkey, but their political salience has varied significantly over time. Both nationalists and Sunni authorities have often treated Alevis as objects of suspicion.[44]

Alevi political activism has manifested itself primarily through support for secularist candidates.

Despite the comparable sizes of Mexico and Turkey, the relationship between majority and minority faiths has taken contrasting paths in the last thirty years. The rapid growth of Protestant denominations in Mexico has been a source of concern for Catholic authorities, but only in the late twentieth century has the absolute number of Protestants become significant beyond a few regional enclaves.[45] The long-standing tensions between Protestants and Catholics in southern Mexico have had important consequences for local politics and affected the mobilizing efforts of individual bishops,[46] but these have not consistently affected the national arena. In the Turkish case, the Sunni-Alevi cleavage is poorly mapped, since the census does not distinguish between the two communities, but there is no sign of significant numbers of conversions from one denomination to the other. The cleavage is nevertheless politically relevant, as it correlates with partisan preferences, and episodes of conflict between Alevis and Sunnis have had tragic consequences, particularly during the early 1990s.[47] Despite these trends, religious politics in both countries have been dominated largely by a secular-religious divide rather than one between members of different faiths.

Religiosity and Secularization

Religiosity is another potentially significant factor shaping the emergence of religious parties. Unfortunately, data on religiosity are not available for much of the period covered in this study; the WVS data cover only the period after 1990. There is no reason to expect that religiosity was lower in Mexico in the past than it has been over the previous twenty years; indeed, it may have been higher in regard to religious attendance. In contrast, it is conceivable that the transnational Islamic revival of the last quarter of the twentieth century has affected Turkey and led to an increase in popular religiosity.[48] However, the declines in religious attendance observed from 1990 to 2007, along with stable numbers in regard to trust in religious communities and belief in their public relevance, suggest that the revival has had a limited impact.

Table 2.2 summarizes polling data from five waves of the WVS between 1990 and 2012. The data present the averages from all the waves in which particular questions were asked. Some, such as attendance, were included in all waves, while others, such as frequency of prayer, were included in only one. Thus, it is somewhat difficult to assess trends over time. However, those indicators for which there is consistent measurement do not indicate major changes in religiosity in either country. Religious attendance in Mexico, for

TABLE 2.2: RELIGIOUS ATTITUDES IN MEXICO AND TURKEY, AVERAGE
SCORES, 1990–2012

	Mexico (%)	Turkey (%)
Attend religious services weekly or more often	47.6	36.0
Pray outside services daily	70.0	80.1
Believe in God	94.8	92.6
Religious person	71.9	77.2
Confidence in churches	73.3	69.3
Religious leaders should not influence votes*	29.9	9.6
Better if more religious people in public office	38.6	47.1
Nonbelievers are unfit for public office	30.7	53.6

Source: World Values Survey data, available at http://www.worldvaluessurvey.org/wvs.jsp.
* Respondents disagreed or strongly disagreed.

example, actually increased from 43.1 percent in 1990 to 56.0 percent in
2000, dropping back to 46.2 percent in 2012. Confidence in churches follows a similar pattern, rising from 76.0 percent in 1990 to a peak of 80.7
percent in 2000 and then dropping to 64.2 percent in 2012. The first five
questions describe religious behaviors and respondents' beliefs and attitudes
toward religious leaders and help us gauge general popular religiosity. The
next three questions inquire specifically about the intersection of religion and
politics and thus bear directly on the viability of religious political mobilization. Unfortunately, these last questions were asked in Mexico only in 2000
and 2005 and in Turkey only in 2001 and 2007.

Measures of religiosity are notoriously imprecise and difficult to compare
across traditions. Given these limitations, answers to the first five questions
in Table 2.2 suggest that overall levels of religiosity in the two countries are
rather similar. Both countries have an overwhelming number of believers and
self-described religious persons. While weekly religious attendance is slightly
higher in Mexico, Turks are somewhat more likely to pray outside religious
services, differences that probably reflect the contrasting ritual practices of
Catholicism and Islam rather than any inherent difference in levels of religiosity. A substantial majority of respondents in Mexico and Turkey have a lot
or quite a lot of confidence in their religious communities. These parallels
suggest that, if aggregate levels of personal religiosity drive religious mobilization, both countries should manifest similar degrees of mobilization.

In contrast, answers to the next three questions in the table show important differences regarding the political implications of religion. Although majorities in both countries objected to religious influence on voting behavior,
almost a third of Mexican respondents disagreed or strongly disagreed with
the idea that this influence is undesirable. In contrast, Turks overwhelm-

ingly and consistently reject this kind of involvement. In contrast, religiosity among politicians is slightly less desirable in Mexico than in Turkey, and Turks are significantly more likely to object to nonbelievers holding public office. The data therefore suggest that, at least since 1990, Mexicans have more pro-clerical political attitudes, while Turks are stronger supporters of lay involvement in politics.

These differences in the relative support for clerical and lay political activism are in many ways at the heart of this book's argument about the effects of religious community structures, and it is highly unfortunate that the surveys cover only the post-1990 era. Civilization-based theories argue that the relative weight of clerical and lay authorities is fixed and built into religious traditions: Catholicism is inherently clerical, while Sunni Islam is not. In contrast, this book argues that the salience of clerical and lay authority is historically contingent, with the level of coordination and mobilizing capacity of each group changing over time. Chapters 3 and 4 thus explore this in significant detail.

Economic Development

Patterns of economic development followed parallel trajectories in Mexico and Turkey during most of the period covered by the case studies. As seen in Figure 2.1, GDP per capita in both countries was virtually identical from 1960, when both had GDP per capita barely above three thousand in constant U.S. dollars (value in the year 2000), until 1975, when both reached nearly five thousand. After that, differences begin to emerge, but they tend to be temporary oscillations: Turkey experienced a recession in the late 1970s, while Mexico did in the early 1980s, and both countries had periods of rapid growth and sharp recession during the 1990s and early 2000s. Starting in the mid-2000s, however, the Turkish economy grew rapidly (with a sharp contraction associated with the 2008 global financial crisis), while Mexico grew much more sluggishly (and experienced the same contraction). As a result, Turkey was substantially wealthier by 2017, with a GDP per capita of nearly fifteen thousand U.S. dollars compared to nearly ten thousand in Mexico.

The strikingly parallel trajectories until the mid-2000s were driven by fundamentally similar processes. Mexico and Turkey remained largely agrarian societies into the early twentieth century, when postrevolutionary state builders became active in promoting rapid industrialization. Statist models of development called for public-sector investment in infrastructure and industry, a process that in effect channeled resources away from the countryside and toward growing urban centers. In addition, state-led modernization

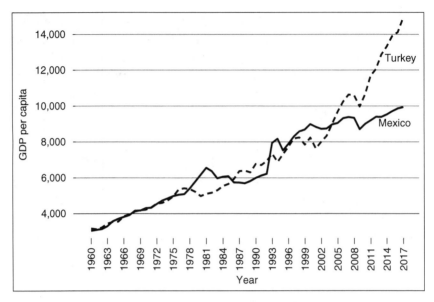

Figure 2.1 GDP per capita in Mexico and Turkey, 1960–2017 (constant 2000 U.S. dollars). (*Source: World Bank 2019.*)

radically expanded the resources available to governments and created large public sectors, which became crucial sources of support for de facto single-party states.[49]

The late 1940s and 1950s were a period of sustained growth. Both countries moved away from the more assertive statism of the interwar era, allowing for the gradual expansion of a private sector that nonetheless retained a substantial public sector and strong regulatory bureaucracies. The countryside, large swaths of which had remained beyond the scope of earlier developmental projects, was increasingly transformed by its interaction with international markets. In the 1970s the oil embargo and the subsequent spike in oil prices affected the countries differently. Turkey, as a net importer, was adversely affected, while Mexico, a net exporter, received a sudden windfall. However, both countries relied on foreign debt to finance mounting expenditures. The debt crisis then struck both countries in the early 1980s, prompting drastic shifts toward liberalization and a sharp reduction of the public sector.

Sudden economic liberalization led to significant social dislocation and protests but eventually gave way to sustained, if uneven, economic growth starting in the mid-1980s. In the mid-1990s both countries once again experienced sharp recessions characterized by sudden devaluations and reductions in middle-class living standards. Mexico recovered promptly from the peso crisis, with new growth facilitated by its entry into the North American Free

Trade Agreement (NAFTA) and the dramatic expansion of its trade with the United States. In contrast, Turkey limped out of the recession and entered another in 2001, driven in part by persistent deficit spending and failure to meet the demands of international lenders. However, by 2003 both Turkey and Mexico were experiencing economic growth, with the former expanding faster than the latter. By 2008 the countries had nearly identical per capita GDP, driven by export-oriented manufacturing and a liberalized economic arena. As noted, Mexico's growth stalled amid a worsening security environment, while Turkey continued along a clear upward trajectory. It bears repeating, however, that the current distinction is of very recent vintage.

In regard to the arguments that this book advances, the process of economic development, especially the subsequent liberalizing economic reforms, had a powerful impact on the resources available for nonstate collective action. The limitations of state-led development schemes associated with secular establishments contributed to the success of religious mobilizers. Perhaps more important, the growth of private-sector businesses created pools of resources that many groups, including religious activists and political entrepreneurs, could draw on in their struggles against authorities entrenched in bureaucracies and ruling parties.

Geopolitical Context

Turkey and Mexico have both been deeply shaped by their proximity to global powers based in Europe and North America. Their influence has been felt in a variety of ways, as geographic proximity first made Turkey and Mexico the targets of expansionist policies and then facilitated their increasing participation in international trade. Overall, there is a striking similarity in the countries' interactions with their powerful neighbors, which have ranged from conflict and competition-driven modernization in the nineteenth and early twentieth centuries, through anticommunist cooperation during the Cold War, to growing economic and institutional integration in the post–Cold War period. These trends have had similar impacts on religious communities in the two countries.

Early encounters were often devastating and played a prominent role in processes of state formation. The Mexican-American War of 1846–1848 cost Mexico virtually half its territory, and victors of World War I dismembered the Ottoman Empire. These episodes triggered efforts to strengthen the state through dramatic reforms, many of which aimed to replicate institutions and policies used by global powers. However, the conflicts also provided ample material for crafting anti-Western nationalist doctrines. Many of these were adopted by religious leaders and activists, who emphasized the religious differences between their countries and those of their antagonists and urged resistance to Western-style state-building reforms. This early nationalist-religious convergence thus became a prominent characteristic of reactionary movements during the state-formation period in the late nineteenth and early twentieth centuries. As late as World War II, significant sectors of each country displayed pro-German sentiments, largely a result of their suspicions of the Allied powers.

The Cold War dramatically reversed these trends. Despite historic antagonisms and flirtations with socialism in the 1930s, both countries aligned themselves with the Western bloc against a perceived communist threat, though they did so in different ways. While Mexican governments repeatedly spoke against communism and persecuted communist sympathizers domestically, they resisted developing closer military ties to the United States and sought to avoid entanglement in foreign wars. In contrast, Turkey embraced Western powers and joined the North Atlantic Treaty Organization (NATO) in 1952, becoming a key part of the alliance's eastern border. Despite these differences, in both countries government fears of leftist subversion became a prominent feature of national politics. This had direct consequences for state-religion relations, as the anticommunist struggle encouraged cooperation between state and religious authorities. Many state representatives saw religion as a useful antidote to atheistic Marxism. In turn, religious leaders gradually overcame their distrust of the modern state, increasingly seeing it as an important bulwark against left-wing revolutionaries. However, this cooperation remained asymmetrical, with state authorities retaining a dominant position and setting explicit and implicit limits to autonomous religious intervention in the political arena.

The post–Cold War era brought yet another international configuration with parallel consequences for the two countries. Rapidly expanding international trade fostered closer links between Turkey and Europe and between Mexico and the United States. Already-established patterns of migration to the United States and Europe sustained enormous expatriate communities and generated substantial flows of remittances. In both countries, growing economic integration was given a solid institutional foundation during the mid-1990s. In January 1994 Mexico became part of NAFTA, leading to dramatically greater levels of trade with its northern neighbor. By 2010 the United States took in 74 percent of Mexican exports and provided 61 percent of its imports. Nativist posturing during the 2016 election in the United States generated some friction but did not immediately alter the reality of growing economic integration. The relationship between Turkey and Europe has been comparably dramatic. Turkey established a Customs Union agreement with the European Union (EU) in December 1995. By 2010 trade with the EU represented 46 percent of total Turkish exports and 39 percent of its imports. Turkey became an official candidate for EU membership in 1999 and assertively sought to achieve membership during the early 2000s.[50] The process proved difficult because of numerous objections from various EU member states; it had largely stalled by the end of that decade and had collapsed by 2017.[51] Nevertheless, it had an impact on Turkey's religious politics—for example, by fostering an environment conducive to the enhancement of the Christian minority's rights.[52]

Thus, despite recent negative trends, a prolonged period of constructive international engagement eroded the traditional xenophobic postures of religious actors, many of whom cautiously embraced globalization and closer relationships with Europe and the United States.[53] In both cases, political parties that historically engaged in religious mobilization frequently became the chief supporters of ongoing economic integration and international cooperation in ways that often improved the rights of religious minorities.

Regime Type

The political institutions that have governed Mexico and Turkey since the mid-twentieth century produced flawed electoral regimes that can be described in similar terms. At the same time, the two countries have had very distinct experiences with democracy and democratization. While Turkey transitioned rapidly to multiparty competition in 1946, Mexico moved much more gradually and entered plausibly democratic terrain only in the early 1990s. Moreover, while Mexico's liberalization has been continuous and monotonic, Turkey experienced several reversals, mostly via military coups followed by relatively rapid restoration of civil governments, and a dramatic and sustained decline starting in 2014. These contrasting regime trajectories are described in Figure 2.2, which presents both countries' regime scores as described by the Polity V project.

Despite their many differences, both regimes remained rigorously committed to holding periodic elections, the results of which determined the distribution of power in the legislature and the executive branches of government. Until the 1990s elites in Mexico manipulated competition to shape outcomes before elections took place, ensuring their continuity in power, while Turkish elites relied on the presence of reserved domains of power to guarantee that elected governments did not pursue policies that went against their interests.

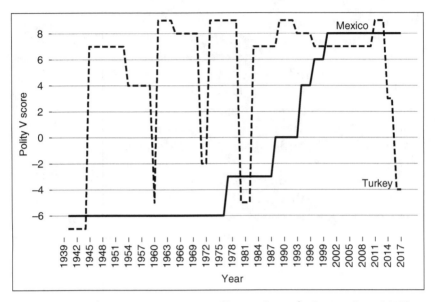

Figure 2.2 Polity V scores, 1939–2017. (*Source: Center for Systemic Peace 2018.*)
Note: The Turkey score is modified to account for the 1960 coup.

Even though the single-party Kemalist regime came to an end in 1946–1950, the electoral transition was not matched by an equally important restructuring of the state apparatus, particularly the military, which retained substantial independence from the elected government. These sectors acted as veto holders over policy decisions. Although this role was informal during the first decade after the transitions, the 1960 coup and the new constitution that emerged from it enshrined the role of the military as a guardian of Atatürk's legacy and the Turkish nation. Since then, Turkish governments have had to operate with the military openly looking over their shoulders and demonstrably willing to intervene when civilian authority was deemed to have failed in its governing role. With the notable exception of the post-2014 period, the democratic troughs visible in the Turkey series in Figure 2.2 represent episodes of direct military intervention. More important, the peaks that identify the intervals of civilian rule should be qualified by the presence of powerful reserved domains that operated beyond government oversight.

The limits of democratic institutions in Mexico were far more visible during much of this period. In contrast to the Turkish case, the inauguration of multiparty competition in 1939 did not lead to alternations in power. The ruling party continued to use its dramatic resource advantage, as well as more direct forms of manipulation and intimidation when necessary, to maintain its grip on the vast majority of elected offices. However, multiparty elections were held continuously throughout the following six decades, and opposition parties always occupied a small number of seats in the legislatures and had a relatively free hand in the electoral strategies they could pursue. Another key to the success of the ruling party was its commitment to nonreelection, which prevented individuals from becoming entrenched in office and allowed the party to circulate resources, accommodate rising politicians, and prevent internal schisms. Thus, Mexico in many ways pioneered the institutions and mechanisms of hegemonic electoral authoritarianism. When the resources available to the state began to decline as a consequence of liberalizing policies during the 1980s, the electoral system became gradually more competitive, culminating with the handover of the presidency in 2000 to an opposition party that had pursued it for more than sixty years.[54] Since then, and despite its shortcomings, Mexico's regime has remained persistently democratic by conventional standards.

Both Mexico and Turkey held multiparty elections regularly throughout the second half of the twentieth century, but their claims to democratic status were undermined by a variety of formal and informal political arrangements. The restrictions applied in each country were clearly different: reserved domains of power in Turkey and a heavily tilted electoral playing field in Mexico. The case studies in Chapters 3 and 4 therefore take these differences into account when examining patterns of religious mobilization.

Regulation of Religion

A final important point of comparison between Mexico and Turkey derives from their patterns of state regulation of religion. During most of the period covered by the cases studies, both countries formally maintained what Ahmet Kuru calls assertive secularism, a situation in which states seek to exclude religion from the public sphere.[55] Until the late 1990s, leading politicians in Mexico and Turkey recurrently presented themselves as guardians of the secular state, advocating and personifying a privatized form of religiosity. Yet the specific institutions that structured this exclusion, as well as their mode of implementation, varied substantially between countries as well as over time.

The Mexican Constitution of 1917 contained powerful language that deprived religious communities of any corporate identity and required direct state supervision of all public religious activities. As noted previously, efforts by anticlerical politicians to enforce these articles met with stiff and often violent resistance from the Catholic Church and lay activists. In particular, the Cristero War (1926–1929) made clear to both sides the costs of continuing aggression. Attempts to enforce the most draconian provisions were abandoned after the 1930s, but the articles remained in place until 1992. In addition to leaving churches without legal standing, these articles deprived religious officials of the right to vote or stand for office, banned religious orders, and severely restricted religious influence in education and the media. The presence of these articles kept churches operating in a legal vacuum and vulnerable to pressure from local, state, and national authorities. The 1992 reforms did away with some of the most severe but less frequently implemented provisions while leaving in place a more limited number of less intrusive but more effectively implemented restrictions.

The Turkish case is also rich in ambivalences. The three Turkish constitutions have consistently enshrined secularism as a guiding principle of the state and established severe penalties for any group seeking to undermine it or providing support to those who do. Atatürk repeatedly modified the Constitution of 1924 and put in place a series of secularist policies governing everything from appropriate headgear to civil marriage. Some of the most severe restrictions were abandoned in the late 1940s—for example, by allowing the use of Arabic in the call to prayer and permitting some forms of religious education—but the Constitutions of 1961 and 1982 retained a formal commitment to Atatürk's vision of secularism. Thus, according to Article 14, basic rights cannot be exercised in ways that threaten the secular character of the republic, and Article 68 requires all political parties to commit to upholding secularism. Article 174 prohibits any modification of Atatürk's reform laws, but conflicts over these provisions, particularly those regulating the use of headscarves, continue to shape Turkish politics. Moreover, Turkish governments have increasingly incorporated Sunni Muslim identity as part of their legitimizing strategies, most famously through the articulation of the Turkish-Islamic Synthesis doctrine following the 1980 coup.[56]

Translating these complex institutional realities and histories into standardized indicators of state regulation of religion is a difficult and inevitably contentious task. Nevertheless, scholarly attempts to generate standardized measures of state regulation of religion consistently yield similar scores for both countries. Jonathan Fox's Religion and State (RAS) data set, arguably the most ambitious effort to fully describe global patterns of state regulation of religion, notes these similarities. For 1991, the year prior to implementation of liberalizing reforms in Mexico, the RAS assigns Turkey a score of 41 and Mexico a 39 for the additive index of state regulation of the majority religion.[57] After 1992 the score for Mexico drops to 19, indicating a substantial liberalization while maintaining the country as the most restrictive in Latin America after Cuba. Describing the situation in the twenty-first century, Brian Grim and Roger Finke's Government Regulation of Religion Index gives Mexico a 3.1/10 and Turkey a 5.1/10, scores that are highly comparable to those produced by the RAS.[58]

While both countries engage in substantial regulation of religion, there are notable differences in their specific institutions and policies that bear directly on patterns of religious mobilization. In Mexico, the Catholic Church lacked any formal legal recognition and Catholic education was severely hampered until 1992. In contrast, the Turkish state has adopted a variety of policies intended to ensure that its preferred vision of Islam is actively promoted among Turkish Muslims, to the point that a recent study describes it as regime of "religious majoritarianism" rather than a conventional secular state.[59] Thus, all legally sanctioned religious officials are employees of the Diyanet, which manages all mosques, hires all preachers, runs pilgrimages, and monitors religious education, among other powers.[60] Among this bureaucracy's core tasks is ensuring that Turks are educated regarding the true nature of Islam, giving the state a prominent role in shaping religious orthodoxy. Moreover, by the 1980s the Turkish government had come full circle from its restrictions on religious education and made it mandatory for all Muslims in public schools.

These endorsements by the Turkish state have been as much about state control over religion as about supporting a particular religious community.[61] In promoting its interpretation of Islam, the state repeatedly purged its bureaucracies and armed forces of suspected Islamist activists and repeatedly shut down religious organizations with agendas perceived as incompatible with its own notions of Islam and secularism. These forms of repression and regulation have been far less prominent in Mexico, where officials have generally limited themselves to vocal criticisms of religious authorities, particularly when they were seen to overstep their authority by opining about social, economic, or political affairs. In this sense, assertive secularism has taken a different form in each of these countries, though neither has been friendly to religious mobilization by nonstate actors.

Summary

The parallels between Mexico and Turkey in their level of religious pluralism, secularization, economic development, and geopolitical situation, as well as their comparable albeit distinctive regime types and modes of state regulation of religion, facilitate structured comparison. Despite the great distances that separate these two countries and the lack of sustained contact between them, their shared features enable both iterated congruence testing and parallel process tracing.

These similarities do not mean that these factors are in any sense controlled for or can be safely ignored. Indeed, there are important differences
between the two countries. Both have similar levels of religious pluralism,
for example, but minorities in Mexico have emerged only recently and experienced dramatic growth in the last two decades, while those in Turkey have
remained stable throughout the entire period covered by this study. Similar
levels of personal religiosity and trust in religious authorities coexist with
clear differences in attitudes toward clerical and lay political involvement.
In terms of political institutions, while both countries have combined multiparty elections with constraints on democratic outcomes, these restrictions
have taken notably different institutional forms. Both countries engaged in
substantial restrictions on dominant religions, but Turkey developed a far
more robust apparatus for governing the provision of religious services. These
differences play a central part in the arguments presented in this book, and
remaining alert to them is crucial to a proper understanding of the cases.

Conclusion

This chapter provides the necessary methodological and empirical background for a constructive comparative analysis of Mexico and Turkey. The
first section discusses the theory-oriented goals of the case studies and the
specific qualitative methods used to attain them. The second examines
the historical trajectory leading up to the period covered by the case studies,
describing the striking parallels between Mexico and Turkey and introducing key actors and historical trends that remained relevant after the inauguration of multiparty competition. The third covers the criteria for case selection, examining the similarities and differences between the cases along
several dimensions associated with potential alternative explanations. The
purpose of this effort is to provide a well-defined background against which
the relationship between political institutions, community structures, and
religious mobilization strategies can be highlighted. We now turn to the case
studies.

3

The Emergence and Transformation
of Religious Political Mobilization in Mexico

Devout Catholics fueled electoral opposition in Mexico during much of the twentieth century, but the style and intensity of their political engagement varied substantially over time. The ebb and flow of Catholic political mobilization can be illustrated by the trajectory of José González Torres, a conservative Catholic intellectual with an illustrious leadership record in confessional associations. Over his lifetime he was national president of the Asociación Católica de la Juventud Mexicana (ACJM), general secretary of the Unión Nacional de Padres de Familia (UNPF; National Union of Parents), president of the professional branch of Acción Católica Mexicana (ACM; Mexican Catholic Action), and president of Pax Romana, the international Catholic university.[1] González Torres joined the Partido Acción Nacional (PAN) in 1941 and rose through its ranks to become party president in 1959. He held the post for three years, marking the high tide of doctrinal Catholic influence within the party. A power struggle within the PAN resulted in his loss of the position in 1962, but, partly in compensation, he was selected as the party's presidential candidate in 1964. After reaching these heights, his influence, and that of his faction, fell into a steady decline. For decades, those who advocated for more explicit engagement with Catholicism lost internal debates to pragmatic liberals and ambitious neophytes. González Torres finally left the party in 1990, joining the much smaller and more stridently conservative Partido Demócrata Mexicano (PDM; Mexican Democratic Party). The PDM had performed unexpectedly well in the early 1980s but failed to maintain its momentum after 1988. Despite the support of disaffected PAN cadres, including that of González Torres, the PDM collapsed and disappeared in the mid-1990s. González Torres died in 1998 and never saw the PAN capture the Mexican presidency at the turn of the century.

The political career of González Torres highlights many distinctive features of Catholic partisan engagement in Mexico in general and in the PAN in particular. Persistent but often marginalized, Catholic activists typically entered electoral politics through alliances with other forces but occasionally attempted to organize their own political vehicles. Their favored party was the PAN, which contested virtually all national elections after its founding in 1939. Indeed, for the first four decades of its existence, the PAN was able to capture only a handful of legislative seats. Its ability to endure this long period on the margins of politics was in no small part a consequence of its ties to religion: Catholic identity underpinned much of its early appeal, Catholic doctrines served to legitimize its proposals and socialize its cadres, and Catholic associations provided critical resources.[2] Yet ties to religion were not always a boon for the PAN. Many of the most difficult moments faced by the party—particularly schisms that cost it prominent leaders and electoral opportunities—were also partly shaped by debates over its identity, doctrine, and ties to religious groups.

As the final stages of González Torres's career highlight, the PAN was not the only possible path for Catholic partisan engagement. Devout political activists who could not, or would not, work within the PAN sometimes organized their own electoral vehicles. The PDM and, some decades earlier, the Partido Fuerza Popular (PFP; People's Strength Party), an organization intimately linked to the reactionary Unión Nacional Sinarquista (UNS; Sinarquista National Union), sought to channel the energy of Catholic opposition in more assertive ways. Despite some temporary and local successes, these smaller parties failed to find secure electoral footing and ultimately collapsed.

Finally, the trajectory of González Torres also confirms that while the broad trend has been away from assertive religious mobilization, the path has not been smooth or uncontested. From the 1940s until the 1960s the PAN edged toward an explicitly confessional identity, maintained close ties to Catholic associations, and drew heavily on Catholic doctrine to shape its programs. At the same time, the smaller PFP pursued full-fledged assertive religious mobilization. By the late 1960s the PAN had weakened its ties to religious associations and reduced the salience of its doctrinal appeals, while the PFP had effectively disappeared. Over the next two decades the PAN continued to draw selectively on religious doctrine and increasingly depended on the devout reputations of its candidates and its good relations with the

Catholic hierarchy to appeal to religious voters. The PDM emerged in 1979 to capture the votes of disaffected conservative Catholics who had been previously mobilized by the PFP and the UNS; but after an auspicious beginning these groups suffered a series of defeats and collapsed in the 1990s. During that decade, the PAN became a powerful electoral competitor in part by sidelining its religious doctrine and ties to confessional associations while its candidates appealed to Catholic voters on the basis of shared personal beliefs, a strategy exemplified by Vicente Fox's successful presidential campaign.

Why was religious political mobilization in Mexico more salient during some periods than others? In this chapter, I show how political entrepreneurs tied to the PAN and other parties mobilized religion and why their efforts to mobilize religion varied over time. I argue that the evolution of religious mobilization strategies responded to changes in Mexico's political institutions—ranging from its electoral laws to its regulation of religion—as well as its Catholic community structure, specifically the growing capacity and coordination of bishops at a national level, alongside an increasingly vibrant but fragmented lay associational sphere. Each of the three sections in this chapter focuses on a specific historical period punctuated by major changes in Mexico's political and religious environment. Table 3.1 describes the periods by noting the key religious parties operating at the time, the main features of the religious community structure, the most notable political institutions governing elections and religion-state relations, and the level of religious mobilization by each relevant political party.

The first section covers the period from the founding of the PAN in 1939 to 1961. In terms of religious community structure it begins before the inauguration of the Second Vatican Council, when the lay Catholic community centered on the hierarchy-sponsored ACM, with the UNS as its temporary rival. Political institutions reflected the single-party hegemony of the PRI, sustained in part by a restrictive single-member plurality electoral system, and the modus vivendi, a pattern of informal tolerance and accommodation between state and Catholic authorities. The next section covers the period from 1962 to 1979, which is characterized by the growing organizational capacity of bishops and the fragmentation of the lay organizational arena once dominated by Catholic Action. In terms of political institutions, electoral reforms created more space for opposition parties but did not challenge PRI hegemony, and the informal accommodation between church and state endured despite some notable challenges. The period ends with a major electoral reform and Pope John Paul II's first visit to Mexico. These events set the stage for examination of the final period, the decades from 1979 to 2000, which is marked by gradual democratization, the formalization and liberalization

TABLE 3.1: RELIGIOUS POLITICAL MOBILIZATION BY OPPOSITION
PARTIES IN MEXICO, 1939–2000

Period	Parties	Religious community structures	Political institutions	Level of mobilization
1939–1961	PAN PFP-UNS	• Limited capacity for collective action by clergy • Height of ACM • Rise and decline of UNS	• Single-party hegemony • SMP elections, no compensation • Modus vivendi, informal tolerance between church and state	PAN: High PFP-UNS: High
1962–1978	PAN	• Reorganization of Bishop's Conference • Decline of Catholic Action • Rise of progressive associations	• Single-party hegemony • SMP with weak compensation • Informal tolerance between church and state	PAN: Medium
1979–2000	PAN PDM	• Consolidation of Bishop's Conference • Decline of progressive associations • Rise of conservative associations	• Gradual democratization • Mixed electoral system with PR component, improvement in electoral monitoring • Constitutional reforms formalizing religion-state relations	PAN: Low PDM: High

of religion-state relations, and the growing effectiveness of the clerical hierarchy within an increasingly plural Catholic community. During this time the rapid rise and decline of the PDM contrasts with the mounting electoral victories of the PAN, with the latter's capture of the executive branch marking the end of political Catholicism's long trajectory in opposition.

Each of the three empirical sections begins with a brief outline, followed by a discussion of the structural properties of the Catholic community and the political institutions that governed religious political engagement during that period. It then proceeds to analyze how structural and institutional features encouraged or discouraged particular forms of religious mobilization by the PAN and other religious political parties, while noting how these causal factors interacted with other variables such as changing economic conditions and growing religious diversity. The concluding section provides an overview of the findings from the Mexican case. It highlights the consistent correspondence between the strategies adopted by party leaders and the structures and institutions that constrained them. It closes by considering broader temporal dynamics, including the different paces of change produced by structural and institutional shifts and the way that misalignments between them can produce partisan crises with significant consequences for religious political mobilization.

Emergence and Crisis of Assertive Religious Mobilization (1939–1961)

The 1940s and 1950s in many ways marked the peak of assertive religious mobilization in Mexican politics. During this time, two important political organizations mobilized religion: the PAN and the UNS-PFP. The PAN was formed in 1939 as a coalition of liberal and Catholic political entrepreneurs who saw in the crisis of the late Cárdenas presidency an opportunity to redirect the energies of the revolution in a more conservative direction.[3] The first generation of Panistas, as its members are often called, displayed important differences over the proper role of Catholicism in the party and its efforts to mobilize voters.[4] Over its first decade the party increasingly relied on religious mobilization, driven by the growing influence of Catholic activists. By the early 1950s the party was largely driven by its Catholic faction, with its members wielding significant influence throughout the organization.

In contrast to the PAN, which was always organized as a political party, the UNS emerged as a mass movement. At its height it had hundreds of thousands of members and was capable of organizing mass demonstrations that effectively took over towns and cities in central Mexico.[5] Moreover, the UNS had little doubt about the role of religion in its mobilization strategies, and it appealed openly and directly to highly conservative versions of Catholic identity and social doctrine.[6] However, the translation of this movement's energy into the electoral arena proved a difficult and contentious task.[7] Its main electoral vehicle at that time, the PFP, was never able to gain a substantial portion of the vote, and by the 1950s the UNS-PFP movement had been effectively driven from national politics and reduced to a regional player with little electoral influence.

To explain these outcomes, one must analyze the structure of Mexico's Catholic community and the rules that governed political competition. Both the temporary dominance of religious factions in the PAN and the failure of the more openly religious UNS-PFP resulted from the combination of highly restrictive political institutions and well-coordinated lay associations during the 1940s and 1950s. The high level of coordination found among the laity and the relative passivity of the clerical hierarchy, a legacy of active confrontation with the state during the 1920s and 1930s, encouraged religious activism among Catholics. Lay associations produced activists eager to mobilize Catholic identity and doctrine in the political arena. At the same time, the highly restrictive electoral arena made it impossible for niche parties such as the UNS-PFP to gain a foothold in the elections, in part by encouraging religious-opposition voters to coordinate around the larger PAN. At the same time, the failure to gain significant numbers of seats also limited the attractiveness of the PAN, depriving it of support among pragmatists whose primary goal was obtaining places in the legislature. As a result of this combination of institutional and structural factors, the energies of Catholic activists increasingly operated as a lifeline for the PAN, while the UNS-PFP withered.

Religious Community Structures and Political Institutions

By 1939, the year the PAN was founded, decades of Catholic activism and resistance in Mexico had produced a broad range of confessional associations, varying dramatically in size, geographic scope, formality, and primary constituencies.[8] Above these stood the clerical hierarchy, which despite the conflicts and crises of the previous three decades retained its formal leadership over the religious community. However, it was severely weakened by decades of conflict with the state and suffered from chronic shortages of personnel. Into the vacuum left by its weakness stepped in lay associations, which can be broadly classified into three main types: the mainstream associations tied to the national branch of Catholic Action, ACM; the formal associations that remained outside the mainstream framework, such as the Unión Nacional de Estudiantes Mexicanos (UNEC; National Union of Mexican Students); and the informal groups that operated in the rural center of the country, such as the UNS. Each of these had a distinct profile, geographic base, and broadly different views regarding the appropriate role of religion in Mexican politics. Moreover, they tended to align themselves differently in the political arena. The hierarchy did not officially endorse any political party, but some individual bishops and priests encouraged and supported the conservative opposition. Formal, urban associations also tended to support the PAN, while informal, rural ones supported the UNS-PFP. Consequently, gradual changes to their coherence and influence played a central role in shaping religious mobilization.

During the 1940s and 1950s, Mexican bishops operated with little formal organization and thus exhibited a very limited capacity for collective action.[9]

Insofar as they had a coherent agenda, bishops focused primarily on securing and maintaining a tolerable mutual accommodation with the state, replenishing clerical ranks dramatically depleted by decades of violence, and consolidating their influence over the laity.[10] The first goal was achieved through the ongoing modus vivendi with the government of President Ávila Camacho, which left anticlerical laws unenforced in exchange for the clerical hierarchy's abstention from political activism. In this context of cautious adjustment and accommodation, many members of the hierarchy went further and succeeded in developing a functional relationship with sectors of the ruling party.[11] This situation allowed the church to recruit new priests and reactivate parishes that had lain dormant for years because of the lack of clergy. More tenuously, it facilitated reinvestment in religious education, particularly through the creation of independent religious schools.

While the modus vivendi and costly conflicts of the postrevolutionary period left the clergy with few options to intervene in politics, the same could not be said for the laity. In the eyes of many lay Catholic activists the modus vivendi was a shameful institution that sustained the illegitimate oppression of Catholicism by a radical secularist clique. Even among those who accepted the importance of rebuilding the resources of the organized church, many felt that it was incumbent on lay Catholics to represent its interests during this period of temporary incapacity. As part of its efforts to prevent this discontent from having potentially destabilizing political consequences, the hierarchy found it necessary to encourage the transformation of the lay associational sphere into a coherent bloc that it could monitor and direct. Its successes and failures in this regard played a central role in shaping the broader Catholic community structure.

The first set of lay associations was composed of groups that the bishops effectively incorporated into the Catholic Action framework. Catholic Action, which was actively promoted by the Vatican under Pope Pius XI (1922–1939), sought to incorporate the laity into encompassing mass organizations that would facilitate social and political engagement while assuring its obedience to the clerical hierarchy. Many of the Mexican organizations brought under its umbrella could trace their roots back to the final years of the Porfiriato, and not a few of their members had directly or indirectly supported the Cristero War of 1926–1929.[12] The devastation caused by that conflict provided the initial impetus for the hierarchy's efforts to reorganize and consolidate lay associations. As early as 1929 it promoted the coordination of lay associations under ACM. Among those groups that were successfully integrated was the ACJM, a youth organization dating back to 1912 that had trained many leading activists and played a particularly prominent role in supporting the Cristeros.[13] In addition, numerous women's and workers' groups formed in the corporatist spirit of Leo XIII's *Rerum Novarum* (1893) found themselves under increasingly explicit clerical direction, which often entailed substantial ideological shifts and internal reorganization.

The process of incorporation was gradual, but by 1939 only a few formal, urban organizations remained outside this centralized framework. Among the most influential of these was the UNEC, founded in 1931, which organized university students and was more progressive and less hostile to the principles of the Mexican Revolution.[14] Under the sponsorship and protection of influential Jesuit priests, it retained a degree of autonomy that granted it greater doctrinal flexibility than many of its counterparts. This allowed it to play a more salient role in the establishment of the PAN in 1939, when the religious character of the party was still contested. The UNEC was consistently under pressure to integrate into the encompassing ACM framework and was eventually brought under its umbrella in 1949. Many of the PAN's founders came from the UNEC,[15] and during the 1940s and 1950s the party recruited heavily from the ACM and its affiliates, which enjoyed a substantial presence across much of the country.

Informal and rural organizations proved more difficult to incorporate, particularly those operating in the heartland of the Cristero War, the Bajío region, which included the populous states of Jalisco, Guanajuato, Michoacán, and Querétaro. Many of these groups engaged in guerrilla operations against the government throughout the 1930s and maintained a secretive cell structure that made them resistant to formal incorporation. Once again Jesuits forged links where the hierarchy could not, and their efforts to reorganize these quasi-insurgent groups and redirect them toward civic-social activism made some progress in the mid-1930s. However, they remained only indirectly linked to the hierarchy. Their openly antiregime profile and ties to armed groups made explicit incorporation under ACM, or even the establishment of open ties to the church hierarchy, impossible. These groups provided the foundations for the UNS, which was formed in 1937 as a way of facilitating coordination, creating a unified lay leadership, and giving the church hierarchy a measure of influence over their activities. The UNS thus stood out as a significant outlier in the broader schema of religious organization in Mexico, one that became increasingly troublesome for the hierarchy as it expanded exponentially and became more outspoken about political engagement. The PFP, as the political branch of the UNS, drew the overwhelming majority of its voters from the politically engaged factions of this movement. Yet the institutional constraints imposed by electoral rules directly affected the electoral consequences of these structural features.

Mexico's political institutions posed a number of serious challenges to religious participation in the electoral arena. For example, until 1945 the responsibility for running and supervising elections was solely in the hands of municipal authorities,[16] with little or no supervision of their activities. This created enormous opportunities for fraud at all stages of the electoral process, since governing party candidates often forged alliances with local officials.

The advantages of establishment candidates were enhanced by the substantial capacity of the ruling party. President Calles's efforts to consolidate the revolutionary cadres into a single dominant party, founded in 1928 as the Partido Nacional Revolucionario (PNR), combined with President Cárdenas's transformation of the organization into a mass corporatist one that included branches for peasants and workers, had made the ruling party into an extraordinarily effective electoral machine. Renamed the Partido de la Revolución Mexicana (PRM) by Cárdenas, it proved able to hold together a broad ruling coalition and mobilize voters with great effectiveness across the entire national territory. A rigid no-reelection rule facilitated the rotation of party cadres and hindered the entrenchment of local power holders by making long-term political careers contingent on the support of the party leadership, thus reducing the likelihood of significant within-party splits.

These already-imposing barriers to successful political opposition were made more severe by the electoral institutions that governed competition. The electoral system consisted of single-member plurality (SMP) elections, long favored by dominant parties for the difficulties it poses for resource-poor opponents.[17] In Mexico during the 1940s the consequences were doubly severe; to win seats, opponents had to defeat the candidates of a powerful and organized ruling party, in districts where the latter maintained strong ties to nonindependent electoral monitors. The system thus forced underfunded parties such as the PAN to engage in asymmetrical competition with powerful local candidates, which it could hope only to contest rather than win in a very select number of districts in which its supporters were clearly clustered.

A small, first step toward greater electoral competitiveness took place in 1945, when an electoral reform law appeared to breathe new life into the opposition. In a bid to gain some control over local politics and prevent the more transparent forms of electoral fraud that tarnished its image in 1943,[18] the PRM-dominated legislature modified elections in two crucial ways. First, it placed responsibility for elections in the hands of the federal government, depriving municipal authorities of their control over the process. Second, it formalized the requirements for party registration, eliminating local organizations and demanding that parties establish a substantial nationwide presence to participate in elections. Specifically, it required that, to register, parties must have at least thirty thousand members distributed across two-thirds of Mexican states.[19]

These changes did not go as far as those the PAN and other opposition groups had been advocating, which included the establishment of an autonomous electoral oversight body and the move to proportional representation.[20] Nevertheless, they temporarily strengthened the PAN, which saw the new federal oversight as an improvement over the absolute discretion of local authorities. Moreover, as the second electoral force in the country, the PAN became a natural focal point for opposition consolidation. Even the UNS initially benefited from the change, which allowed its pro-participation faction to initiate proceedings to organize the PFP. However, these reforms ultimately failed to provide a sustainable basis for electoral competition. The PAN soon saw its expectations of increased prominence corrected by the enduring advantages of the governing party, since 1946 renamed the Partido Revolucionario Institucional (PRI; Institutional Revolutionary Party). The PFP faced an even more disappointing debacle and lost its registration in 1948. The specific consequences of political institutions and religious community structures were mediated by the strategies adopted by party leaders and the tensions these generated within their organizations.

Patterns of Religious Mobilization

The combination of a fractured but lively associational environment, a tentative and delicate accommodation between church hierarchy and state, and restrictive electoral institutions had a direct impact on patterns of religious mobilization by the PAN and the UNS-PFP. The PAN was empowered by the nationwide network of formal Catholic associations, on which it came to depend for support once it became clear that, despite its position as Mexico's second-largest party, political institutions would keep offices scarce. As this reliance grew, the PAN deepened its informal ties to Catholic Action, maintained a doctrine that emphasized its Catholic roots, and gradually moved toward more explicit appeals to Catholic identity. The PFP in turn was weighed down by its dependence on the UNS, a movement with limited appeal beyond its regional base and a poor relationship with the Catholic hierarchy. Given these impediments to the development of broader support among either mainstream voters or other Catholic activists, the PFP leadership was forced to constantly remobilize its core constituency by emphasizing its Catholic identity and adherence to reactionary versions of Catholic social doctrine, adopting a strident tone that made it virtually impossible to capture elected offices.

The trajectory of the PAN from 1939 to 1961 was characterized by the growing influence of Catholic activists at the expense of liberals and pragmatists. The PAN began as a broad coalition of all three groups, united by their opposition to President Cárdenas and held together by the political savvy of the founder of the PAN, Manuel Gómez Morin, who had an extensive personal network linking him to many of the regime's most significant opponents.[21] The founding coalition included Catholic students and activists who had fought with him against the project of socialist education, middle- and upper-class professionals who resented the president's moves toward socialism, and politicians of various stripes who had been marginalized by the administration.[22]

The leading voice among this first generation of religious Panistas was Efraín González Luna. He provided Gómez Morin with a powerful political ideology that complemented Gómez Morin's commitment to producing an intellectually rooted, coherent alternative to Cárdenas and his socialist project.[23] For the first years of the party's existence, González Luna and his supporters viewed electoral participation with suspicion, advocating instead an extra-electoral focus on capacity building and raising public awareness.[24] They feared that electoral participation would weaken the party's ideological commitment and dilute its organic ties to like-minded religious associations.[25]

The 1946 party program was the first fully developed electoral manifesto put forth by the PAN. Its platform represents a balancing act among the various groups in the party. It argues for the need to reform church-state relations and enhance religious freedom, but these positions are presented obliquely and embedded in broader arguments about essential liberties. "Institutions of faith" are included together with the family, labor, and cultural organizations as a type of fundamental association meant to enable the "fulfillment of [Mexicans'] material and spiritual destiny" but unable to do so because of existing regulations.[26]

By the late 1940s, the Catholic faction's fears regarding electoral engagement had largely abated as a result of deepening links between the PAN and religious associations and the effect of restrictive political institutions. Concretely, repeated participation in elections had demonstrated that the PAN was the second-largest party in Mexico, but the failure to capture more than a handful of legislative seats eased concerns about co-optation.[27] Most pragmatic seat seekers and many liberals left the organization, allowing Catholic activists to move rapidly up the ranks.[28] Reflecting their increasingly secure position within the party, Catholic activists such as González Luna shifted their position to favor electoral participation, framing participation as a moral duty rather than as a means of gaining political power.[29]

The leadership of the party changed to reflect the new influence of religion within the PAN. Gómez Morin stepped aside in 1949, and the résumés of the next three presidents of the party signaled the growing influence of religious activists in the party. The first, Gutiérrez Lascuráin (1949–1956), had been a leader in the ACJM; the second, Ituarte Servín (1956–1958), was a prominent member of ACM and the president of the Unión de Católicos Mexicanos (UCM; Union of Mexican Catholics). The pedigree of the third, González Torres (1958–1961), is discussed earlier in the chapter.[30]

During this time there was also a surge in religious rhetoric and an ambition on the part of many new members to redirect the party toward a more openly religious identification. Christian Democracy became the banner of choice for this group, which maintained strong links to Venezuela's COPEI, at the time a conservative Christian Democratic party, as well as Christian Democratic organizations in Germany.[31] They forcefully demanded the explicit and public acknowledgment of links to Catholic identity and doctrine.[32] In their eyes, the future of the party lay in political mobilization through direct religious appeals, partnerships with domestic and foreign associations guided by similar principles, and forcefully articulated and religiously grounded critiques of the secular establishment.

The party platform was modified to highlight the growing importance of religion. References to the need for constitutional reform and religious freedom became lengthier and more explicit. Most striking, however, are changes in the tone of the party's discourse: The program describes the status quo as a cause for "mutilations and persecutions" that give freedom of worship a "monstrous and delinquent character." Similarly, in rejecting any notion of favoritism for one church or another, it references conflicts that have "bloodied and continue to darken our lives" and contribute to the "tearing apart of Nation and State."[33] These powerful phrases marked the most striking attempt by the PAN to craft an explicit Catholic identity.

However, many of its most prominent members actively resisted the attempted confessional turn of the PAN. Key party leaders blamed poor electoral performance on the party's growing emphasis on Catholic identity and doctrine, and by 1961 the PAN was approaching electoral competition with much less enthusiasm.[34] González Torres remained a staunch defender of religious mobilization and committed participation, citing the sacred duties of the organization,[35] but the party had serious difficulties finding the candidates and resources necessary to compete. Problems deepened after the PAN attempted to force its representatives to surrender their seats to protest electoral fraud, an effort that led to the expulsion of four recalcitrant party members.[36] Furthermore, increasingly prominent cases of official intimidation had substantially raised the costs of participation.[37] In 1961 the party was able to run candidates in only 53 percent of districts, a substantial decline from the 86 percent that had been covered in 1958. The disappointing results of this limited effort were evident, and the party obtained only 8 percent of the vote and five delegates to the national legislature, representing the first decline in the PAN's vote share since 1946 and its first ever decline in seats.

The PAN was not the only organization seeking to mobilize religion during this period. The UNS entered the electoral arena in 1945 by registering its first electoral vehicle, the PFP. Its members had come under increasing pressure from the church hierarchy, which took exception to its intemperate manifestations, penchant for incendiary rhetoric, and insistence on attacking the relatively friendly government of Ávila Camacho. This drove a deep wedge between many UNS cadres and Catholic bishops.

In the early 1940s disagreements over the appropriate stance to take in regard to the church and the governing party provoked a series of crises within the UNS, ultimately leading to formation of the PFP. The bishops did not hesitate to use their influence to push the organization away from explicitly political causes, and a significant number of Sinarquistas heeded its warnings.[38] However, an important faction opted to break its links with religious associations dominated by the hierarchy and promote an explicitly political project. This strategy was made possible by the relative isolation of the UNS from the Catholic hierarchy and by the appearance of electoral opportunity created by the 1943 reform. The followers of Manuel Torres Bueno leveraged their remaining strength to register the PFP as their political vehicle, despite the loud objection of other factions of the UNS.[39] The resulting break was acrimonious and revealed the factious and personalistic character of the UNS leadership. By 1946, when the break was completed, the politically oriented part of the movement was significantly reduced in size and influence and even more isolated from other Catholic groups and organizations elsewhere in the country.

The PFP, with its restricted geographic scope and contested support base, fared worse than the PAN once it became clear that political institutions would not allow substantive electoral gains. Competing with both the hegemonic PRI and an increasingly religious PAN, it obtained a minuscule percentage of the nationwide vote and a single representative. The demise of the party unfolded rapidly after that. Its strength was highly concentrated in the Bajío region, where it made some inroads at the municipal level. Yet in an effort to regain national relevance, the PFP recruited aggressively, organized large marches in its zones of influence, and staged protests and demonstrations against presumed electoral fraud in Mexico City. At one of these events, activists read harsh speeches against the revolutionary regime and placed a hood over the head of a statue of Benito Juárez. This demonstration caused the government to accuse the PFP of sedition, revoke its registration as a political party, and launch a broader campaign against the UNS. Despite staging demonstrations against these policies in the Bajío, the UNS failed to prevent the rapid decline of the movement.[40] The PFP was unable to regain its registration, and the UNS was left without a political party.

The period from 1939 to 1961 marked the high tide of assertive religious mobilization in Mexico. The PAN and the PFP offered contrasting versions of a Catholic political project, with the former drawing on Catholic Action and its affiliates while the latter attempted to mobilize supporters of the UNS among the peasantry of the Bajío. By any standards both the PAN and the PFP were minor parties, securing only small fractions of the vote and minimal numbers of legislators. Although the PFP was clearly a niche party, the PAN had been organized as a proto-mainstream organization, albeit one still torn by its profound and growing reliance on religious activists.

Both of these organizations depended on the existence of substantial Catholic associations with some autonomy from the Catholic hierarchy. Although individual bishops provided occasional support for these parties, the Catholic hierarchy as a whole generally objected to their attempts to mobilize religion in a systematic and explicit manner. While the PAN drew on a nationwide network and avoided direct confrontations with the hierarchy, the PFP depended on a single association with a troubled relationship to the broader Catholic Church. These differences in their bases of religious associational support proved fateful for their development, particularly in light of the limited electoral opportunities created by Mexican political institutions.

The single-member plurality electoral system forced opposition candidates to compete head to head against a hegemonic party whose candidates drew heavily on the resources of the state. In a tilted playing field, this virtually ensured that neither the PAN nor the PFP would secure a sufficient number of seats to be attractive to pragmatic politicians. However, while the PAN developed a nationwide presence and a close relationship to Catholic Action, which provided a consistent base of support and helped it endure the long electoral drought, the PFP depended on its core of UNS members, whose confrontational tactics constantly complicated the party's efforts to expand its appeal or challenge its eventual exclusion.

The Perils of Transformation (1962–1978)

The 1960s and 1970s were a period of crisis and contestation, with advocates of contrasting approaches to religious mobilization competing for influence in a rapidly changing social and political environment. For the PAN, the period was one of reform, debate, and conflict. The internal divisions between the liberal and religious wings of the party, which had been building up during the previous decades, came to the fore in 1962–1963. This conflict marked a watershed, as recruitment patterns shifted away from reliance on religious associations and appeals to Catholic identity were abandoned or reembedded in the discourse of human rights. Yet the next decade witnessed the reemergence of a sharp distinction between a doctrine-oriented abstentionism and a more pragmatic participationism. Catholic activists increasingly saw elections as compromising the party's doctrinal coherence and broader mission, an attitude that gradually isolated them from a party base that remained oriented toward elections. By 1976 these divisions threatened to dismember the PAN.

The same period represented a long nadir for the UNS and its political offshoots. The group was reduced to a regional movement whose commitment to sociopolitical transformation was increasingly under fire by the very religious community it claimed to represent. In this context, the movement increasingly found itself without the means to organize local labor unions and peasant cooperatives, let alone a national party.[41] Although the symbols and legacy of the Sinarquistas remained relevant in the Bajío, their electoral manifestations were virtually without consequence. Although a change in leadership within the movement led to an attempt to enter the electoral arena once again in the 1970s, the inhospitable political environment and the lack of an adequate associational base presented insurmountable obstacles.

Consistent with the causal argument advanced in this book, the timing of these crises reflected ongoing changes in the structural and institutional conditions in Mexico: the dramatic transformation of the Catholic community brought about by the Second Vatican Council (1962–1965) and the reform of electoral institutions in 1963. By formally accepting and incorporating principles such as human rights and the separation of church and state, Vatican II paved the way for the unequivocal endorsement of democratic politics, although these opportunities were not consistently seized. It also brought about the end of the encompassing system of lay organizations built around Catholic Action. This was gradually replaced by a variety of organizations with myriad voices, ranging from revolutionary socialism to promarket liberalism, all claiming to draw on Catholic ideas and doctrines for inspiration. At the same time, it encouraged bishops to strengthen their coordinating institutions, particularly the Conferencia del Episcopado Mexicano (CEM; Mexican Episcopal Conference). Thus, just as lay Catholic Action was diminishing in its capacity and salience, the clerical CEM was emerging as the effective core of organized Catholic life in Mexico.

The electoral reform installed a weak compensatory mechanism that softened the disproportionality of the single-member plurality system. By this means, the governing party aimed to provide the opposition a modicum of voice while guaranteeing the continuing acquiescence of the legislature. The reform had only a limited impact on the UNS, which was too distant from the legislature to effectively benefit from these small concessions. In contrast, it brought about an immediate adjustment by the PAN and contributed to undermining the shaky liberal-Catholic and pragmatic-doctrinaire coalitions that sustained the party.

Religious Community Structures and Political Institutions

The Second Vatican Council had a dramatic impact on religious mobilization in Mexico, as it did across the Catholic world. By abandoning organicist notions of state-society relations that had been prominent in its earlier social thought, encyclicals such as *Pacem in Terris* (1963) diminished the sense of inherent illegitimacy that many devout Catholic activists associated with secular postrevolutionary governments. By emphasizing the need to combat economic inequality and social injustice, documents such as *Gaudium et Spes* (1965) opened the door to cooperation with a broad range of groups in society. Vatican II and the subsequent Latin American Bishops Conference in Medellín (1968) also opened the way for religious activists to make claims regarding redistributionist and interventionist policies traditionally associated with secularist and leftist movements. This is not to say that the ideas of Vatican II favored reconciliation between Catholic thinkers and Mexican political practice. In most cases the new thinking reinforced long-standing polemics of the PAN against government policy, perhaps most notably in the areas of political rights, religious freedoms, and education. Thus, *Dignitatis Humanae* (1965) advocated a notion of religious freedom that clashed directly with the assertive secularism embodied in Mexican laws, a point widely understood among the Mexican laity and clergy.[42] What it did do was initially empower those who sought to articulate original political arguments that drew on Catholic doctrine.

Equally important but less often appreciated was Vatican II's impact on the structure of the Catholic communities in Mexico and elsewhere. The foundations for this transformation lay in documents such as *Gaudium et Spes*, which emphasized the legitimacy and importance of activism grounded in the individual moral conscience of members of the laity. This subtly undermined the form and mission of Catholic Action and its affiliated associations, which had been based on the principles of hierarchy and corporatist organization.[43] Vatican II also significantly expanded opportunities for lay participation in the life of the church as deacons and catechists, although these opportunities were unevenly implemented across dioceses.[44] These were profound changes, and the lay associational sphere in Mexico was dramatically transformed over the course of the next decades.

Before Vatican II, the well-coordinated system centered on ACM had been produced and sustained in large part by the support given to it by the hierarchy, which insisted that it constituted the sole legitimate means for lay participation in civil society. This support was gradually replaced by a much less coordinated universe of Catholic organizations, ranging from businessmen's unions to ecclesial base communities (CEBs), only weakly linked to one another and often upholding very different understandings of the implications (if any) of Catholicism for politics.[45] Initially, this process appeared to strengthen the lay associational sphere, giving progressive groups such as the Secretariado Social Mexicano (SSM; Mexican Social Secretariat) and Centro Nacional de Comunicación Social (Cencos; National Center for Social Communication) a far more prominent role and voice in religious affairs.[46]

Ultimately these developments caused friction between progressive and conservative communities and further accelerated the fractionalization of the lay Catholic community. The ACM withered, experiencing a sharp decline in membership and the rapid erosion of its once hegemonic position. This meant that instead of a narrow lay leadership that had once been able to shape the agenda for Catholic political involvement, there now emerged an increasingly pluralistic environment in which Catholic voices could be heard advocating policies along the entire political spectrum. The transformation of Christian Democracy is an example. During the previous decade, it had been a banner for the traditionalist right, but now it gradually became associated with the ideas of its reformist and moderate left. Groups such as the Instituto Mexicano de Doctrina Social Cristiana (IMDOSOC; Mexican Institute for Christian Social Doctrine) emerged as influential centers for progressive Catholic thought, advocating the values of solidarity and political pluralism. These centripetal trends were reinforced by variation in the decentralization of dioceses, and those that allowed greater participation by laity in church affairs often fostered a greater level of local political activism, typically with a progressive bent.[47]

In the midst of this diversification of lay Catholic voices, the CEM underwent its own quiet transformation.[48] While preserving the formal autonomy of bishops, it encouraged them to reengage with the lay community and to increasingly discuss and coordinate their efforts at the national and international levels. During this time, new branches were added that aimed to engage with the needs of groups such as students and indigenous communities, and the permanent secretariat began formulating clear stances on pertinent public issues. The increasing organizational capacity of Mexican bishops did not put an end to the diversity of their positions;[49] instead, it created spaces where diversity could be managed, processed, and ultimately transformed into consistent policy statements.

The bishop's formal status as head of the Catholic community was thus made more effective by internal reforms that the church in general and the ecclesiastical hierarchy in particular had undergone since the Second Vatican Council. The *Christus Dominus* decree in 1965 had already called for the reorganization of bishops to facilitate collective action, emphasizing the need to strengthen national Episcopal conferences. In response, the CEM spent much of the 1970s putting its house in order.[50] This entailed both the expansion of its members' capacity for collective action—for example, through the rationalization of its organizations and the reorganization of its territorial distribution[51]—and the pruning of internal dissenters.[52] The dissenters included groups on the right and left of the spectrum—that is, those who rejected the reformist trends and those who took them further than the hierarchy was willing to tolerate. Exemplifying the reaction to the second group was the bishops' attitude toward the SSM. In 1969 the CEM revoked its role as official spokesman for the hierarchy. Over the next decade, the CEM pursued a strategy of sanctions and incentives designed to weaken the organization while encouraging it to adopt more moderate positions.[53] Their enhanced capacity allowed bishops to be more effective at determining the legitimacy of specific manifestations of Catholic religious discourse in the public sphere.

As the CEM became increasingly capable of coordinating collective action, it resisted calls for political engagement that might drag it into a disadvantageous conflict with the state.[54] Indeed, during this period many bishops developed increasingly cooperative ties with the state, not least as a result of the greater flexibility afforded to them by the Vatican II framework.[55] Thus, the 1960s and 1970s became a period of internal reform and capacity building, during which the CEM shunned explicitly political arguments and devoted its resources to consolidating its position at the center of the increasingly diversified set of Mexican Catholic networks. These structural changes were not the only challenges to established patterns of religious mobilization, however, as the development of religious mobilization was also shaped by discreet changes in electoral institutions.

The dramatic changes in the religious community coincided with apparently minor but actually quite significant changes in electoral rules. The PAN had long called for electoral reform, but until the 1960s there were only cosmetic modifications to the 1946 law.[56] Under pressure to improve the quality of its representative institutions, the Mexican government opted to expand opportunities for opposition participation. In 1961 the regime signaled its willingness to compromise with the PAN regarding the establishment of new electoral procedures. Adolfo Christlieb Ibarrola, a protégé of Gómez Morin and a prominent figure in the pragmatic wing of the party, was selected to join the official committee discussing the reforms. The result, passed into law in 1963, established a two-tier system for electing candidates. While districts would still elect representatives following the SMP method, parties that obtained at least 2.5 percent of the vote nationwide would be entitled to five "party deputies," with an additional deputy for each 0.5 percent scored above this threshold, up to a maximum of twenty, who would be selected from the top losers in the SMP contests.[57] In exchange, the law prohibited seat-winning parties from boycotting the legislature, with the penalty being deregistration.[58]

The new electoral law was never applied as written, however, because the state opted to reinterpret its norms and extend representation to registered parties that had not crossed the 2.5 percent barrier. The Partido Popular Socialista (PPS; Socialist People's Party) and the Partido Auténtico de la Revolución Mexicana (PARM, Authentic Party of the Mexican Revolution), two puppet parties that endorsed the PRI's presidential candidates, were granted representatives despite falling significantly below the threshold. This elicited protests from the PAN, which insisted on strict application of the law. The maximum number of seats allowed through the compensation system was twenty, so the new version of the rules in fact posed a serious challenge for the largest opposition party, which was relatively disadvantaged in relation to both the hegemonic PRI and its semiautonomous supporters. For example, in 1967 the PRI obtained 83.8 percent of the votes and 82.8 percent of the seats, while the PAN secured 12.4 percent of votes but only 9.5 percent of seats. In contrast, the PPS obtained 2.2 percent of votes and 4.8 percent of seats, and the PARM, 1.4 percent and 2.9 percent. The only party significantly disadvantaged by the new system was the PAN, and the mirage of multipartyism gave the system a gloss of legitimacy that undermined the opposition's efforts to bring about fundamental reform.

Yet the disadvantageous disproportionality and the danger of legitimizing the regime were not the only concerns for the PAN. The incorporation of minor parties into the legislature despite their inability to cross the 2.5 percent barrier, which the PRI argued was in keeping with its spirit of enhancing proportionality, was perhaps most troubling because it signaled the extent to which electoral results were still driven by the preferences of the ruling party rather than by the application of publicly known rules. An even more unequivocal signal of this underlying feature of electoral law was the sudden decline in SMP victories for the PAN following the modification of the law. Even under the dismal conditions of the 1961 election, the party had been recognized as the absolute winner in five districts. Despite the superior effort put forth in 1964, the party secured SMP victories in only two districts. In 1967 this number would drop to one, and in 1970, to zero. The dominant party had found a way to avoid having to sacrifice any of its own candidates and still maintain opposition participation in the legislature. The way in which party leaders adapted their style of religious mobilization in the face of these changes, like their responses to religious reforms associated with Vatican II, gave rise to significant intraparty contestation.

Patterns of Religious Mobilization

The structural and institutional changes of the early 1960s had notably different effects on the PAN and the UNS. For the PAN, the electoral reform initially favored a moderate shift toward pragmatic electoral strategies at the expense of religious mobilization. Yet over the next two decades the rise of new religious associations and evolving patterns of religious authority, together with the continued difficulties posed by the electoral system, revived debates over the proper role of religion and doctrine within the party. In doing so, it pitted a new progressive religious wing against a rising coalition of liberal pragmatists and economic conservatives. For the UNS, in contrast, the period was characterized by electoral impotence, deepened by its continuing difficulties with the electoral laws and an increasingly hostile Catholic associational environment.

The UNS wrestled with contradictory incentives, moving back and forth between attempts to engage in electoral politics and isolationism. The growing influence of progressive Catholicism did little to reinforce the appeal of the traditional, nationalist, and reactionary UNS. In response it attempted to increase its influence by sponsoring labor unions and peasant cooperatives, but these efforts generally met with failure, even in the Bajío region.[59] In 1963 the group reacted to electoral reforms by attempting to form an alliance with a conservative-nationalist proto-party known as the Partido Nacionalista Mexicano (PNM; Mexican Nationalist Party). However, as occurred for many of the initiatives launched by the UNS during this period, the effort came to naught as the government revoked the party's registration and declared that it lacked the necessary requirements for electoral participation, even after it had captured three seats in the legislature.[60]

Perhaps the most interesting detail in this otherwise fruitless episode has to do with the role of formal electoral reform in prompting strategic adjustment by intransigent political groups. The quasi-autarchic UNS of the 1960s appears as a least-likely case for responsiveness to formal electoral reform, but it nevertheless clearly reacted to the modest adjustments in the formal institutional context.[61] A leadership change in 1970 led to further attempts to engage in the electoral arena, but these remained frustrated by the movement's inability to meet party registration thresholds.

Within the PAN, 1962 marked the eruption of the long-building reaction against religious influence and the difficulties it had generated for the party. Adolfo Christlieb Ibarrola headed these efforts.[62] A member of the UNEC in his youth, he represented a sector of the party that, without questioning the importance of religion, rejected assertive religious mobilization.[63] He publicly challenged the notion that a Mexican party could unfurl an explicitly religious banner without becoming openly entangled with the Catholic Church, to the detriment of both.[64] He proposed a clear division of labor, in which the PAN proposed a platform indirectly informed by Catholicism but did so without formulating open appeals to Catholic identity or flaunting its partnerships with religious associations.[65]

At this crucial juncture, individual members of the Catholic hierarchy seized on the opportunity provided by Christlieb to reaffirm the distinction between political and religious arenas and thus both reassert its claims to the nonpolitical character of Catholicism and reclaim its hegemony over explicitly religious action. In a newspaper interview conducted a few months after the PAN's national convention, Bishop Méndez Arceo declared:

> Frankly, I dislike the concept of Christian Democracy. The social doctrine, the strictly social, corresponds to civil society. . . . For that reason, may I add, I find that the position of Christlieb Ibarrola hits the mark, in that it has straightforwardly articulated the non-interference of the Church in his party, in all parties.[66]

The bishop's public aversion to assertive religious mobilization was grounded in the previously mentioned pattern of accommodation between church and state emerging in Mexico during that time.[67] The ability of liberals to redirect the PAN away from assertive religious mobilization was thus enhanced by the support of religious authorities. Many prominent Catholic activists in the party, faced with stinging rebukes from the very groups they aimed to defend, became increasingly marginalized, and in 1963 they presented their collective resignation.

The electoral reform thus initially contributed to reconsolidating the party, but by 1968 concerns regarding manipulated elections and fraud became increasingly severe. That year, elections for municipal and state legislative elections in Baja California were widely condemned as fraudulent, with the governing party denying the PAN a range of hard-fought electoral victories.[68] Christlieb's protests and demands for an investigation were abruptly rebuffed,[69] demonstrating that the government had no intention of allowing the system to become anything but a mechanism through which it could control electoral outcomes and pick and choose its opposition.

These developments had a direct consequence for the attractiveness of the PAN to religious activists. Participating in elections, once a badge of moral courage,[70] now acquired a dubious tone. For religious activists eager to challenge the legitimacy of the regime, this was no longer a particularly tempting proposition, and the recruitment of new religious activists to the PAN diminished sharply.[71] In contrast, for those who privileged gaining access to government office but were unable or unwilling to join the PRI, the PAN once again became a feasible alternative. The ensuing changes in patterns of recruitment would dramatically alter the balance of power between Catholic-doctrinaire and liberal-pragmatic party members in the long run.

Members who had joined the PAN during 1947 to 1962, the period of greatest confessional influence, held much of the party's leadership during the following decades. Yet new party members were increasingly drawn from the ranks of business entrepreneurs and other economic conservatives with few ties to religious associations.[72] The stage was thus set for confrontations between rising pragmatists who wanted to ensure that their resources were used to achieve the greatest electoral effect and entrenched Catholic ideologues for whom electoral participation was but part of a broader project aimed at transforming Mexican society.

The contested status of religious doctrine during this period is visible in the statements put forth by the PAN. The platform for the period 1970–1976 maintained its predecessor's explicit critique of the extralegal arrangements that characterized church-state relations but abandoned much of the hyperbolic language of the prior era. It shifted emphasis to underscore that the PAN sought freedom of conscience for both believers and nonbelievers and did not seek any type of privileges for specific creeds. However, in deference to the firm doctrinal commitments of its members, its critical posture remained front and center, with the party condemning the "simulation and hypocrisy that greatly weaken the moral energy of a free society" and the "shameful extralegal tolerance" to which religious bodies were subjected.[73]

Differences regarding mobilization strategies reinvigorated the old debate between liberal participationists and religious abstentionists. Until the early 1970s, their leaders were able to collaborate to avoid crises. For example, in 1970 the party came close to boycotting the election when participationists secured only 51 percent of convention members' votes. Indeed, their endorsement was obtained thanks only to the selection of Efraín González Morfín, leader of the religious-doctrinal faction, as the party's presidential candidate. From this position, religious activists could use a vigorous election campaign as a platform from which to promote their doctrinal positions. In exchange for this opportunity, González Morfín supported José Ángel Conchello, leader of the pragmatist-liberal faction, in his successful bid for the party presidency in 1972.[74]

But tactical accommodation did little to ease discontent with an electoral system prone to manipulation by the government or ameliorate the growing distance between progressive Catholics and pragmatic conservatives. Discontent with the electoral system was widespread in the party and played into the arguments of religious abstentionists. Conchello conceded that the electoral reform of 1963, particularly its manipulation by the regime, had increased skepticism in the electorate regarding the representation of minorities.[75] However, he argued that growing discontent with the system actually played into the hands of the PAN, which had increasing opportunities to force the government to accept its electoral victories. Moreover, the leftist policies of the Mexican government after 1972 provided the PAN with the support of an increasingly alienated business community, allowing the party to launch a vigorous electoral campaign the following year. While Conchello applauded these developments, González Morfín saw in them a threat to the party's doctrinal commitments.

The conflict between the two tendencies came to the fore in 1975, when a bitterly divided party assembly supported González Morfín's bid to replace Conchello as party president. Conchello proceeded to construct a parallel structure within the party and publicly criticize the decisions taken by the new president.[76] These actions forced González Morfín to renounce the presidency by the end of the year. In response to their failure to secure control over the party, the abstentionists refused to support the presidential candidate proposed by Conchello and a majority of PAN members at the 1976 convention. Exploiting procedural rules and their majority positions in the National Executive Committee, they successfully impeded the election of an official candidate, forcing the party to abstain from the presidential contest that year. After thirteen consecutive hours in session and seven rounds of voting, the convention broke down into a virtual brawl with no decision having been reached.

The crisis had a direct impact on the electoral fortunes of the party. After a decade of running candidates in more than 90 percent of districts, in 1976 it participated in only 67 percent. In 1973 the party had secured 16 percent of the vote. Three years later it was able to capture only 8.5 percent. The most dramatic consequence was the absence, for the first time since 1946, of a PAN contender for the presidency. As the debacle unfolded, the party undertook a series of policies aimed at reducing the damage. Conchello and his most active supporters were suspended from the party for two years.[77] By 1978 the party remained weakened and seriously divided. Much of the leadership remained in the hands of the religious-abstentionist wing associated with González Morfín, but his position was endorsed only by a minority among the rank and file, who bitterly resented their role in the crisis. Conchello's supporters remained active within the party and agitated for a return to the electoralist policies that had led to sustained growth in the early 1970s.

The crises experienced by religious mobilizers during the 1960s and 1970s reflected the transformations taking placed within the Catholic community as well as the challenges posed by restrictive and manipulative political institutions. As a result, the PAN, despite its experienced cadres, substantial roots in civil society, and network of lay Catholic support, experienced serious schisms. The UNS, crippled by its ongoing conflicts with both church and state, failed repeatedly in its attempts to reenter the electoral arena.

These developments reflected the tension between a diverse set of Catholic civil-society associations, with members eager to promote doctrinally committed visions of politics, and a political system that severely restricted their ability to do so. Fears of manipulation by the regime pushed many Catholic activists to seek alternatives to party organization, weakening the party's religious associational links. For those who were already invested in the PAN, restrictive electoral laws made it necessary to work together with liberals and conservatives to remain competitive. The party's limited electoral successes, the unwillingness of the hierarchy to engage effectively in partisan politics, and the open manipulation of the electoral process by the ruling party made it increasingly difficult to sustain the resulting coalition. Thus, while religious doctrine continued to play a central role in the party's mobilization efforts, it faced increasing resistance within the party.

Religious Revival and Selective Mobilization (1979–2000)

During the final two decades of the twentieth century Catholicism reemerged as a significant issue in Mexican politics, buoyed by the electoral success of the PAN, the emergence of a new conservative party with ties to the UNS, and the rising profile of Mexican bishops. The PAN gradually adopted a new style of religious mobilization, appealing indirectly to Catholic identity, narrowing the role of Catholic doctrine, and diversifying its associational ties. Operating in an increasingly competitive electoral environment, it sought to present itself as the party of democratic reform and the focal point for the anti-PRI vote.[78] Religious associations were marginalized by growing secular sources of support, and social doctrine became primarily an instrument for the socialization of party elites.[79] At the same time, the PAN candidates appealed to Catholic identity to differentiate themselves from the PRI. The electoral triumph of Vicente Fox in the 2000 presidential election, which included the occasional striking use of Catholic symbols but only limited references to religious doctrine or associational links, marked the culmination of this process.

The UNS, after thirty years of electoral frustration, found an outlet in the PDM, which steadily gained adherents during the 1980s and even expanded beyond its regional base in the Bajío region. The PDM successfully attracted several prominent Panistas disenchanted by their party's abandonment of doctrine. However, it never obtained more than a handful of legislative representatives. Its limited appeal to the mainstream electorate, strained ties with the hierarchy, and the growing importance of a presidential race in which it could not hope to compete made it difficult for the party to remain relevant in the 1990s.

The increasing salience of religious mobilization in the 1980s and its partial decline in the 1990s resulted from changes in Mexico's political institutions and its Catholic community. A series of electoral reforms begun in 1977 expanded opportunities for electoral opposition. By lowering the barriers for representation, they allowed marginal actors such as the PDM to gain access to the legislature. To the PAN, they offered an increase in the size of its legislative contingent and the opportunity to compete for higher offices. The consolidation of these reforms through the establishment of a credible electoral commission in the 1990s favored opposition parties capable of contesting high-profile races, such as governorships, SMP seats, and especially the presidency.

At the same time, the enhanced capacity of Mexican bishops, the conservative turn following the election of Pope John Paul II, and the successful negotiation of long-awaited constitutional reforms put the Catholic hierarchy solidly at the helm of the Catholic community. During the 1980s this growing influence led some bishops to engage in contentious political action, most notably by lending their moral support to the struggle against electoral fraud, which in turn led to accusations of partisanship. In the 1990s concerns about the potential costs of politicization brought a shift away from confrontation. The CEM repeatedly signaled its preference for negotiation over confrontation and thus provided indirect support for the PAN and sidelining of the more assertive PDM.

Religious Community Structures and Political Institutions

The last two decades of the twentieth century witnessed a fundamental readjustment of state-church relations in Mexico, including the first substantial overhaul of state secularism. These formal changes reflected an equally profound transformation unfolding within the global Catholic Church. After two decades of upheaval and adjustment following the Second Vatican Council, the 1980s witnessed a new and distinctive reassertion of clerical influence. While the preconciliar Catholic Church had hesitated to accept the legitimacy of the secular state and dealt with political authorities by means of informal and conditional arrangements, the new approach was built on the separation of secular and religious authority, whereby the preconciliar church understood its role to be one of moral supervision. The consolidation of this postconciliar model of church-state relations had a direct impact on the possibilities for religious political mobilization in Mexico, as indeed it did across much of the Catholic world.[80]

In Mexico, the new period was inaugurated in a dramatic fashion in 1979, when the recently elected Pope John Paul II began the first of his five visits to Mexico. His public appearances drew enormous crowds and demonstrated that the Catholic Church could still energize broad swaths of the Mexican population, surprising a secular establishment used to low rates of public participation. This no doubt imbued the entire Catholic community with new confidence and had a direct impact on the ongoing debates and struggles within the community.[81] In particular, John Paul II spoke against the perceived excesses of liberation theology and encouraged a move toward more centralized patterns of religious authority. Speaking to a gathering of

Mexico's priests, John Paul II emphasized the unique and irreplaceable role of the clergy, thus placing limits on the more controversial extensions of lay activism favored by some progressive bishops,[82] and he called for refocusing on pastoral duties, reminding clergy that they "are not social or political leaders or officials of a temporal power."[83] This segregation of religious and political powers enhanced the influence of the bishops, who, by asserting their distance from political power, in fact reaffirmed their claim to authority over religious activism in the public sphere.

The reaffirmation of clerical leadership, together with the restructuring of the Catholic Church during the 1970s, meant that by 1980 the CEM was in a much better position to take the helm of public Catholic discourse. Its growing ability to intervene in public debates coincided with growing disenchantment with politics as usual. The economic crisis of the early 1980s contributed dramatically to eroded popular confidence in the regime led by the PRI. Perhaps most dramatically, the earthquakes that devastated Mexico in 1985 and the poor government response led to vigorous action by the Catholic community.[84]

Given this context, individual bishops became increasingly willing to use their authority to intervene directly in political disputes during the following decade, even as they were careful to frame their positions in doctrinal and religious terms. Several bishops became explicit in their criticism of corruption and fraud and repeatedly called for the state to remain neutral in electoral contests.[85] Moreover, key voices in the CEM overtly criticized the constitutional articles governing religion, taking over a role that had traditionally been associated with the PAN and lay groups in civil society. Actions by the bishops included hosting workshops to train citizens in democratic practices, such as how to challenge electoral fraud, and publicly criticizing the liberal economic policies of President Ernesto Zedillo's administration.[86] Although most bishops explicitly rejected overt partisanship, a few individual bishops went as far as to make thinly veiled statements in support of PAN candidates.[87]

Even as the CEM grew more effective, it faced an increasingly complex political environment as a result of the arrival of Girolamo Prigione, whom John Paul II appointed as his representative in Mexico. Until Prigione's arrival, the position had not wielded significant power in Mexico.[88] Prigione changed that dramatically, occupying the post from 1978 to 1997, far longer than any predecessor, and developing strong relationships with a broad segment of Mexico's political elite, most notably President Salinas.[89] The emergence of Prigione as the de facto representative of the Catholic hierarchy in the eyes of the political establishment, as well as many of the Catholic

Church's secular opponents, pushed the CEM to become more active to protect its autonomy and provide support for the Vatican when Prigione's visibility forced their hand.

The evolution of the hierarchy was accompanied by other important changes within the broader Catholic community that contributed to the transformation of Catholic political engagement. The post-1979 period witnessed growing diversification of lay activism, most notably through dramatic expansion of conservative lay groups directly engaged in politics. The most important of these was ProVida, a pro-life group formed in 1978 that gradually emerged as one of the most vocal and visible organizations in debates around reproductive rights in Mexico. The explicitly political quality of its goals—resisting the liberalization of abortion laws—marked a change from the formally apolitical, spiritual, and social agendas that had characterized mainstream Catholic lay organizations since the 1940s. Until the 1970s abortion had been uniformly illegal across Mexico, with exceptions in the case of rape or to protect the life of the mother.[90] During that decade, concerns about population growth and emergence of feminist voices led to loosening some restrictions in particular states. Debates around these issues were initially muted and driven by the proclivities of regional politicians.[91] However, by the early 1990s ProVida's electoral activism had contributed to putting the item on the legislative agenda of several states, particularly those in which the PAN was gaining political power. For secularist and feminist groups, the growing visibility of religious mobilization to oppose abortion posed a major challenge and raised the stakes in electoral contests.

Overall, the impression among the public was one of a highly active church hierarchy and a growing conservative Catholic movement, much more connected to mundane affairs and willing to take public stances on the contentious topics sweeping Mexico at the time.

The climax of this growing Catholic political engagement was the long-awaited reform of Articles 3, 5, 24, and 130 of the constitution. The manner in which this was achieved highlighted the new relationship between the Catholic Church and the Mexican government.[92] Though publicly framed as a response to growing religious pluralism, the reform was widely seen as a concession by the state to the Catholic hierarchy.[93] The PAN, which had doggedly pursued this reform since its foundation and presented similar legislation in 1987, played a very minor role in the actual reform, which was ultimately negotiated between President Salinas and the papal nuncio.[94] The Catholic Church was a major beneficiary of the reform, which allowed it to openly offer religious education, legalized monastic orders, and enabled it to own assets necessary for the performance of its functions.[95] Thus, despite some misgivings, the CEM ultimately issued a statement that many inter-preted as an endorsement of the reforms.[96]

However, increased exposure also brought important setbacks for the hi-erarchy in its efforts to maintain a unified front and affirm its strictly super-visory role in Mexican politics during the 1990s. The CEM as a whole and the majority of bishops were consistently concerned about the negative effects of partisan engagement.[97] Two events were particularly notable in demon-strating the potential risks of open involvement in public affairs. The first was the death of Cardinal Posada Ocampo, who was killed during a shoot-out between drug gangs at Guadalajara airport. The murky circumstances surrounding his death caused some bishops to openly question whether the government had been involved, which in turn prompted the CEM to issue a public statement in which it accepted the official account of the events.[98]

Even more disruptive was the Zapatista uprising in Chiapas, which high-lighted the continuing divisions within the church. Through a combination of dramatic civic and military actions and savvy engagement with the media, the Ejército Zapatista de Liberación Nacional (EZLN; Zapatista National Liberation Army) drew international attention to the plight of marginal-ized indigenous communities in southern Mexico. Its efforts in this area brought the group into contact with progressive members of the clergy and laity, many of whom sympathized with the movement's emphasis on social justice.[99] Thus, while largely secular in nature, the revolutionaries established a friendly relationship in Samuel Ruiz García, the bishop of San Cristóbal de las Casas.[100] Bishop Ruiz was a long-standing advocate of the more progres-sive readings of Vatican II and had been the subject of disciplinary actions by the Vatican for his closeness to liberation theology. Ruiz's prominent role as mediator between EZLN and the government heightened his profile and breathed new life into schisms that many in the hierarchy had considered suc-cessfully overcome. The bishop, who faced both overt and discreet criticism from many of his peers, was ultimately protected by the formal autonomy of his position, a powerful reminder that bishops' capacity for collective action, like their coordination with the Vatican, rested largely on a delicate structure of voluntary compliance that could be endangered by excessive politiciza-tion.[101]

In this context of internal tension and high public exposure, the CEM retreated from direct political engagement until the vigorous 2000 contest for the presidency effectively forced its hand. Despite this retrenchment, the bishops remained effectively at the head of the Catholic associational sphere and thus managed to provide religious legitimacy for the democratic process, indirectly supporting the PAN's efforts while avoiding open entanglement with specifically partisan forces. In these efforts the bishops found unexpected support from changes to the electoral rules, even though institutional incentives did not always align neatly with their preferences.

In addition to the changes taking place within the Mexican Catholic Church and its relationship with the state, the period from 1978 to 2000 also witnessed the fundamental restructuring of Mexico's electoral institutions. Unlike earlier instances of limited reform, such as the 1963 changes to electoral and party laws, the state's series of reforms carried out during the last two decades of the century added up to a real instance of regime change. This had a series of important but contradictory effects on religious mobilization. On the one hand, the legislative electoral environment became more permissive, encouraging the entry of more explicitly religious groups into the political arena. On the other hand, by making bigger prizes available for the opposition, particularly the presidency, they encouraged more effective coordination around mainstream platforms. Thus, the possibility of gaining seats by appealing exclusively to a narrower, more religiously oriented portion of the electorate improved but ran up against incentives to form broad coalitions to contest higher offices.

The reform process began in the aftermath of the 1976 elections. The presidential contest of that year proved an embarrassment to the PRI. The PAN was paralyzed by internal crisis, and the remaining parties supported the establishment candidate. As a result, the PRI was deprived of the nominal legitimacy provided by multiparty competition. For a government that proclaimed itself firmly committed to democratic practices and electoral legitimacy, the situation was unacceptable.[102] Moreover, it was dangerous, as it suggested that the opposition might shift away from relatively benign electoral strategies to the subversive activities associated with guerrilla movements.[103] The renewal and consolidation of the party system became an important element in President José López Portillo's agenda. Buoyed by the discovery of new oil reserves during his first year in office and confident in the enduring popularity of his party and the marginality of the opposition, López Portillo accepted the need for more fundamental reform.

In 1977 the governing party passed the Ley Federal de Organizaciones Politicas y Procesos Electorales (LOPPE; Federal Law on Political Organizations and Electoral Processes). This reform package represented a dramatic attempt to transform the electoral institutions in Mexico. The law had two primary components. First, in an effort aimed primarily to draw the left into the electoral arena, it eased requirements for party registration. Second, and crucially for the PAN, it discarded the much maligned party deputy system in favor of a new compensatory mixed electoral system. While the majority of seats would still be drawn from single-member districts, one-fourth of seats in the lower house (one hundred) would now be distributed in proportion to overall votes among parties that had won fewer than sixty SMP seats. Other reforms expanded the availability of mass-media space for opposition parties, and all registered political parties were given a presence on the electoral oversight body.[104]

The law was adjusted throughout the 1980s and early 1990s in ways that reflected the diminished confidence of the PRI in its ability to obtain overwhelming vote majorities. In 1986 the number of proportional seats was doubled, but these were made available to all parties that secured between 1.5 percent and 51 percent of the vote. An additional clause guaranteed the largest party an absolute majority in the legislature. In 1989 the system was changed again, with proportional seats distributed differently depending on whether the winning party obtained less than 35 percent, 35–60 percent, or more than 60 percent of votes. The awkwardness of the process led to the adoption of a standard mixed system in 1993, with proportional seats distributed independently of the SMP results.[105] The Senate undertook a similar set of reforms, culminating in the introduction of a proportional representation (PR) component that brought greater procedural symmetry in the two legislative chambers.

The LOPPE signaled an enormous expansion of electoral opportunities that would clearly enhance the PAN's ability to capture seats. Nevertheless, the party was initially wary of the new law. Still recovering from the shock of the 1976 schism, formally led by beleaguered doctrinaire activists, and with a vivid memory of the disappointments of the 1962 electoral reform, the PAN leadership did not support the LOPPE. Its leaders correctly assessed the initial intent of the PRI, which was to maintain control over the legislature while providing enough rewards to keep the opposition engaged.[106] Indeed, the law was openly designed to prevent coordination by the opposition.[107] Since 1945 party registration laws had required parties to maintain a presence across much of the national territory. By encouraging opposition parties to focus their resources on competing with each other for PR representatives, it diverted them from the more abundant, but also more expensive, SMP constituencies.

The Federal Code of Electoral Institutions and Procedures (COFIPE; Código Federal de Instituciones y Procedimientos Electorales) law of 1990 moved the country toward an effectively autonomous electoral court, the Tribunal Federal Electoral. This was a substantial improvement over the previous institutions, whose partiality was vividly exposed by the electoral contest of 1988. Although the 1990 version of the law kept the minister of the interior, a presidential appointee, as head of the commission, the credibility of the reforms led to a dramatic expansion in turnout in the 1994 presidential election. In 1996 these trends were further strengthened when the head of the tribunal was formally replaced by independent authorities selected by the legislative branch. These changes, together with the transformation of the Mexican economy, had a significant impact on the plausibility of competing for higher office.[108] The 1988 election demonstrated the competitiveness of presidential races. That year the PAN captured its first governorship, in Baja California, and repeated its victory by capturing Guanajuato in 1991 and Chihuahua in 1992. Throughout the 1990s it gradually acquired a substantial presence in the Senate, where proportional reforms that favored larger opposition parties were incorporated in 1993 and 1996.[109] As elections for these offices heated up, their more restrictive electoral conditions dampened popular enthusiasm for marginal parties that were effectively excluded from the possibility of gaining them.

Patterns of Religious Mobilization

The expansion of electoral opportunities and the growing organizational capacity of the Catholic hierarchy brought about a transformation of religious politics in Mexico during the last two decades of the twentieth century. Electoral reforms created new opportunities for contestation, with the PAN rising to become an increasingly meaningful competitor for the PRI and a new UNS-sponsored niche party participating in elections during the 1980s. However, while the UNS remained committed to assertive religious mobilization, the PAN increasingly moved toward a new selective style of mobilization that combined indirect appeals to religious identity with tacit support from the Catholic hierarchy while relying less on Catholic social doctrine or lay associations.

After decades of marginalization, the 1977 electoral reform led the UNS to register a new electoral vehicle. It did so under a newly available "conditional registry," which required it to obtain at least 1.5 percent of the vote to retain legal status. In the 1979 election, the new PDM crossed this threshold with a relatively comfortable margin, securing 2.2 percent of the vote and ten seats. The PDM subsequently maintained a consistent fraction of the vote, obtaining 2.3 percent in 1983 and 2.7 percent in 1985. This stability masks a robust growth in its absolute number of supporters, which nearly doubled from 1979 to 1985, making it one of the most rapidly expanding parties during these years. Nevertheless, despite its avowed intention to become a competitive party nationwide,[110] the PDM never managed to make substantial gains beyond its traditional strongholds or appeal to groups that did not have a prior affinity for the UNS.[111]

Religious mobilization played a central role for the PDM. A 1989 survey of party members revealed that 40 percent were affiliated with religious associations and 80 percent claimed to attend mass "without fail."[112] Moreover, the PDM openly embraced the conservative interpretation of Catholic social thought that had characterized the UNS for decades. Although its platform was focused primarily on secular concerns regarding economic and political reform, it also contained notable references to religious freedom and religious education, as well as a strong dose of anticommunist statements drawn from the preconciliar Catholic tradition.[113] In addition, virtually all polled militants named adherence to Catholic social doctrine as a reason for membership in the party.[114]

The PDM approached the 1988 election with high expectations, but the unexpected competitiveness of the presidential race effectively sidelined the party,[115] which obtained less than 1.5 percent of the vote and lost its legal registration. Lacking committed supporters beyond its UNS base, and with little institutional support from the Catholic hierarchy or other lay associations, the PDM proved unable to recover from this first real test.

The PAN's adjustment to the new electoral environment was equally rapid but far more fruitful in the long run. The post-1976 settlement between religious and pragmatist factions of the PAN collapsed almost immediately, as rank-and-file members pressured a reluctant leadership to engage in a full-fledged electoral effort. Supporters of doctrinal-based mobilization attempted to resist their demands, but weakened by the debacle of 1976, they had no real alternatives to offer their fellow party members. González Morfín left the party in 1978, along with other prominent members from the party's progressive religious wing.[116] In the 1979 election, the PAN, still recovering from these divisions, secured only 10.8 percent of votes, well below its result in 1973. However, this effort was still enough to secure forty-six legislative seats, which, because of the party list system, could no longer be suspected to have been selected by the PRI.

The PAN's ability to benefit from the new electoral opportunities was dramatically improved by a severe economic crisis and the nationalization of the banks in 1982. Mexican business, particularly in the economically expanding areas in the north of the country, began to shift seriously toward the opposition, supporting the PAN and providing it with a supply of candidates and financial resources much greater than it had ever possessed. These Neopanistas, as they came to be known, were scarcely moderates,[117] but they were certainly not interested in revisiting stale doctrinal battles and did not depend on religious associations to carry out their campaigns.[118] Riding on this influx of dedicated capital and candidates, the PAN's presidential candidate obtained 16.4 percent of the votes in 1982. Legislative results were even more encouraging, with the party obtaining 17.5 percent of votes and fifty-one seats in the lower house.

During the next decade the Neopanistas' resources were sometimes reinforced by religious activism, but in contrast to earlier periods this was no longer driven by the party itself. The 1986 gubernatorial election in Chihuahua became emblematic of the new role of religious mobilization in electoral competitions. The PAN candidate, Francisco Barrio, was a newcomer to the party and a prominent business executive. Although church officials denied being partial to any party, numerous public statements left little doubt about which candidate they favored, with the bishop of Ciudad Juárez declaring to the press that people voted for the PRI only because "they benefit economically from the current regime, because they are under strong pressure from labor leaders or peasant associations . . . or finally due to a profound ignorance or lack of awareness of what has happened in Mexico over the last decades."[119] When the PRI declared itself the winner by an implausibly large margin, Catholic churches in Chihuahua read a homily by the archbishop in which he declared that mass would be suspended the following week in protest.[120] This was a direct reference to the events that had marked the beginning of the Cristero uprising sixty years earlier. The Mexican government promptly requested that the Vatican prevent the archbishop's threat from being carried out. The Vatican veto, delivered by Papal Nuncio Girolamo Prigione, provoked substantial discontent among local bishops,[121] but it also served as a demonstration of the authority of the hierarchy over rank-and-file priests and activists, many of whom had been eager to force a direct confrontation with the regime.

The PAN's presidential candidate in 1988, Manuel Clouthier, was also a Neopanista and in many ways exemplified the emerging style of mobilization. Drawn into opposition politics by the nationalization of the banks in 1982, he was a political newcomer with substantial personal wealth. He was a committed conservative with links to Catholic organizations such as the Movimiento Familiar Cristiano (MFC; Christian Family Movement) and had strong ties to an increasingly vocal set of secular civil-society organizations representing conservative economic interests.[122] In the lead-up to the election, he relied on his personal connections to mobilize followers for confrontational mass demonstrations, relegating the official party apparatus to the sidelines.

Clouthier's style in many ways became a model for later elections, but the events of the 1988 campaign ultimately overshadowed his candidacy. The PRI experienced its first substantial split, as its left wing, under the leadership of Cuauhtémoc Cárdenas, rejected the ruling party's newfound commitment to liberal economic policies.[123] These defectors, joined by a broad coalition of leftist parties and civil-society organizations, mounted a powerful challenge to the PRI, forcing the party to begin a painful process of internal reorganization.[124] The official victory of the PRI candidate, Carlos Salinas, was broadly considered fraudulent and attained at the expense of Cárdenas. As the conflict escalated, Clouthier supported protests against the electoral result, issuing calls for civil disobedience that were sufficiently disruptive to merit criticism from Catholic bishops.[125]

Crucially for the PAN, the unexpectedly competitive election deprived the PRI of its legislative supermajority, which, given the new government's ambitious plans for liberal economic reform, meant that it would have to seek the support of the conservative opposition. The PAN took full advantage of this juncture, using its newfound leverage to demand greater electoral transparency and recognition of its electoral victories. A major triumph was the official recognition of its success in the 1989 governor's race in Baja California, representing the first opposition capture of a governorship in six decades. In 1995 Vicente Fox won another governorship for the PAN in Guanajuato, a position he had narrowly lost in 1991 amid accusations of fraud by the PRI. In 1991 the PAN also obtained its first seat in the Senate. Elections for this upper chamber, which had been strictly first past the post, were subsequently reformed in 1993 and 1996 to increase its proportionality, with substantial benefits for the PAN.[126]

The policy of collaboration with the government, despite its clear benefits, troubled many longtime members, for whom working with the PRI was anathema. This led to the formation of a recalcitrant faction within the PAN, the Foro Democrático (FD; Democratic Forum), which called for a return to doctrinal principles. The group included notable religious members such as González Schmal, linked to the tradition of González Morfín, and González Torres, the historic leader of the Catholic wing during the 1950s.[127] After a prolonged period of internal debate, most of the leadership of the FD left the party in 1992. After failing to launch an independent party, several joined the PDM, which shared many of the premises of the doctrinal wing of the PAN.[128] The resulting conservative coalition was known as the Unión Nacional Opositora (UNO; National Opposition Union). Lacking an organized base, its presidential candidate, an ex-Panista, obtained only 0.28 percent of the vote. The utter failure of this effort signaled the implausibility of launching an effective niche party on the right, given institutional incentives and structural constraints.

The PAN, which had been outflanked by PRI-led constitutional reforms and the restoration of Mexico's relations with the Vatican, attempted to sustain its appeal to Catholic voters by reaffirming its religious identity: in 1993 the party accepted an invitation to become a permanent observer at the Christian Democratic Organization of America and in 1998 joined the broader Christian Democratic International. These shifts were justified by the ideological affinity between the PAN and Christian Democracy,[129] but there is little to suggest that these affinities had not existed, or been less salient, in the 1960s. Rather, with the influence of religious activists in its ranks reduced and the Catholic hierarchy firmly at the helm of religious activism, the party leadership was safe to make appeals to Catholic identity that had limited significance regarding policy commitments. Thus, although party elites identified themselves as conservative on issues of personal morality and economic policy, PAN voters in the 1990s tended to be spread out along the ideological spectrum.[130] Insofar as it retained its relevance, religious doctrine was used as a means of maintaining the internal coherence of the party.

Vicente Fox, who leveraged his successful capture of the governorship of Guanajuato to become the PAN's candidate in 2000, replicated many of the tactics pioneered by Clouthier. He was independently wealthy, supplemented the PAN's limited mobilizing infrastructure with a substantial inflow of external resources, and did not hesitate to distance himself from the party leadership when it proved necessary for his candidacy. To mobilize voters, Fox relied primarily on a massive, expensive media campaign. This was largely funded through para-party organizations such as Amigos de Fox, which raised enormous sums from local and international sources, often in ways that violated laws governing fund-raising.[131]

At the same time, Fox made significant efforts to signal his personal religiosity. In sharp contrast to the doctrinal treatment of religion that had characterized PAN campaigns earlier in the century, and echoing Clouthier's emphasis on personal traits and resources, his appeals were framed as a personal, emotional connection to Mexican tradition.[132] These included the use of the image of the Virgen de Guadalupe in his campaign, which generated cautious criticism from the Catholic hierarchy.[133] He met with more success when he sent a letter to the leaders of several churches in which he made ten promises, including his willingness to defend life from conception until natural death, along with the easing of restrictions on media access for religious associations.[134] These were presented to the public as personal stances, reflecting the beliefs of the candidate rather than doctrinal positions developed by the party.

In keeping with its efforts to guide voters without openly endorsing any particular party, the CEM issued an extensive message titled "From the Encounter with Jesus to Solidarity with All: The Encounter with Jesus Christ, Road to Conversion, Communion, Solidarity, and Mission in Mexico at the Threshold of the Third Millennium."[135] This forty-thousand-word document expounded the hierarchy's vision of the role of the Catholic Church in Mexican society, with particular emphasis on its role as the social and cultural foundation of the Mexican nation. This concept of the nation is juxtaposed with that of a state that imposed an alien ideology that suppressed Mexico's Guadalupean-Catholic identity.[136] When it turns to politics, the document does not hesitate to speak of a looming "democratic transition" and warn against the possibility of electoral fraud.[137] Despite the absence of open partisan endorsement, Vicente Fox and the PAN seized on these and other statements as declarations of church support for their political project, a point that was largely agreed on, though harshly criticized, by candidates from the PRI and Partido de la Revolución Democrática (PRD; Party of the Democratic Revolution).[138] The mechanisms of indirect religious mobilization, planted since the 1980s, were thus fully established by the time of Fox's campaign.

The reconfiguration of religion-state relations, the consolidation of political competition in a mixed electoral system, and the concentration of religious authority around the Catholic hierarchy checked the rise of assertive religious partisanship and led to the consolidation of the new model of indirect religious mobilization in Mexico. The changes in the Catholic community structure were most visibly embodied by the growing willingness of bishops, especially the papal nuncio, to speak out about politics but also by the visibility of politically engaged Catholic groups in civil society. The constitutional reforms negotiated by President Salinas and Papal Nuncio Prigione, and the notable exclusion of the PAN from the process, were both fruit and evidence of this process.

In the new structural and institutional environment, Catholic bishops represented by the CEM, despite their persistent diversity of views and the challenges posed by a rapidly evolving sociopolitical environment, were increasingly able to act as key arbiters of the legitimate use of religious claims by Catholic actors. In this capacity, they were able to admonish or encourage specific instances of political speech that drew on religious doctrines, identities, and associations.

The effects of these trends on patterns of Catholic political mobilization by political parties were unambiguous. By 2000 the PDM was largely forgotten and the PAN was a broad party that enjoyed the open support of conservative lay activists and the discreet favor of some prominent members of the Catholic hierarchy. The PAN's conservative doctrinal positions on cultural and moral issues and its informal links to Catholic organizations, while a far cry from the assertive patterns of religious mobilization that had characterized its early years, aroused suspicion among secularist groups. However, even among its opponents, few considered it an existential threat to democracy or even to the secular state.

Conclusion

As the analysis in this chapter shows, patterns of religious political engagement in Mexico changed substantially during the second half of the twentieth century. The PAN moved away from assertive religious mobilization based on explicit Catholic doctrines and deep ties to Catholic association toward a strategy that relied on indirect ties to Catholic associations and the inclusion of religious principles as secondary components of its political agenda. It thus became an effective competitor at the national level and contributed to Mexico's democratic transition in 2000. In contrast, organizations such as the PFP and the PDM, which remained committed to assertive religious mobilization, were swept from the electoral arena despite minor and temporary successes.

The process of transformation was neither the inevitable consequence of a teleological process of secularization nor the idiosyncratic product of individual personalities. Instead, it reflected the shifting opportunities and constraints generated by evolving religious community structures and political institutions. The rising pluralism of lay Catholicism and the growing capacity and coordination of the clerical hierarchy increased the costs and risks of assertive religious mobilization while enabling limited religious mobilization. Political institutions, including both electoral laws and regulations that shaped religious political engagement, which had unintentionally enabled partisan religious mobilization in the mid-twentieth century, increasingly discouraged the integration of religious and partisan activism and eventually came to facilitate lay activism outside the electoral arena. By analyzing each period separately, the chapter demonstrates the congruence between structures and institutions, on the one hand, and patterns of religious political mobilization, on the other.

The evidence also shows, however, that the evolution of religious political mobilization in Mexico was not a smooth process. Institutional incentives were sometimes reinforced by shifts in community structures—for example, when electoral reforms and changing attitudes among religious authorities facilitated the transition away from assertive mobilization in the early 1960s. Yet even during that felicitous instance the losers in the resulting realignment resisted their marginalization, as evidenced by the defection of influential young activists from the PAN. At other times, institutional changes took place during periods of greater turbulence within the religious community, contributing to more dramatic conflicts, such as the profound crisis that pitted the PAN's doctrinaire leadership against its rising pragmatist factions in the 1970s. Some trends were reversed—for example, when the rise of conservative religious associations and the loosening of electoral restrictions in the 1980s empowered assertive religious mobilization by the PDM, only for the trend to collapse in the 1990s as the institutional environment shifted in favor of mainstream parties and the Catholic hierarchy recoiled from the perceived costs of excessive political engagement.

The conflicts, crises, and reversals that accompanied the evolution of religious political mobilization in Mexico point to the importance of temporal dynamics such as speed and sequence to this type of process. Structural changes, such as those wrought by the Second Vatican Council or the conservative turn led by Pope John Paul II, did not unfold instantaneously, and their impact on political party strategies was mediated by their even more gradual effect on the preferences and capacities of the clerical leadership and the formation and decay of lay associations. Opportunities created by institutional reforms might be seized quickly or slowly depending on the coherence of the party leadership, which in turn depended on the consequences of prior institutional reforms.

As a result, while many features of the broader process, particularly structural ones such as the growing effectiveness of the hierarchy and pluralism of the laity, displayed notable similarities across the Catholic world, one should not expect that religious political mobilization will evolve in the same way across countries. Even when these structural changes are accompanied by comparable institutional adjustments—for example, when countries converge on modes of religion-state relations that grant substantial autonomy to religious communities or adopt comparable electoral regimes—the effects of these changes may vary significantly depending on their prior histories of religious political engagement or on the speed at which religious and partisan actors adapt to these trends.

Finally, a critical difference between religious political parties is the extent to which they are in a position to shape the structural and institutional environment in which they operate. During the period covered by this chapter, the PAN was not in a position to shape the Catholic community or, at least until the 1990s, to have any say in the institutional environment in which it operated. Yet the PAN's capture of the Mexican presidency in 2000 had the potential to transform it from a rule taker to a rule maker by putting the resources of the state at its disposal. As Chapter 5 demonstrates, however, the autonomy and capacity of the Catholic community along with the institutions governing religion-state relations it inherited from the PRI regime substantially limited its ability to redirect patterns of religious activism or push for institutional reforms that would have yielded potential electoral benefits.

4

The Contentious Evolution of Religious
Political Mobilization in Turkey

In 1969 a young engineer named Necmettin Erbakan sought a seat in Turkey's National Assembly. Erbakan had entered politics through the Union of Chambers and Commodity Exchanges as an advocate for small Anatolian businesses. He captured the chairmanship of the organization in 1967, but the government of Süleyman Demirel, concerned about his opposition to state-championed Istanbul-based companies, forced him to step down. Undeterred, Erbakan then sought to secure the nomination for a legislative seat in Konya, a religious and conservative district in south-central Anatolia, through Demirel's Adalet Partisi (AP; Justice Party). He was refused the nomination.[1] Seeing his political future within the AP blocked, Erbakan drew on his ties to the İskenderpaşa religious community and, with its backing, launched an independent bid for the Konya seat. He won it.[2]

The ties between politics and religion woven by Erbakan proved longlasting. That same year, Erbakan launched Milli Görüş (MG), a political movement that proposed an agenda of national renovation through a combination of economic and religious reforms. Most strikingly, MG embraced assertive religious mobilization in the electoral arena and thus broke with the conservative Turkish establishment by appealing explicitly to Muslim identity and advocating a distinctively Islamic political ideology. The MG quickly became a focal point for religious party organization. After arriving at the National Assembly, Erbakan gathered sixteen like-minded legislators and formed an assertively religious political party, the Milli Nizam Partisi (MNP; National Order Party).

The organization was short-lived. A coup in 1971 closed the party, which the military accused of going against the secular foundations of the Turkish state. However, when elections were reinstated the following year, Erbakan reentered politics through the new Milli Selamet Partisi (MSP), which achieved modest but consistent electoral success and became a coalition partner in governments led by larger parties on both the left and the right. However, escalating political tension between nationalists, Islamists, and leftists culminated in another coup in 1980, which banned all existing parties, including the MSP. Once again, the MG returned to politics after the restoration of electoral competition in 1982. This time the organization was the Refah Partisi (RP), which maintained the pattern of assertive political mobilization of religion that had characterized the MNP and the MSP. However, in contrast to the earlier parties, Erbakan's RP was able to grow consistently over the next fifteen years.

In 1996 the RP captured a plurality of seats in the Turkish National Assembly, and after complex negotiations, Erbakan became prime minister in 1997. Assertive religious mobilization had brought him to the height of his political influence, but it was once again a secularist reaction by the military that brought him down. The generals issued a public memorandum that threatened direct intervention unless Erbakan stepped down. The RP was subsequently shut down by the judiciary, which found it guilty of undermining the secular nature of the Turkish republic. That debacle was a watershed moment for Erbakan and the MG. An attempt to reorganize the party under a different label, the Fazilet Partisi (FP; Virtue Party), proved short-lived, as the successor party failed to match the RP's electoral success and was shut down after one election cycle.

Erbakan would never be prime minister again. However, in many ways the genie was out of the bottle: Religious mobilization had proven that it could provide the foundations for electoral success. When a severe economic and political crisis ravaged public confidence in Turkey's mainstream parties in 2001, the space was opened for Erbakan and his followers. However, after the closure of the FP, Erbakan's supporters split. A hardline faction led by Erbakan remained committed to assertive religious mobilization and formed the Saadet Partisi (SP; Felicity Party). In contrast, advocates of more restrained religious mobilization, led by the charismatic RP ex-mayor of Istanbul, Recep Tayyip Erdoğan, formed the Adalet ve Kalkınma Partisi (AKP), and this second faction seized the opportunity and captured a majority of seats in the National Assembly. Erbakan remained in politics until his death in 2011, a witness to the rise of the AKP and its unmatched record of electoral success. His last party, the SP, never crossed the vote threshold necessary to secure seats in the National Assembly.

Erbakan embodies the successes and limitations of Turkey's assertive religious parties. As his trajectory illustrates, patterns of religious political mobilization in Turkey have evolved substantially during the second half of the twentieth century. This chapter shows that this evolution directly reflected changes in Turkey's political institutions and the structure of its religious community. In contrast to the Mexican case, in which a single party remained the dominant agent for religious mobilization, Turkey witnessed the rise and fall of several major and minor parties that relied on some combination of appeals to sectarian identity, links to religious associations, and references to religious doctrine. Moreover, while in Mexico the general trend was toward less religious mobilization, Turkey exhibited significant fluctuations between periods of higher and lower religious mobilization. Party leaders, candidates, and activists recurrently revised and debated religious mobilization strategies in response to the gradual but virtually continuous rise of autonomous lay associations as well as sudden changes to political institutions resulting from military interventions.

The story of Erbakan and the MG is embedded in a broader pattern of evolving religious mobilization. In the 1950s, before Erbakan entered politics, the Demokrat Partisi (DP; Democrat Party) dominated the electoral arena, in part through its deft use of limited religious mobilization: the party maintained some ties to religious associations and made limited use of religious rhetoric but avoided explicit appeals to religious identity or reliance on doctrine. During that same decade, the Millet Partisi (MP; Nation Party) attempted to pursue assertive religious mobilization by combining explicit references to religion, calling for doctrinally informed legal reforms, and seeking ties to religious communities but failed to gain traction in the electoral arena. In the 1960s the AP largely replicated the DP strategy while offering limited opportunities for advocates of assertive religious mobilization such as Erbakan. In the early 1970s, Erbakan's MSP became the first party to achieve electoral success through assertive religious mobilization that combined appeals explicitly to Islamic identity, visible ties to religious associations, and proposals that drew directly on religious doctrines and ideas.

In the early 1980s the Anavatan Partisi (ANAP; Motherland Party) pursued limited religious mobilization but cultivated ties to elite religious associations, while the RP built on the MSP style of assertive religious mobilization. By the mid-1990s, the ANAP had largely abandoned religious mobilization while the RP had enhanced its religious appeals by deepening its partnerships with religious associations.[3] When the RP was closed down by its secularist opponents in the military and the judiciary, the FP sought to replicate its patterns of religious mobilization, meeting with less electoral success but the same secularist reaction. From its remnants arose two parties with contrasting approaches to religious politics: Erbakan's SP pursued assertive religious mobilization, while Erdoğan's AKP opted for a more limited strategy that combined associational linkages with qualified appeals to religious identity.

This assortment of partisan actors, pursuing mobilization strategies that range from limited to assertive in rapid sequence and even in parallel, provides a fertile environment for testing the congruence between religious community structures and political institutions, on the one hand, and patterns of religious mobilization, on the other. They also facilitate the exploration of the causal mechanisms behind variation and the temporal features of adaptation and continuity in the face of changing incentives.

Like the chapter on Mexico, the remainder of this chapter is divided into three empirical sections and a conclusion. Each of the first three sections focuses on a particular time period, summarized in Table 4.1. The periodization is built around the incidence of major changes in the institutional and structural foundations of religious mobilization. The first stretches from the inauguration of multiparty competition in 1946 to the 1960 military coup. During this time, political institutions were highly restrictive, and autonomous religious associations began to expand but remained weakly coordinated. The second period covers 1961 to 1980, characterized by a more permissive political environment, as well as an increasingly robust and diverse associational setting. The third period, 1981 to 2002, was shaped by greater state engagement in religious affairs and the introduction of new electoral constraints, as well as by the rapid and substantial expansion of religious associations. The period ends with the electoral victory of the AKP in 2002.

Each empirical section begins with a brief overview of the patterns of religious mobilization during the period. Then it describes the condition of religious community structures and the political institutions that most directly affected religious mobilization. It then focuses on mechanisms, presenting a detailed account of how party leaders and candidates shaped, contested, and modified their approaches to religious mobilization in response to structural and institutional constraints. As these discussions show, various shifts in the dominant style of religious mobilization were far from smooth. In addition to reiterating and clarifying the observed correspondence between causal factors and outcomes within each time period, the conclusion therefore explores

TABLE 4.1: RELIGIOUS POLITICAL MOBILIZATION BY OPPOSITION
PARTIES IN TURKEY, 1946–2002

Period	Parties	Religious community structures	Political institutions	Level of religious mobilization
1946–1960	DP MP	• Emergence of local religious associations • Growth of Nurcu and Nakşibendi religious communities	• Highly disproportionate electoral system • Limited liberalization of assertive secularism, including educational reforms • Control over formal religious sphere by the Diyanet state bureaucracy	DP: Low MP: High
1961–1980	AP MSP	• Continued growth of local religious associations • Pluralization of Nurcu and Nakşibendi communities • Emergence of MG	• Proportional electoral system • Greater associational rights and protections • Establishment of NSC and Constitutional Court	AP: Low MSP: High
1981–2002	ANAP RP FP SP AKP	• Expansion of Nurcu communities, particularly the Gülen movement • Pluralization of MG • Growth of religious business sector and formation of MÜSIAD business association	• Turkish-Islamic Synthesis promoted by state • Expansion of public religious education • Legalization of Islamic banking • Proportional representation with 10% vote threshold	ANAP: Low RP: High FP: Medium SP: High AKP: Medium

broader temporal dynamics, including questions of sequencing, legacy, and speed of change.

Beginnings of Religious Mobilization (1946–1960)

The 1940s and 1950s were a period of limited religious mobilization in Turkish politics, which nevertheless contrasted with the assertive secularism of the single-party era that preceded it. The first successful postrevolutionary opposition party in Turkey, the DP, brought together a coalition including landlords threatened by land reform, businessmen wary of statist policies, peasants impoverished by wartime scarcity, and religious conservatives who resented the imposition of assertive secularism. In Şerif Mardin's influential formulation, the DP was able to attract and maintain the support of a broad "periphery" that had been sidelined by the urban, military-bureaucratic elite represented by the ruling Cumhuriyet Halk Partisi (CHP).[4]

Religious mobilization played a controversial role in the DP's campaigns, and scholars still dispute the relevance of Islam for the party.[5] On the one hand, its leaders, most notably Prime Minister Adnan Menderes and President Celâl Bayar, were consistently outspoken regarding the DP's commitment to the principle of *laiklik*, the Turkish version of state secularism akin to the French *laïcité*,[6] and framed its efforts to relax some restrictions on public religious expression in terms of liberal rights.[7] On the other, prominent members included severe critics of Atatürk's reforms, such as Fehmi Ustaoğlu, who openly called for a return to Islamic values in politics.[8] Local party congresses routinely produced documents that called on the party to stand as a representative of religious identity and justify its policies in religious terms.[9] Overall, DP candidates in national elections generally opted for limited appeals to religious identity, and the party's informal links to religious associations, such as its references to religious doctrine, were discreet and kept at a distance by the party leadership.

The period also witnessed attempts to engage in more assertive forms of religious mobilization. The most successful was the MP, which appealed more explicitly to religious identity, referred to Islamic principles, and maintained close ties to an outspoken segment of the Nakşibendi religious community. Despite attracting some prominent candidates and avoiding immediate closure, the MP never managed to become a central player in Turkish elections, and its influence diminished until it was banned in 1953.

To understand the DP's success and the MP's failure, we must consider the role of institutional incentives and religious community structures.

Religious Community Structures and Political Institutions

On the eve of the formation of the DP in 1946, the Sunni Muslim community in Turkey was formally organized around the Diyanet İşleri Başkanlığı (DİB; Directorate of Religious Affairs), referred to by convention as the Diyanet. This arm of the Turkish state, formed in 1924 as a replacement for the Ottoman-era caliphate and the Ministry of Islamic Law and Foundations, was tasked with administering formal religious functions and guiding religious practices. In practice, it managed all mosques and appointed all imams, preachers, and other religious functionaries.[10] From the point of view of the architects of Turkish secularism, the Diyanet was conceived as an instrument for the modernization and rationalization of Islam and as a critical tool for shaping and managing religious sentiments and behaviors among the population.[11] However, even during the early years of the Turkish Republic, when secularist reforms were most intensely implemented, the Diyanet was largely staffed by religious officials who had been trained under Ottoman rule and who accommodated, rather than embraced, secularist reforms.[12]

Moreover, despite the ambitious reforms the Diyanet was tasked with implementing, the available resources were quite limited, particularly because the CHP had placed religious endowments under a separate bureaucratic office and severely restricted the viability of religious education.[13] Indeed, the Diyanet did not even own the mosques it administered. Moreover, the Diyanet did not have a substantial voice in policy making. Instead, it was tasked with implementing policy proposals emanating from elsewhere in the state, often designed by staunch secularists. Much of the population resented and opposed these policies, which seriously impeded their efficacy and caused many to be rolled back or abandoned.[14] By the late 1940s, after decades of halfhearted attempts to implement externally mandated reforms in the face of public opposition while being starved of resources and labor, the Diyanet was in a state of severe weakness and disrepair.[15] It leadership sought to enhance its diminished powers by appealing to the Kemalist establishment, positioning itself as a potential bulwark against popular superstitions and communism.[16] It was in no position to facilitate opposition to political mobilization.

Beyond the weak formal structures of the Diyanet, the Sunni community was primarily organized around neighborhood and village groups, occasionally linked by a small number of informal networks, most notably the Nakşibendi community and the emerging Nur movement, known as the Nurculuk, which were not sophisticated organizations. Rather, they sustained and aggregated a variety of local notables and networks, bonding them by mutual recognition and a shared idiom. Neither the local- nor the national-level groups had a legally recognized existence since the 1938 Law of Associations banned, among others, "groups based on religion, sectarianism or mystical orders . . . , groups whose goal is to destroy the territorial integrity of the state and political and national unity [and] groups that are secret or that conceal their goal."[17] From the perspective of the secular leadership of the country, religious movements effectively violated all three of these restrictions.

In 1946 the government passed a new Law of Associations in anticipation of the transition to real multiparty competition, which limited government control over civil society while maintaining restrictions on group participation in political activities.[18] This liberalization produced real changes in religious organization in Turkey.[19] The most notable was a substantial expansion in the number of associations, which increased from 0.6 per million people in 1946 to 7.3 in 1950. This expansion continued through the 1950s, reaching 45.4 per million inhabitants in 1955 and 184 by 1960. Initially, the overwhelming majority of these new associations were local, task-specific bodies, particularly mosque-building groups, which later expanded to include religious schools, Qur'an courses, and philanthropic societies.[20] These highly fragmented local religious associations played only a secondary, supporting role in the electoral success of the DP, facilitating mobilization and recruitment in the countryside but remaining distant from the heads of the party.

Equally important for the future development of political Islam in Turkey was the gradual institutionalization of Turkey's larger religious movements, particularly the Nakşibendi, a deeply rooted religious brotherhood,[21] and the Nurculuk, an emerging religious community organized around the charismatic figure of Said Nursi.[22] Progress on this front was slow during this period. Even after the associational reform, their situation remained ambiguous at best, as they lacked legal recognition and their leaders were often subjected to persecution. Prominent Nakşibendi leaders were arrested for performing unauthorized religious services,[23] and Said Nursi was sanctioned by state authorities on various occasions.[24] However, the gradual expansion and consolidation of these networks of networks played a central role in the subsequent development of religious communities and political parties in the country.[25] They contributed to the establishment of structural foundations for eventual party mobilization by organizing lodges, schools, and prayer and discussion groups, among a myriad of other forms of local organization. In particular, they facilitated the channeling and coordination of resources that had until then remained dispersed at the village level.

In addition to acting as coordinating mechanisms, their greater scope allowed Nurcus and Nakşibendis to contribute to the emergence of a particular approach to religious mobilization. Having witnessed decades of repression and having benefited directly from partial liberalization, their leadership was highly conscious of the potentially devastating impact of a secularist reaction by the state. The Nurcus and Nakşibendis were thus cautious in their attitude toward political mobilization. Said Nursi favored the development of broad coalitions in the political arena, hoping to avoid polarizing the country along a religious-secular cleavage.[26] The Nakşibendi community, lacking a single, dominant figurehead, showed a greater variation of responses to political Islam but was generally disinclined to directly challenge *laiklik*.[27]

The moderating impact of these networks contrasts with the more radical activism associated with other religious groups, notably the Ticani religious community. Among the most important actions undertaken by the Ticani was reading the call to prayer in Arabic in the National Assembly in 1949, the defacement of monuments to Atatürk in 1951, and the demonstrations during the funeral of Marshal Fevzi Çakmak, leader of the MP, on April 12, 1950, when his "coffin was snatched from the gun carriage and carried on the shoulders of the crowd led by chanting imams."[28] This last event involved a large crowd, which closed cinemas and theaters and called on radio stations to stop broadcasting music. In all three cases, political reaction was swift and resulted in the arrest of numerous participants, as well as the hardening of secularist institutions—for example, through Law 5816, passed in 1951, which criminalized attacks against Atatürk's memory. Members of the Ticani order were pursued under its auspices, leading to incarceration of its leader, Kemal Pilavoğlu, and the dramatic decline of the order.[29] These events, taking place at the crucial moment of transition, appeared to justify the prevailing attitude among most Nurcus and Nakşibendis against direct political engagement and discouraged calls for rapid, fundamental reform.

As the failure of the Ticani political project illustrates, political institutions played a central role in restraining religious political mobilization during this period. The willingness and ability of secularist officials to impose severe costs on religious mobilizers, exacerbated by the enduring uncertainty regarding the government's commitment to democratization and the entanglement of party and state that resulted from twenty-five years of CHP rule, posed a number of challenges to the peaceful and effective incorporation of religious groups into the political arena. In this context, two sets of institutional constraints contributed directly to the emergence of a conservative coalition that included, but was in no way dominated by, religious activists.

The most obvious constraint on religious mobilization derived from the red lines drawn by the Kemalist regime during the transition period (1946–1950). Political liberalization in Turkey was a top-down process spearheaded by President İnönü and bounded by the preferences of the military, bureaucracy, and ruling party.[30] Secularism, specifically the regulation of religious expression in the public and political spheres, quickly emerged as one of the most important of these red lines. Previous responses by the Kemalist establishment to any suggestion of religious reaction, such as the dramatic prosecutions and policy reforms that followed the Menemen Incident, the murder of a gendarme lieutenant by religious extremists,[31] set a strong and highly credible precedent regarding its willingness to defend the secular nature of the republic.[32]

A more subtle but equally important set of incentives derived from the electoral system, which was highly disproportionate and converted small electoral advantages into enormous differences in seats. From 1946 until 1960, Turkey used a multiple, nontransferable vote (MNTV) electoral system, in which voters could cast votes for as many candidates as there were seats in the district. Formally, voters were allowed to split their tickets and vote for fewer candidates than there were seats available in a district, features intended to enhance the representative quality of the results. In practice, the electorate overwhelmingly relied on preprinted ballots issued by the political parties and thus voted straight-party tickets, transforming the system into a simple plurality with multimember lists.[33] The result was an overwhelming degree of disproportionality in favor of the largest party. Thus, in 1954, 57.5 percent of the national vote secured an astounding 93 percent of legislative seats for the DP.

By delivering overwhelming majorities to whoever could capture a plurality of votes, the system encouraged the DP to adopt a centrist platform. More precisely, it strongly discouraged religious groups that clearly preferred the DP to the CHP from shifting their allegiance to any explicitly religious party: if successful at the polls, such a party would capture the entirety of government and threaten the bureaucracy and the military, potentially triggering deliberalization and repression; if unsuccessful, it would split the conservative vote and deliver a massive victory to the CHP. Dramatic electoral disproportionality thus steered all but the most radical conservative voters toward the center-right, occupied in this case by the DP.

Patterns of Religious Mobilization

The limited resources and low organizational capacity of the Sunni religious community and a highly disproportionate electoral system generally discouraged assertive religious mobilization. The DP repeatedly balked at making direct appeals to the religious identity of voters, and its leadership never relied on theological or doctrinal arguments to defend its policy proposals. Although it was content to recruit religious activists with ties to groups such as the Nurculuk and Nakşibendi communities, these links remained weak and distant from the party leadership.[34] How political institutions and religious structures produced specific patterns of religious mobilization can be best appreciated by examining the party's responses to the various challenges it faced in its early years—that is, at the time when its attitude toward religious mobilization was taking shape.

When it was inaugurated in 1946, the DP faced a complex situation created by twenty years of single-party rule, which generated uncertainty about the viability of emerging as a real opposition party. The CHP was effectively cojoined with the state apparatus and felt confident that it could dictate the precise limits of the political opening. Indeed, the ruling party hoped that the opposition would be moderate and retain a minority status for "forty to fifty years."[35] To ensure conformity with Kemalist principles, formation of the new party was entrusted to well-known and highly regarded members of the governing party with a long track record of commitment to Mustafa Kemal, most notably Celâl Bayar. To win elections, the CHP relied on its established reputation and voters' familiarity with the party.

Faced with the possibility of being regarded as puppets of the CHP, the DP leadership actively sought to demonstrate its distinctiveness. Given the CHP's notorious distaste for public Islam, appeals to religious identity were considered a potential means to this end. Press organs affiliated with the DP began to discuss the moral superiority of the party in regard to the Kemalist establishment, and the first DP convention included an extended discussion of the possibility of introducing courses on religion. As a result, as early as 1946 the DP was accused of "injecting religious propaganda, such as the promise to introduce the Arabic script and allow the reading of Ezan [call to prayer] in Arabic" into its electoral appeals.[36]

The rapid growth of the DP in the countryside led President İnönü to open the door to moderate reform, particularly in the area of education. The National Assembly modified the religious education law in 1948–1949, including the establishment of imam training schools, known as Imam Hatip schools, and the foundation of the Faculty of Divinity in Ankara. This convergence on a centrist platform left little distance between the parties with regard to religious policy,[37] while the continuing presence of Kemalist hardliners left little doubt that further relaxation of secularist norms would be hard-fought and that attempts at fundamental reform were potentially threatening to the democratic system as a whole.

This convergence created a dilemma and potential opportunity for religious activists who were seeking to directly challenge the CHP. In 1948 religious members of the DP who considered that coordination between Bayar and İnönü compromised the principles of the opposition came together to form the MP.[38] Its leader was Fevzi Çakmak, a well-known hero of the liberation war and devout Muslim. The MP appealed directly to voters' religious identity and maintained publicly visible ties to religious associations.[39] Among its central goals was "to uplift moral standards by strengthening the family and by giving the youth a nationalistic and religious education."[40] Concretely, the MP was most assertive in calling for the relaxation of secularist norms, including permission to wear the fez, and the expansion of religious education.

This conservative challenge initially appeared as a real threat to the DP, as MP members briefly equaled DP members in the assembly after a second wave of defections in 1949.[41] However, the electoral system ultimately blunted its impact. In the lead-up to the election, it became increasingly clear that the MP was having difficulty convincing the already-mobilized anti-incumbent voters to switch allegiances from the DP. The organization was able to win just under 4 percent of the vote in the crucial 1950 elections, and because of the disproportionality of the electoral system, this translated to a single seat in the 487-member National Assembly. Electoral rules thus ensured that only the DP would emerge as a viable challenger to the CHP. In the aftermath of the election, the MP suffered a wave of defections. Its remnants were banned in 1953 for "political use of religion" and reformed in 1954 as the Republican Nation Party but had even less electoral success.[42]

The 1950 contest was a watershed for the DP: the party captured 53.3 percent of the vote and, thanks the disproportionate electoral systems, 83.8 percent of seats. As a result, Adnan Menderes, the charismatic leader of the DP, became prime minister of Turkey. In the aftermath of its massive electoral victory, the DP came face-to-face with the reality of governing and the need to satisfy its broad constituency. It embarked on a series of legal initiatives and reforms aimed at the partial liberalization of the religious sphere. These included amending Article 526, which allowed the call to prayer to be read in Arabic; lifting the ban on religious radio programs, allowing the Qur'an to be read on the airwaves; and shifting voluntary public religious education from opt-in to opt-out, virtually ensuring that the overwhelming majority of Turkish children would receive it.[43] It also considered enhancing the resources and autonomy of the Diyanet, although these proposals remained largely unimplemented.[44] The CHP, struggling to recover from its dramatic fall from power, adopted an intransigent position and systematically criticized the DP's permissive religious policies, although these reforms were largely in keeping with the limited liberalization endorsed by the CHP during its final years in government.

These reforms proved sufficient to earn the DP the enthusiastic support of religious leaders such as Said Nursi and several influential Nakşibendi figures.[45] However, other religious activists operating in Turkey's fragmented religious environment were not satisfied and considered that the DP was not doing enough to roll back *laiklik* and restore Turkey's Islamic identity. The Ticani community engaged in a campaign of vandalism against images of Atatürk. Around the same time a new style of religious activism also came to the fore, led by a cluster of religious-political periodicals that called for the reincorporation of Islamic values and ideas into politics.[46] Although many of these had links to peripheral, short-lived parties, others had direct links to the more religious members of the DP. This emerging religious movement, which brought together traditional religious actors and a new generation of activists, put pressure directly on the party to cater to its preferences.

The fragmentation and weakness of the incipient religious movement greatly reduced its efficacy and left it in a vulnerable position. An assassination attempt against the influential secularist journalist Ahmed Emi Yalman in 1952 proved to be the trigger. The attack was widely understood to have been religiously motivated, and the DP drew a sharp distinction between mainline parties and radical political actors.[47] In the aftermath of the assassination attempt, DP members who had expressed assertively religious views were expelled from the party, including Ustaoğlu, who had recently published a series of provocative articles in *Büyük Cihad*, one of the prominent antisecularist periodicals.[48] A large-scale campaign of repression, including the arrest of various prominent activists and the closure of religious-political periodicals, effectively razed the foundations of the more outspoken wing of the rising religious movement. The relative ease with which the DP cut off the more activist elements in its religious base highlights how the limited mobilizing capacity of Islamic activists allowed the DP to remain committed to a limited style of religious mobilization.

The expansion of religious associations throughout the 1950s subtly strained this situation. Most associations remained small, local affairs— schools, mosques, and neighborhood charities—but there was also a notable expansion of the larger, informal communities. The Nurculuk became prominent enough to provoke concerns among hardline secularists, and Said Nursi was put on trial and not allowed to enter Ankara.[49] However, highlighting the equivocal attitude of the DP toward religious activism, Nursi was also personally courted by Menderes, the leader of the party.[50] Even more important, conditions were established for the publication of his main text, the *Epistles of Light.*[51]

This equivocation was also pronounced with respect to the Nakşibendi. Members of the order were often able to secure employment in the Diyanet and its mosques.[52] However, a prominent Nakşibendi sheikh, Suleyman Hilmi Tunahan, was arrested and tortured in 1957 and died a few months after his release.[53] In a symbolically charged display, his followers attempted to bury him in the garden of Istanbul's Fatih Mosque, an effort ultimately blocked by police.[54] The rapid expansion of Turkey's religious constituency thus put pressure on the DP to demonstrate its commitment to religion.

During the same period, the consolidation of the electoral environment also began to cause difficulties. Embattled by a declining fiscal and economic situation in the late 1950s,[55] Menderes prominently advertised his administration's involvement in the construction of fifteen hundred mosques and his personal gift of one hundred thousand Turkish lira for a mosque in Istanbul.[56] More spectacularly, Menderes's survival of a plane crash at Gatwick Airport outside London in 1959 was used in propaganda to suggest divine sanction for his government.[57] The ensuing demonstrations of public religiosity, many of which were attended by prominent DP members, produced a spectacle suggestive enough to cause substantial unease among both local and foreign observers.

At the same time, consistently disappointing results at the ballot box, made even more lopsided by the mechanical effect of the electoral system, convinced many members of the CHP and its allies in the military that they had limited chances to capture the government by electoral means. Combined with the DP's willingness to pass laws that directly challenged their ability to criticize the government, these persistent electoral defeats drove the CHP opposition to believe that its influence would only diminish with time. The turn toward sedition in the armed forces was felt as early as 1957, when nine army officers were charged with conspiracy (and then promptly released by Menderes, who did not want to test the loyalty of the military), but became increasingly urgent over the next two years. In this polarized atmosphere, the DP launched a partisan investigation into the ties between the CHP and the military, endowing the committee charged with its execution with extraordinary powers. An announcement that the commission would publish its results earlier than expected ultimately convinced the military to overthrow the government. The May 27, 1960, coup was not primarily a response to the DP's shift in favor of more direct appeals to religious identity, but this had doubtlessly contributed to the growing polarization of the country.[58]

Limited religious mobilization during the period from 1946 to 1960 was the result of fragmented religious community structures and restrictive political institutions. The secular state's control over formal religious bodies through the Diyanet and related institutions, together with the weakness of informal religious communities, left few organizational resources available to partisan actors interested in mobilizing religion. Moreover, incentives for anything beyond limited religious mobilization were tempered by the electoral system and fears of a secularist reaction. Although the mobilizing power of religious appeals was demonstrated early on, prompting convergence of the CHP and the DP on a moderate reform platform, efforts by a rising religious movement proved possible to ignore and suppress. In part, this reaction was facilitated by disproportionate electoral rules that handed overwhelming majorities to the mainstream DP and severely punished smaller organizations catering to more devout voters, such as the MP.

The resulting pattern of selective religious mobilization by a mainstream party was gradually undermined by shifting structural conditions. The growing resources of religious associations, though still limited during this period, increased the influence of religious leaders and encouraged minor adjustments to the DP's religious mobilization strategy. Ultimately, the exclusive quality of the electoral system brought about the end of the system by systematically keeping the CHP from power. This pushed its leadership to support a military coup that dramatically altered the institutional environment.

The Rise of Assertive Religious Mobilization (1961–1980)

The two decades following the May 27 coup witnessed a dramatic transformation of religious mobilization in Turkey. The most dramatic events of the immediate postcoup era involved the closure of the DP and the execution of its political leadership, including Prime Minister Menderes, Finance Minister Hasan Polatkan, and Foreign Affairs Minister Fatin Rüştü Zorlu. In addition, the coup resulted in the purge of hundreds of military officers, judges, prosecutors, and university faculty.[59] To cement their achievements, the architects of the coup implemented a series of profound political reforms aimed at minimizing the possibility that another party might gain the power that the DP had accumulated. These reforms included substantial modifications of electoral institutions that made them markedly more proportional and permissive, making it harder for any single party to achieve a supermajority in the National Assembly. A new Constitutional Court could throw out legislation deemed unconstitutional, and media and universities were granted substantial legal protection and autonomy. Finally, a new bill of rights enhanced the rights of individuals and groups.[60] These reforms, crafted by a committee led by academics sympathetic to the military, had profound consequences for Turkish politics, many of which were unintended. Most pertinently, combined with increasingly robust religious networks and associations, these reforms facilitated the emergence of assertive religious mobilization.

Despite these dramatic changes, the shift from limited to assertive religious mobilization did not occur overnight. For nearly a decade, patterns of religious mobilization remained very similar to those prevalent in the DP era. Despite the substantial changes in the electoral systems and constitutional reforms intended to diminish the relative importance of political parties in national life, the AP was largely successful at reestablishing the broad-based, peripheral coalition that had led the DP to power.[61] Like its predecessor, it also managed to appeal to religious voters—as evidenced by its strong showing across rural Anatolia—without pursuing assertive mobilization. Among the few notable differences was the AP's more open relationship with particular religious associations,[62] but even here the difference was one of degree rather than kind.

Not until 1970 did a new party emerge that could effectively seize the political opportunities created by the institutional and religious changes taking place in the country. Necmettin Erbakan's short-lived MNP signaled the emergence of a new style of religious mobilization. Its successor, the MSP, successfully established itself as a serious political contender and consolidated the new style of religious politics. These parties forged much closer links with religious associations than the DP or the AP, directly appealed to voters' Sunni Muslim identity, and called for policy reforms that drew directly on their interpretation of Islamic principles. By leveraging all three dimensions of religious mobilization, the MSP became Turkey's first enduring assertive religious party.

The shift from one model to another responded to the mismatch between limited mobilization strategies and the opportunities made available by the institutional framework and the structure of religious communities. The continuing expansion and consolidation of religious networks and associations, which benefited from the growing economic integration of conservative Anatolian merchants and peasants, created a power base that was not efficiently leveraged by DP-style religious mobilization. At the same time, electoral reforms put forth after the 1960 coup dramatically diminished the costs of supporting an independent religious party. While these had been initially tempered by fears of a prompt authoritarian reversal, the new proportional representation system in fact made it possible to participate in elections without undermining potential conservative allies, since support could always be negotiated in the postelection legislature.

Religious Community Structures and Political Institutions

The 1960s and 1970s witnessed the continuing growth and diversification of Turkish religious associations. The new legal frameworks created by the

Constitution of 1961 greatly facilitated this process by providing a variety of guarantees of associational rights, allowing large and small religious communities to build mosques, sponsor charities, and invest in education. The trajectory of the largest religious movements in Turkey during this period, such as the Nurculuk and the Nakşibendi, was also one of growing pluralization, albeit structured by the presence of recognized leaders and authorities that gave these movements a measure of coherence and articulation.

Said Nursi's death in 1960 was a catalyst for the transformation of the Nurculuk from a relatively univocal group to an increasingly pluralistic religious community.[63] In an effort to prevent the disintegration of the movement, Nursi's closest disciples formed a Board of Trustees to act as the authoritative voice of the Nurculuk after his passing. Several members advocated strict control over the dissemination of Nursi's texts, arguing that the unique bond between reader and text could be best preserved through an oral tradition in which written documents were individually crafted and handmade.[64] However, by the late 1960s this status quo was increasingly challenged by a new generation committed to expanding awareness of Nursi's teachings. In 1967 a group of educated Nurcus started a new publishing house that turned out a religiously oriented periodical, *İttihad* (Union). Military authorities closed down this magazine following the 1971 coup, but it was promptly replaced by the newspaper *Yeni Asya* (New Asia).[65] This was the beginning of an explosion of activity in the media, which would grow rapidly over the next three decades. This pluralism was also furthered by the rapidly increasing number of reading circles (*dershaneler*). While many were under the indirect supervision of established movement leaders, others were only nominally under the oversight of the Board of Trustees. Increasing availability of Nur texts, along with members committed to expanding the movement's presence across the country, resulted in the emergence of hundreds of Nurcu reading circles. The participative quality of these associations, in which local leaders took up positions of authority, virtually ensured that diverse voices would emerge under the broad umbrella of the movement.

Crucially, however, growing pluralism was constrained by the presence of broadly recognized movement elites, who also acted as points of reference for the Nurcu community as a whole. While encouraging discussion and cooperation, the Nurculuk also emphasized the importance of hierarchies, and new communities were typically built around the leadership of a particular learned individual. Fethullah Gülen, who led the community in Izmir during the 1960s before becoming the leader of a global religious movement, is but one prominent example. As the movement became increasingly involved in formal business, media, and educational ventures, these individuals frequently came to occupy positions of authority within these associations as well, giving their charismatic authority a new measure of legal recognition.[66]

Many of these dynamics were also visible within the Nakşibendi community. Under the leadership of Mehmet Zahit Kotku, the order became an increasingly influential player in Turkish politics.[67] He encouraged the reengagement of the order with secular concerns by emphasizing the importance of combining spiritual and material well-being and encouraged followers to pursue and secure success in this world as well as the next. As a formal leader of the Nakşibendi and head of one of its most influential communities, the Iskenderpaşa congregation, he was in a position to exert significant influence. In the long run, this was enhanced by the success of his methods, which saw him emerge as the religious mentor of such prominent politicians as Necmettin Erbakan, Turgut Özal, and Recep Tayyip Erdoğan.[68] Kotku was an advocate of the free market, calling on his disciples to pursue trade and economic autonomy rather than employment in the state bureaucracy.[69] His injunction to engage the world was not entirely new to the Nakşibendi, whose members had provided the leadership to the 1930s revolts against secularization and maintained a prominent presence in the Diyanet. But it was with the blessing of leaders such as Kotku that the Nakşibendis became increasingly involved in a variety of economic and civil-society enterprises.

The Nakşibendi's relationship to the state and market was affected by the 1960 coup and the policies implemented in its aftermath. Concerns among the secularist establishment about the growing influence of religious orders in the Diyanet led to a legal reform in 1965 ruling that only graduates of the state-sanctioned Imam Hatip schools and Faculty of Divinity could find employment there.[70] This law dealt a blow to religious communities such as the Suleymancıs, a subset of the Nakşibendis that had invested significant resources in developing their own private seminaries and whose graduates found employment in the Diyanet. In 1971 private Qur'an seminaries were nationalized, further distancing the Suleymancıs from official religious authority. This effectively encouraged many to turn toward civil society, publishing, media, and other economic activities as a means of expansion.[71] Not all Nakşibendis, however, were equally affected by these laws, as many remained invested in Imam Hatip schools and continued to see in the Diyanet a viable means to remain involved in mainstream religious affairs.[72]

Despite the secularist orientation of the coup leaders, the Diyanet found its authority formalized and even enhanced in the aftermath of the coup. The new regime formally recognized its role in shaping public morality, expanding its influence beyond the narrower role in faith and worship, and recognizing it in the new constitution. Moreover, it promoted a substantial centralization and expansion of the Diyanet's bureaucracy. The aim of these changes was to increase the Diyanet's influence relative to autonomous groups in religious civil society and thus to extend state control over the religious sphere, but it also deepened and strengthened the potential for religious influence within the state.[73]

The political and institutional changes brought about by the 1960 coup went far beyond these reforms. The seriousness of the military's commitment to political change was demonstrated by the treatment afforded to the DP leadership following the coup: Prime Minister Menderes and two key ministers were executed, President Bayar and eleven others received commuted death sentences, and hundreds of others received lengthy prison sentences. These exemplary punishments made a deep impression on the Turkish public.

The coup leaders aimed to remake Turkish politics by crafting a new set of fundamental laws and institutions. The result was the Constitution of 1961, which differed from its predecessor in a number of crucial ways and, unbeknown to its architects, had a direct, positive impact on the ability of parties to pursue new styles of religious mobilization. The new document ultimately made it much easier to form assertive religious parties by increasing the expected benefits of independent religious competition, reducing the costs of breaking away from secular partners, and mitigating the risks of secularist reaction. Yet greater permissiveness was largely an unintended consequence of the reforms. Their central purpose was to prevent the accumulation of power in the hands of a single party that had, in the eyes of the military, enabled the DP to threaten the well-being of the republic. To achieve this purpose, the new document adopted a proportional electoral system, established an upper legislative chamber, set up a Constitutional Court with the power of judicial review, institutionalized the supervisory role of the military by means of a National Security Council (NSC), and formalized and expanded constitutional guarantees of individual and collective rights. All of these reduced the stakes of electoral competition. Whereas in the 1950s capturing a plurality of votes formally granted the winning party power over the entirety of the state and government, proportional representation made it far more difficult for a single party to control the legislature, let alone the judiciary or the military.[74]

By pushing coalition bargaining into the postelectoral phase, proportional representation created incentives for potential coalition partners to maintain autonomy in the electoral arena and negotiate support for the government during coalition formation, or even on an issue-by-issue basis. Given the diversity of the periphery that had supported the DP, the military and its political allies could reasonably hope that this would prevent the emergence of a unified party that could systematically threaten its interests. Although there was some tinkering with the electoral formula as parties sought to secure advantages on the margins,[75] the basic framework remained firmly in place until 1980.

The establishment of the NSC and the Constitutional Court produced a system in which the civilian government operated side by side with an independent military authority and a largely self-selecting judiciary.[76] The upper chamber, with its appointed members and senators for life, provided additional protection for the Kemalist state from unexpected surges of the popular will. The new document thus institutionalized intervention by the state bureaucracy in representative politics. This reduced the likelihood that political conflict would result in a full-fledged coup by multiplying both the buffers and points of contact between the military and the political class.

The 1971 "coup by memorandum," as it was labeled, demonstrated the limits of the new mechanisms. The NSC, dissatisfied with the civilian government's apparent unwillingness to bring about reforms it considered urgent and worried about rumors of coup plotting by junior officers, issued a communiqué in which it demanded the resignation of the government and its replacement by a nonpartisan coalition.[77] While dramatic, this intervention was markedly different from, and far less deadly than, the elimination of the previous political elite associated with the 1960 coup.

Patterns of Religious Mobilization

Why did it take ten years for the new, assertive style of religious mobilization to emerge? One reason is that religious mobilization in the 1960s, like virtually every other aspect of political life, took place in the shadow of the May 27 coup and its aftermath. Political risk calculations were directly affected by the tragic fate of Menderes and the DP leadership. The severity of their punishments, particularly the executions, stood in striking contrast to the ambiguous legitimacy of charges leveled against the accused.[78] Many accusations were based largely on hearsay and circumstantial evidence, and even sympathetic observers note that they would not have stood up in most European courts.[79] Others rested on an arguably tendentious reading of the Constitution of 1924, which had vested all sovereign powers in the assembly and stated that representatives could not be prosecuted for their votes. The severity with which the DP was treated dramatically altered politicians' risk calculations, discouraging them from pursuing strategies that might trigger a military backlash, including more explicit forms of religious mobilization.

However, even in the first few years after the coup, parties had clear incentives to engage in religious mobilization. With multiple potentially viable political actors competing to secure the support of the ex-DP voters, religious networks could provide much-needed support. Moreover, while its leadership was decimated, the DP's enormous provincial and subprovincial resources, including its activist networks and infrastructure, remained in place. Three tentative successor parties to the DP emerged after the restoration of electoral politics in 1961 by aggregating largely intact regional clusters of DP groups.[80] These groups' links to religious associations were a significant part of the DP's broader organizational legacy, and the new parties competed to curry their favor. As the would-be successors to the DP maneuvered to position themselves as the preferred partner for the Nurculuk, the Nakşibendi, and other religious communities, these religious communities acquired new leverage in dealings with potential political representatives.

Two contradictory forces thus came to bear on political parties pursuing religious mobilization in the 1960s. On the one hand, they were constrained by the credible willingness of the NSC and the secularist judiciary to impose severe punishment on those who threatened the established order and its Kemalist foundations. On the other hand, the possibility of inheriting the DP's infrastructure pushed them to form alliances with rising religious movements that could tilt the field in favor of one party or another.

During the 1960s the AP, first under Ragıp Gümüşpala and then under Süleyman Demirel, emerged victorious from the competition to become heir to the DP. The AP forged more significant ties to the Nurcus and Nakşibendis than Menderes and the DP had maintained.[81] The AP government gave movement members greater access to public resources and defended their members and organizations from secularist demands emanating from the state.[82] Yet even as the AP mobilized religion through associational linkages, Demirel cultivated a progressive, secularist-friendly image. He had been educated in the United States and worked in a multinational company; his best-known public post had been head of the State Water Resources Development Agency, which strengthened his technocratic credentials. After Gümüşpala died in 1964, Demirel rose through the party ranks by displacing more traditional-conservative competitors such as Sadettin Bilgiç.[83] Under his leadership, the party opted not to engage in direct appeals to Muslim identity and entirely avoided referring to religious doctrines. Like Menderes before him, Demirel instead relied on the liberal language of individual and associational rights enshrined in the new constitution to carve out legal room for public manifestations of piety.

The sweeping victory of the AP in the 1965 elections, in which it obtained 52 percent of the votes and 53 percent of National Assembly seats while support for other major right-of-center parties declined sharply, appeared to confirm the success of its overall approach and solidified its claim to the DP mantle. However, electoral victory also paved the way for greater dissent within party ranks. The main point of contention was economic policy, but even this division had a distinctive religious dimension. Under Demirel, the AP opted to pursue rapid modernization through foreign investment and thus favored large industries and businesses based in major urban centers, which enjoyed the international connections and orientations needed to realize Demirel's vision. This came at the expense of small businessmen, artisans, and merchants, who felt distinctly vulnerable to competition from multinationals and state-supported industries. Crucially, this increasingly alienated petite bourgeoisie was the most religiously conservative part of its constituency. During the AP's first two years in power, overall economic growth partially compensated for the distributive effects of economic policies. However, as the economic climate turned more challenging in 1967, contention became more acute.

Demirel's policies provoked the crystallization of a clear nationalist-religious faction within the AP.[84] A first challenge by conservative delegate Osman Turan was effectively rebuffed in 1967.[85] In the 1969 elections the AP again secured a majority of seats, but this time with only a plurality of votes and with a sharply diminished voter turnout.

Necmettin Erbakan's MNP and its successor, the MSP, ultimately seized these opportunities to engage in assertive religious mobilization. Like Demirel, Erbakan was an engineer by training with work experience in the West, in his case in Germany,[86] but unlike Demirel he combined his technical credentials with an abiding commitment to conservative Islamic principles. Drawing on these two elements in his background, Erbakan openly challenged the notion that the Muslim world had to choose between "Mecca and mechanization," as advocates of modernization claimed,[87] arguing that Turkey could and should industrialize on its own cultural and religious terms. His overt appeals to religious identity, incorporation of religion into policy proposals, and well-known personal ties to the Nakşibendi order made him an object of scorn among secularist and leftist intellectuals,[88] but Erbakan and his supporters gradually emerged as a near-permanent feature in the Turkish political landscape.

After entering politics, Erbakan published a manifesto titled *Milli Görüş*, which became the ideological centerpiece of an eponymous social movement and a series of political parties. Erbakan drew on two related networks to establish MG as a social and political force. First, he drew heavily on the personal networks and ideological support of Kotku, the influential Nakşibendi leader.[89] Kotku used his religious connections to support Erbakan's various campaigns, which proved decisive in kick-starting Erbakan's national political career. Second, he leveraged his ties with religiously conservative and economically protectionist elements in the Anatolian business community.[90] After returning from Germany, Erbakan became a prominent figure among the more conservative segment of this group and occupied positions of authority in a variety of business associations during the mid- to late 1960s.

The process began when Erbakan, with Kotku's blessing, ran for head of the Union of Chambers and Commodity Exchanges in 1968. This was a test of the AP establishment's openness to religious activists, and he was running against Demirel's favored candidate. Although successful at the ballot box, Erbakan's election was annulled by Demirel, who argued that there had been irregularities in the process.[91] Undeterred, Erbakan then sought the AP nomination for the Konya electoral province, the heart of arguably the most conservative and religious region in Turkey. Once again, Demirel vetoed his candidacy. However, he could not prevent Erbakan from competing as an independent, which he successfully did. Once in parliament, Erbakan began to coordinate with a set of delegates with ties to the Nakşibendi and Nurcu communities. The result was the formation of the MNP.

The MNP never competed in national elections, as it was banned by the military along with other suspect groups as part of the 1971 military intervention. Erbakan was forced to flee to Switzerland and was initially banned from participating in Turkish politics. However, the group of activists coalescing around the banner remained active. A group of Erbakan's supporters began lobbying military authorities almost immediately to facilitate his return and allow the reorganization of the party.

In October 1972 these came together to form the MSP, which was unambiguously intended as a continuation of the banned MNP. The party was built on virtually identical associational foundations, conservative businessmen and Sufi networks, and retained its calls for the restoration of "national" (*milli*) values and traditions, a transparent allusion to Islamic principles.[92] The policy proposals of the party were also framed in terms of thinly veiled religious arguments, with party members demonstrating sustained interest in topics such as promoting modesty via state censorship.[93]

The 1973 elections demonstrated the effectiveness of assertive religious mobilization, with the MSP securing 11.8 percent of the votes and 10.7 percent of seats. The impact of the electoral system was crucial, resulting in a highly proportional allocation of seats that favored small parties. Moreover, neither of the two largest parties, the AP and CHP, obtained the number of seats necessary to form a viable single-party government. The distrust between their leaderships impeded the formation of a grand centrist coalition, and the MSP thus found itself in the position to play kingmaker.

The MSP seized its success with a combination of political pragmatism and doctrinal rigidity that played to its strengths in the area of religious mobilization. Confident in its ability to use its associational depth to retain voter support, it entered into governing coalitions on three different occasions during the 1970s, once with the CHP and twice with the AP. Each time, Erbakan succeeded in obtaining several ministries for his party, including a position as deputy prime minister for himself. While in government, the party pursued policies including the ban of "pornographic" images and stricter enforcement of alcohol-sale and nightclub regulations.[94] It also used its position in the ministries to reward its religious supporters, strengthening its presence in the state bureaucracy and the Diyanet.[95] In this fashion, the party managed to continue to appeal to religious voters and promote a doctrinally informed policy agenda without formally overstepping the red lines set out by the military.

This pragmatism and willingness to cooperate with disparate political forces caused predictable friction within the party. Many members were particularly uncomfortable with the CHP alliance, which they saw as contrary to the party's principles. This tendency was particularly pronounced among the Nurcus, who had always been divided in their support for the MG project.[96] Nurcu defections became increasingly common, and by late 1977 the overwhelming majority of the contingent had left the party and realigned itself with Demirel.[97] These defections, together with the mixed results of its participation in government, contributed to the decline in support for the MSP in the 1977 elections, in which it received 8.6 percent of votes and 5.3 percent of seats. However, the party retained prominent Nakşibendi support, ensuring that associational links of the party remained firm. The electoral system also proved crucial to the survival of the party. Thanks to its proportionality, the party was able to weather its decline while remaining a crucial player in the legislature.

The late 1970s witnessed an escalation of violence that remains controversial and poorly studied.[98] There is little doubt that politically motivated attacks in Turkey escalated during this period, driven by confrontations between leftists and nationalists.[99] Although the MG, Nurcus, and Nakşibendis were all firmly anticommunist and did not hesitate to voice their condemnation of these movements, they shied away from the strategies of the nationalist Milliyetçi Hareket Partisi (MHP; Nationalist Movement Party) and its paramilitary arm, the Grey Wolves, which carried out brazen violent attacks.

This context produced conflicting incentives for the MSP. On the one hand, it encouraged the party to distance itself from radicals on both fronts to consolidate its standing as a plausible governing partner for the DP or CHP in an otherwise radicalized environment. The commitment to nonviolence that characterized both the contemporary Nakşibendi and Nurcu movements, and their preference for gradual over revolutionary change, provided important support in this direction. Moreover, by remaining in government, the MSP was able to continue to secure state employment for its supporters, which held the additional promise of enhancing its influence in the still largely hostile apparatus of the state.

On the other hand, the MSP also needed to keep itself relevant in an arena that appeared increasingly dominated by leftists and nationalists. One way to do so was to engage in heightened forms of peaceful but explicit religious mobilization. Mobilizing religion in this way was a calculated risk, as the military remained hypersensitive to independent religious activism. The most salient religious demonstration during this period took place on September 6, 1980, when Erbakan and the MSP organized a rally in Konya to protest Israel's decision to make Jerusalem its capital.[100] The event was the largest and most vocal religious demonstration in decades.

On September 12, 1980, only six days after the Jerusalem march, the military intervened directly in Turkish politics once again. Despite the marginal role played by religious mobilization in the violence leading up to the intervention, the Jerusalem demonstration played a prominent role in the justification for the coup.[101] The military declared itself committed to taming not only dysfunctional Turkish politics but also society as a whole. The generals included the safeguarding of secularism, or at least their understanding of secularism, as one of the key features of the new regime. To do so, the new military government proposed a project of fundamental transformation that in many ways closely resembled the uprooting of the political system in 1960.

The transition from the limited religious mobilization of the AP to the assertive religious mobilization of the MSP was gradual, reflecting the establishment and consolidation of permissive political institutions and the steadily growing capacity of religious associations. The AP initially benefited from the continuing weakness of lay associations, which along with the threat of military intervention and the organizational legacy of the DP discouraged risky political strategies and facilitated the re-creation of a broad conservative coalition. Yet over time, this inertia was overcome by the growth of religious community structures as well as incentives emerging from the new political institutions.

During these two decades the Sunni Muslim community in Turkey witnessed the rise of increasingly robust coordinating associations that often operated at a distance from the clerical religious authorities associated with the state's Diyanet. Indeed, religious figures such as Nursi and Kotku encouraged their followers to engage with technology and the market as a means of enhancing their autonomy and did not shy away from ideological confrontation with Kemalists, who saw religion as something that needed to be tamed or suppressed to make way for secular modernity. These religious groups, with their expanding mobilizing resources, provided much of the necessary foundations for the emergence of assertive religious mobilization.

Political institutions made it possible to translate this emerging religious influence into the electoral arena. A greater degree of associational freedom and rights protection gave religious activists more confidence in their ability to operate in public. Moreover, the highly permissive electoral system allowed parties that catered to a minority of the electorate to nevertheless thrive politically. Thus, despite its inherently provocative nature, the MSP was able to remain a significant, legitimate player in Turkish politics throughout the 1970s. It did so not by attracting an enormous number of voters (its vote share hovered around 10 percent of the electorate) but rather by successfully exploiting a fragmented party system and positioning itself as a necessary component of any governing coalition. The institutional and structural environment in which the MSP operated dramatically facilitated the development of this niche-party strategy. Thus, by 1980, when Turkey's escalating domestic strife prompted the military to intervene in politics yet again, the MSP had successfully established assertive religious mobilization as a viable instrument for political contestation in Turkey.

Contested Adaptation and Costly Success (1981–2002)

The last two decades of the twentieth century were marked by the coexistence of groups advocating limited religious mobilization or pursuing assertive religious mobilization. Initially, the division was between Turgut Özal's ANAP, a center-right party, and Erbakan's RP, a MG vehicle that gathered the remnants of the MSP. The decline of ANAP led to an uneasy but electorally successful convergence of both groups within the RP. The process was driven by the dramatic expansion of Islamic associations amid a restrictive political environment. However, a crisis at the end of the 1990s led to the collapse of the RP and ultimately to a schism between its reformist and traditionalist wings.

The ANAP pioneered a new style of selective religious mobilization. Özal seized the opportunities provided by the uncertain postcoup environment to position his party as the leader of a broad conservative coalition and thus took advantage of his close ties to religious associations while abstaining from open appeals to religious identity or putting forth doctrinally driven platforms.[102] Relying on this strategy, the party achieved sustained electoral success in the 1980s. However, its dependence on a single dominant figure ultimately caused the party to fail following Özal's exit from the party and unexpected death.

In contrast, the RP initially attempted to revive the assertive approach that had allowed the MSP to operate as an important political player in the 1970s. The limited electoral success of these efforts led its leadership to realize that electoral success under altered institutional and structural conditions required a rethinking of its religious mobilization strategy. The party supported grassroots religious activism while simultaneously deemphasizing some of the most assertive elements of its religious mobilization strategy, thus developing a dual-track approach that reflected the growing distance between its doctrinally committed members and an increasingly influential set of reformers.[103] Nevertheless, the new strategy led the party to electoral success, and the RP won the most seats in 1995 and formed the first Islamist-led government in Turkey the following year. This achievement was met by a powerful secularist reaction, however: the military toppled the government in 1997 and subsequently banned the RP.[104] The crisis strained the traditionalist-reformist partnership and led to a formal schism in 2002.

The growing salience of religious mobilization was powered by dramatic changes to Turkey's religious community structure and the incentives generated by new political institutions. The rapid expansion of religiously oriented businesses and business associations during this period,[105] along with the consolidation of transnational networks and the growing institutionalization of established religious communities,[106] created an enormous pool of resources for religious activists and their representatives. Institutional reforms largely directed the way in which these changes affected electoral politics. On the one hand, the state developed a new stance that co-opted and legitimized particular aspects of religious doctrine, known as the Turkish-Islamic Synthesis,[107] and empowered the Diyanet to strengthen its implementation. On the other, it adopted restrictive electoral institutions that made it virtually impossible to pursue a niche-party strategy, with a high electoral threshold rewarding preelectoral coalition building and preventing smaller parties from entering office. The effect was to facilitate the normalization of religious appeals while gradually pushing the RP to soften its assertive style of religious mobilization. Even after military intervention brought that party's collapse, these incentives remained in place to shape the strategies of its successors.

Religious Community Structures and Political Institutions

The 1980s witnessed the accelerating expansion of religious associations and the further consolidation of both domestic and transnational religious networks. There was some continuity in form, with broad communities, such as the Nurculuk and Nakşibendi, providing a loosely coordinated framework and common language and more coherent and specialized associations within them, such as the Gülen movement and MG, serving as vehicles for more concrete collective action. However, the scope and resources of these associations were dramatically expanded, and new associational types emerged as important players alongside these increasingly well-established groups. In particular, the expansion of business enterprises owned by religious groups and persons, and their organization through associations such as the Independent Industrialists and Businessmen's Association (MÜSIAD), had a direct impact on religious mobilization.[108] The overall result was an increasingly confident and effectively coordinated religious community with an enhanced capacity for collective action but significant pluralism and no community-wide veto players.

This broad-based transformation of the religious community structure was made possible by a crucial shift in public policy following the 1980 coup: the move away from a centralized, statist economy in favor of liberalizing economic reforms. This facilitated an economic takeoff in the religiously conservative and historically less-developed provinces of central Turkey, a phenomenon often referred to as the rise of the Anatolian Tigers.[109] This process, alternatively described as the emergence of an "Islamic subeconomy" or "Islamic capital,"[110] was characterized by the rapid emergence of small and medium-sized enterprises that embraced an explicit religious discourse and orientation. It was powered by a variety of mechanisms, the relative impact of which remain contested: an improved investment climate for employers of small and medium-sized businesses, remittances from Turkish workers in Western Europe, and newly legalized institutions of Islamic or interest-free banking.[111] Remittances sent by Turks working in Western Europe played a direct role in both the emergence of a religious business sector and the consolidation of transnational religious movements. Religion served as a common bond within the enormous Turkish expatriate community in places such as Germany, and religious associations such as the MG, Nur, and Gülen movements found this to be a propitious environment for expansion and recruitment.[112] These organizations in turn nudged the flow of remittances toward conservative businesses and institutions, thus coordinating investments by conservative Muslims.[113] Their ability to do so was enhanced by the 1983 legalization of interest-free, or Islamic, banking.[114] The formation of the interest-free banks greatly facilitated the effective flow of capital among devout Muslims who had previously been hesitant to put their money in conventional banks or take out loans because of concerns about the legitimacy of interest payments.

These mechanisms facilitated capital accumulation in regions where it had previously been absent, allowing devout individuals and groups to engage in the modern, globalized economy without sacrificing their religious identity. This led to the formation of new, competitive firms in Turkey's historic periphery and directly reinforced existing religious communities and networks.[115] The emergence of this increasingly transnational, but distinctly Turkish, business-associational nexus created a vast new pool of resources that religious parties could potentially tap into.

The community's capacity for collective action was dramatically enhanced by the emergence of new business associations, the best-known and most important of which was MÜSIAD. Formed in 1990 by a collection of young, religious business owners, MÜSIAD rapidly expanded to become a plausible alternative to the well-established Turkish Industrialist and Businessmen's Association (TÜSIAD), which had existed since the 1970s and represented the largest companies in Turkey. In contrast, MÜSIAD emphasized that it aimed to provide a voice for small and medium-sized firms that resented the favoritism and tight links that characterized the relationship between the state and larger companies typically located in or around Istanbul.[116] As part of its effort to reassert its difference from the establishment, it explicitly relied on Islamic referents in its public statements and maintained explicit links to other religious associations.[117] The public policy dimension of its work rapidly transferred onto the political arena, where its members supported rising Islamist candidates against more secular establishment forces.

It was far from obvious, however, whether this new structural configuration would lead to more or less assertive forms of religious mobilization. By delinking economic resources from the preferences of the secularist elite and empowering critics of Kemalist secularism, it potentially increased the expected yields from explicit appeals to religious identities, doctrines, and associations. Yet by encouraging religious activists to become formalized and invested in the global economy, it simultaneously discouraged them from adopting tactics that might prove unduly disruptive or provocative. Moreover, the continuing diversity within the religious community, which included groups with clearly distinct preferences, resources, and organizational styles, suggested the possible emergence of multiple, viable religious parties pursuing different styles of mobilization. Therefore, while the structural transformation of the 1980s and 1990s gave religious mobilization new impetus, it did not in itself provide it with a clear direction.

One of the most striking aspects of the postcoup regime was its embrace of the Turkish-Islamic Synthesis, an ideology that sought to reframe and co-opt religious sentiment as a means of containing leftist activism and enhancing the legitimacy of the state.[118] In practice, the adoption of this framework enabled and legitimized reliance on political parties' appeals to religious identity. It resulted in concrete changes, such as the significant growth of the Diyanet's powers and the even more dramatic, state-sponsored expansion of Imam Hatip schools, whose graduates became an increasingly significant source of votes and activists for religious political mobilizers.[119]

The reforms initiated after the 1980 coup encouraged the formation of broad, centrist parties capable of capturing substantial fractions of the national vote. One of the main goals of the architects of the Constitution of 1982 was to strengthen the state in relation to society as a reaction to the polarization and social conflict of the 1970s.[120] The new document contained a series of institutional reforms intended to bring about this effect, including a 10 percent threshold for parties seeking seats in the national legislature, substantially expanded powers for the NSC, and a strengthened presidency. Jointly, these were intended to prevent the fragmentation of the legislature while increasing the power of unelected and indirectly elected state institutions.

The new 10 percent national vote threshold represented a momentous change for political parties in Turkey. One of the military's central concerns during the 1970s had been the inordinate power wielded by small parties, such as the MSP, in the legislature and the ensuing fragility of governing coalitions. By repeatedly depriving the largest parties of an outright majority and making them dependent on the favor of fringe parties, permissive proportional representation had resulted in weak governments that consistently failed to provide the military with a civilian working partner. The solution to this problem was sought in the threshold, which dramatically limited the ability of small parties to secure any seats in the legislature with which they might hold the government hostage. Under the new constitution, no party that obtained less than 10 percent of the nationwide vote could obtain a seat, even if it won an overwhelming majority in specific electoral districts. The new law thus severely penalized small parties, especially regionally concentrated ones, and encouraged the formation of broad, preelectoral coalitions.

The effect of this threshold on political outcomes was dramatic. Relying on Rein Taagepera's formulas for predicting party sizes,[121] we can estimate that without the threshold Turkish elections between 1983 and 2011 would have created legislatures with an average of 7.25 parties holding at least one seat, average parties holding 13.7 percent of seats, and the largest party holding about 37 percent of seats. These would have been highly fragmented legislatures, even more so than those operating during the 1970s because of the greater number of total seats available in the assembly. Winners would almost certainly have had to form coalitions to govern. Instead, as a result of the 10 percent threshold, the legislatures of that period contained an average of 3.7 seat-holding parties, an average party with 29 percent of seats, and the largest party holding 48 percent of seats. Absent the threshold, single-party government would have been extremely unlikely, but with the threshold, such governments emerged in half the elections (1987, 2002, 2007, and 2011). Moreover, while clearly still capable of producing minority and coalition governments, the electoral system effectively ensured that any government-formation negotiations would take place between large parties representing significant swaths of the political spectrum rather than single-issue or niche associations.

The enhanced powers of the NSC and the indirectly chosen presidency also shifted power away from the elected government and representative institutions. While Turkey remained a parliamentary regime, the presidency was set up to act as a restraint against populist excesses and as a bridge between the NSC and the government. The presidency had limited executive authority, with its new powers instead oriented toward sanctioning and controlling the legislature. The president could also use his power in regard to the NSC to pressure the legislature, since by setting the agenda for the NSC, he could force the Council of Ministers, which is formally responsible to the assembly, to prioritize his concerns.[122] The first postcoup president was General Kenan Evren, leader of the coup. The military therefore understandably considered the presidency a far more reliable institution than the government or the legislature.

Patterns of Religious Mobilization

The most successful political party of the 1980s was the ANAP, which relied on a limited form of religious mobilization based on ties to religious association and discreet appeals to religious identity. Its success was initially a consequence of the military's efforts to directly alter Turkey's political landscape. General Evren did not allow any of the precoup parties or their direct successors to participate in the 1983 election, leaving the field open for candidates backed by the military and those of the ANAP. The ANAP benefited greatly from the eclectic background of its leader, Turgut Özal, who combined ties to the military with credible independent appeal and religious piety.[123] The ANAP's relative autonomy from the generals made it a focal point for critics of the coup, allowing it to benefit from their support without having to directly challenge the military. In this context, the party proved enormously successful, and Özal became prime minister with a solid majority of seats.[124]

Özal pursued a limited mobilization strategy adapted to a restrictive electoral environment in which religious associations were increasingly salient. He used religious referents in many of his speeches but avoided portraying his party as the unique bearer of religious identity. In addition, he maintained well-known links to religious associations that more closely resembled those of the Islamist Erbakan than those of his center-right predecessors such as Demirel and Menderes. Like Erbakan, he had direct ties to Kotku, the influential leader of the Nakşibendi Iskenderpaşa community, who acted as his spiritual mentor. Özal's ability to mobilize religion was also indirectly strengthened by the military's embrace of the Turkish-Islamic Synthesis.[125] This was particularly manifest in the case of educational reform, which ultimately made religious education compulsory.[126] Although these policies were largely driven by the military, their implementation under Özal strengthened his reputation a supporter of the devout religious community.

In summary, Özal and the ANAP benefited from the particularities of the postcoup environment: the threshold delivered a disproportionate number of votes in its favor, state ideology enabled limited religious appeals, and the support of several religious groups, including the Nurcu and several Nakşibendi communities, contributed to its success. However, the ANAP was not the only party attempting to mobilize religion in the electoral arena.

Erbakan's supporters formed the RP in 1983 as a replacement for the MSP and a vehicle for the MG movement. It was prevented from participating in that year's national elections, however, and not until the municipal elections of 1984 was it able to measure its strength at the polls. In that contest, it managed to secure representation in Van and Urfa, but overall it captured less than 5 percent of the national vote, a disappointing result but one that could still be partly attributed to the aftereffects of the coup and particularly to the banning of its most popular candidate, Erbakan.[127]

Over the next three years, the RP sought to gain prominence in an electoral environment dominated by the ANAP, in part by engaging in more assertive forms of religious mobilization. Among the most notable events in the RP's campaign was a demonstration on January 16, 1987, in favor of lifting the ban on Erbakan's candidacy. Held in Istanbul, it drew on the party's enduring connections to religious associations to gather Erbakan supporters and included explicit appeals to religious identity and doctrine.[128] Özal, under pressure from precoup political forces and debilitated by difficulties in Turkey's adjustment to economic liberalization, decided to hold a referendum on whether banned candidates should be allowed to participate in the 1987 national elections.[129] This pitted the ANAP and supporters of the 1982 coup against a broad coalition of forces, ranging from conservative Islamists to social democrats. The referendum passed by a minute margin, with 50.2 percent of valid votes in favor of allowing banned politicians to participate.

The impact of Erbakan's return was not what the RP had hoped for, prompting it to rethink its approach to religious mobilization. The party expected to do well in the 1987 elections, but the results were disappointing. The party secured only 7.2 percent of votes, an improvement over its performance in 1984 but nevertheless well short of the requirements for gaining representation in the national legislature. This failure provoked serious debate within the party. Some members argued for the need to focus on assertive religious mobilization and promote social transformation, while others began to explore the possibility of diversifying the party's support base by deemphasizing openly religious appeals.[130] Neither of these strategies had substantial support, however, and the party gained 9.8 percent of votes in the 1989 municipal elections, which put the threshold tantalizingly within reach.[131] For the 1991 election, the party formed an alliance with the Milliyetci Çalışma Partisi (MÇP; Nationalist Working Party) and the smaller Reformist Democratic Party. Establishing this coalition necessarily entailed some dilution of the RP's distinctive style of religious mobilization. However, the success of this stratagem, through which the coalition partners gained 16.2 percent of votes and sixty-two seats in the legislature, made it a crucial moment for the party. The success of this coalition vividly demonstrated the value of expanding the party's support base, a lesson that would not be lost on younger cadres.

The RP now pursued religious mobilization on a different scale. Its members used the legislature as a new platform, arguing that the party represented a "deeper Turkey" that held Islam as a core referent but was primarily concerned with honest government and liberalized economic development.[132] Its doctrines increasingly emphasized the notion of Adil Düzen (just order), as a way of incorporating religious doctrines pertaining to economic redistribution, financial reform, and public morality into its policy proposals.[133] At the municipal level, the party developed explicit links to local religious groups while emphasizing pragmatic reforms and service delivery.[134] Religious activists managed to form collaborative partnerships that linked RP representatives to women's groups, neighborhood prayer groups, and local businesses, resulting in remarkably effective and resilient instruments for mobilization.[135]

The RP's ability to expand its electoral appeal without losing religious support was greatly facilitated by the other parties of the Turkish right. The ANAP had found itself on the defensive since the 1987 referendum and especially since Özal's ascent to the presidency in 1988.[136] The growing antagonism between Özal and Demirel resulted in a deep split in the center-right. Özal's sudden death in 1993 and his replacement by Demirel as president did nothing to ease the animosity between the ANAP and the successor to Demirel's AP, the Doğru Yol Partisi (DYP), now led by Tansu Çiller. Moreover, the ANAP and DYP competed to position themselves as defenders of moderate—that is, privatized and quiescent—Islam against the more outspoken RP.[137] The purging of religious activists from the ANAP's ranks in the early 1990s, coupled with the DYP's ongoing criticism of religious activism,[138] cost them support among religious voters and Nurcu and Nakşibendi groups.

Benefiting from the missteps of the traditionally dominant center-right, the RP was able to make substantial electoral gains.[139] The municipal elections of 1994 proved to be a second crucial moment for the RP. Its candidates, buoyed by their reputation as effective administrators and credible political outsiders, managed to capture 19.7 percent of the national vote and the mayoral offices in Istanbul and Ankara, along with those in twenty-seven other major cities. Recep Tayyip Erdoğan, newly elected mayor of Istanbul, instantly became a prominent and controversial figure in national politics. The following year the party continued along the road of electoral success, securing 21.4 percent of votes and 158 seats in the legislature, a result that made the RP the single largest party in the assembly. During this time, the RP's campaign brought Islamic identity into its speeches and policy proposals, calling for stronger links to Muslim-majority countries and the protection of the rights of pious individuals.[140] It also stood for economic policies associated with the religious business groups affiliated with MÜSIAD, such as the defense of private enterprise and institutions of interest-free banking.[141]

However, electoral success brought with it a new set of challenges to a party that billed itself as both a pragmatic problem solver and a committed advocate of religious reform. After some maneuvering, and seizing on divisions among center-right parties, Erbakan became prime minister in a coalition with Çiller's DYP.[142] But this tenuous alliance, built largely on the threat of exposing corruption by Çiller's previous administration, clashed directly with its religious mobilization strategy.

Constrained by his coalition partner and wary of provoking an extra-electoral reaction from the NSC, Erbakan sent mixed signals. On the one hand, he spoke warmly of Atatürk, the military, and the recently deceased Özal; more credible was the costly signal of signing a military agreement with Israel.[143] On the other, he pursued a set of largely symbolic efforts aimed at sustaining religious support. Much to the chagrin of the military, which correctly feared it would irk key NATO partners, Erbakan conducted his first foreign policy trips exclusively to Muslim-majority countries, including Iran and Libya.[144] These trips proved largely ineffectual and, in the case of the Libyan venture, deeply embarrassing.[145] Domestically, Erbakan also adopted strategies that did little more than provoke secularist protests. In a typical instance, he invited leaders of various Sufi communities to join him for Ramadan dinner, which was portrayed by media as a symbolic assault by religious forces on the prime minister's residence.[146] The party also made a point of the need to allow women to attend universities while wearing the traditional Islamic headdress, an issue that had already emerged as a point of serious contention.[147] More concretely, the rapid expansion of religious cultural and educational institutions, along with the entry of RP affiliates into the national bureaucracy and military establishments, caused significant concerns in the NSC and other secularist groups in the state and civil society.[148]

Even as Erbakan courted repression from secularist forces, his failures to pursue the religiously infused pragmatism and honest government that were the hallmark of RP's municipal administrations were eroding his base of support.[149] Particularly severe was the Susurluk scandal, which exploded in November 1996 and revealed undeniable connections between Çiller's DYP, police officers, and organized crime.[150] Erbakan sought to minimize its impact, supporting a law aimed at curbing the press's investigation and defending the DYP delegates' parliamentary immunity. This strategy proved costly, with many supporters resenting his inability to deliver on this most basic aspect of ethical politics.[151]

By late 1996 the RP's balancing act aimed at mobilizing religion, appeasing the NSC, and remaining in government had put Erbakan in an increasingly unsustainable position. On February 28, 1997, the military-dominated NSC issued an eighteen-point memorandum advising the RP government to initiate a series of wide-ranging reforms aimed at curbing Islamist activities in the state and society.[152] Known as the "February 28 Process," it was in fact an ultimatum backed by the threat of direct intervention. Faced with this threat, Erbakan signed the document but delayed its implementation. Instead, he tried to negotiate and maneuver himself into a less disastrous outcome. In July 1997, amid escalating threats and protests, he resigned in the expectation that Çiller would be given an opportunity to re-form the government. However, President Demirel, under pressure from the military, gave ANAP's leader Mesut Yilmaz the choice to form a coalition that excluded the RP.

In the months between issuing the memorandum and Erbakan's resignation, the judiciary launched a prosecution of the RP. The basic premise for the judiciary's arguments was that the party's activities threatened the principle of secularism protected by Article 2 of the constitution.[153] More specifically, the court highlighted the party's efforts to permit wearing the Islamic headscarf in universities, its plans to expand religious education, speeches by Erbakan in which he referenced the Constitution of Medina as a model for judicial pluralism, and his iftar with Sufi leaders.[154] These policies neatly mirror the diverse set of religious mobilization strategies used by the RP, covering appeals to identity (headscarves and education), doctrinal references (Medina Act), and associational links (Sufi leaders).

The guilty verdict was handed down on January 1998, and the party was officially closed down. Five party leaders, including Erbakan, were also banned from politics. They were not alone in bearing the brunt of secularist reaction. In December 1997, Istanbul mayor Erdoğan was arrested for reciting verses by nationalist poet Ziya Gökalp at an RP rally, which combined martial imagery with religious allusion in a way that suggested Islamic militancy. A wide variety of businesses owned by religious associations or prominent religious conservatives were shut down, as were dozens of media outlets sympathetic to the RP, including newspapers, television channels, and radio stations.[155]

The years following the soft coup witnessed a growing schism between the traditionalist (*gelenekçiler*) and reformist (*yenilikçiler*) camps that had formed within the RP during the 1990s.[156] The traditionalist group was linked to Erbakan and the MSP old guard, while the latter pragmatic-reformist camp was led by a new generation of leaders clustered around Erdoğan and Abdullah Gül. The choice was between accepting an opposition party role, in which the organization would pursue assertive religious mobilization at the cost of short-term exclusion from government, or the substantial tempering of religious mobilization for the sake of becoming acceptable to the various existing veto-wielding powers.[157]

The stage on which this debate took place was the short-lived FP. The party was formed by ex-RP members and led by Recai Kutan, a founding member of the MSP,[158] but Erbakan operated as the party's de facto head. Initially, its leadership argued that the RP's fate was the result of limitations imposed on Turkish democratic processes and saw participation in democratic institutions as a viable pathway for removing these constraints without sacrificing its religious mobilization strategy.[159] However, the FP was able to secure only 15.4 percent of the vote in the 1999 elections, a notable decline from its 1995 performance. Moreover, when one of its female representatives attempted to wear a headscarf at the swearing-in ceremony, she was ultimately prevented from doing so by shouts and threats from other deputies.[160] The incident led to a judicial process against the FP, with the state prosecutor contending that the party had become a center for antisecular activity.

The poor performance of the party in the 1999 elections and the prospect of prompt closure exacerbated the division between traditionalists led by Erbakan and Kutan and reformists represented by Erdoğan and Gül, with religious mobilization in many ways at the heart of their disagreement. The party faced a stark choice between, on the one hand, striving to consolidate its religious constituency, transforming society from the grassroots, and loosening secularist restrictions and, on the other, working within existing political institutions and presenting itself as a viable governing party before both the NSC and the public at large. At the party congress in May 2000, Gül mounted an official challenge to Kutan's leadership, obtaining 45 percent of the delegates' votes and thus narrowly losing to the traditionalist camp.[161] When the FP was closed down in 2001, it almost came as a relief to many of its members, who seized the opportunity to launch their own political vehicles. Kutan and the traditionalists acted first, organizing the SP, emphasizing their continuity with the MG tradition and its approach to assertive religious mobilization that combined appeals to religious identity, doctrinal references, and ties to religious associations. A month later, Gül formed the Adalet ve Kalkınma Partisi (AKP) as an organization committed to the reformist vision of pursuing change while operating within the existing system.

The religious mobilization strategy that yielded the RP its electoral success was a response to the growing power of religious associations in an institutional environment that enabled religious mobilization but set up a restrictive electoral arena. After several failed attempts to reproduce the MSP's niche-party strategy during the 1980s, the RP adapted to the institutional constraints and moved toward the center while expanding its coordination with religious civil-society organizations ranging from Islamic foundations to small activist groups.[162] This effort was bolstered by its ability to exploit the possibilities created by the principles of the Islamic-Turkish Synthesis and its close relationships with dynamic religious associations and businesses that coordinated a growing conservative elite.[163] Meanwhile, in striking contrast to Özal and the early ANAP, the traditional parties of the center-right overestimated the robustness of their appeal and underestimated the strength of these groups, facilitating their convergence around the RP.

The coexistence of seat-seeking pragmatists for whom securing political power was paramount along with an old guard invested in assertive religious mobilization repeatedly caused strains within the RP. These were eased by electoral success in the early 1990s but became increasingly severe as secularist reaction made clear the cost of achieving electoral success through assertive mobilization. Although the tension was certainly exacerbated by the military and judiciary interventions, it also reflected a substantial division among members of the group regarding the best means for incorporating religion into the political arena. By forcing a choice between two different approaches to religious mobilization, the period of crisis and contestation set the stage for a new, and dramatically successful, approach to religious politics.

Conclusion

The contentious evolution of religious parties in Turkey during the second half of the twentieth century was the result of a complex process powered by gradual changes to its religious community structure and channeled by political institutions. The growing resources and coordination of diverse religious groups, ranging from Nurcu reading circles and Nakşibendi prayer groups to business associations such as MÜSIAD and transnational networks such as the Gülen movement, brought devout constituencies from the margins to the center of political contention over the course of five decades. Yet this gradual and largely linear process of empowerment did not translate to a continuous increase in religious political mobilization, largely because of dramatic shifts in institutional constraints and opportunities faced by religious activists and political entrepreneurs.

The periodic changes to the basic institutions governing religious political engagement in Turkey consistently aimed to contain the emergence of threats to the secularist, Kemalist establishment. The institutional arrangement set up in the late 1940s, designed with the expectation that the governing CHP would remain the largest party after the transition to democracy, was scrapped when the DP began to dominate the assembly, in part by means of limited religious appeals. The system set up to replace it after the 1960 coup made it difficult for any single party to dominate elections and placed substantial limits on the power of the assembly, and it was in turn abolished when it failed to produce stable governments and gave disproportionate power to niche organizations such as the assertively religious MSP. In response, the leaders of the 1980 coup sought to co-opt and leverage rising religious sentiment while containing its partisan expression through a combination of pro-religion policies and restrictive electoral laws. Yet once again these arrangements had unexpected consequences, enabling the rise of an RP that managed to expand its appeal by both deepening its ties to religious movements and expanding its appeal by exploiting divisions among its conservative rivals. The coup by memorandum of 1997 and the banning of the RP cut short its victory but did not address the underlying reality that robust religious mobilization had become a viable path to electoral success.

Given these dramatic shifts in the institutional environment, it is less than surprising that, in contrast to the Mexican case, where organizational continuity meant that debates about religious mobilization took place discreetly within a single party, the Turkish case is populated by a diverse cast of organizations publicly pursuing diverse religious mobilization strategies. Moreover, different modes of religious political mobilization coexisted and were simultaneously pursued by multiple parties. From the struggle of the MP and DP at the dawn of the multiparty era, through the wary coexistence of the AP and the MSP in the 1970s, to the competition between the ANAP and RP for devout voters and resources into the 1990s, the landscape of religious mobilization in Turkey paints a dramatic picture and allows us to assess its congruence with institutional and structural conditions. The picture that emerges is remarkably consistent with the theoretical expectations that guide this project: religious mobilization responded positively to expanding resources and coordinating capacity among religious actors and shifted toward greater assertiveness when political institutions made it more electorally viable.

This striking diversity of religious mobilization and the responsiveness of religious political entrepreneurs to the incentives generated by structural resources and institutional constraints strongly support the notion that modes of religious mobilization are not driven by fixed doctrines. At the same time, paying attention to the temporal dynamics that characterized how religious activists and party leaders responded to these changes makes it clear that individuals, communities, and organizations are invested in particular styles of mobilization. The delays in adaptation, along with the contentious character of strategic shifts, show that how religious parties respond to shifting incentives is highly contingent on the outcome of struggles between the diverse factions that constitute them. The decade-long lag between the institutional reforms of 1960 and the formation of the first durable, assertive religious party in 1972 is particularly striking and was largely driven by the ability of the AP to capture and repurpose the mobilizing infrastructure developed by the DP. Even Erbakan first attempted to operate within the AP before launching the MG and his own electoral vehicles. Similarly, the RP took a decade, three full electoral cycles, to learn how to benefit from the rules set up following the 1980 coup. As it had for the AP, this delay was driven largely by the organizational inertia of its predecessor, the MSP, for which assertive religious appeals to a minority of voters had yielded substantial political gains.

5

From Words to Deeds

The Challenges of Incumbency

The victories of the PAN in 2000 and the AKP in 2002 were the culmination of decades-old struggles to secure political power, but they also set in motion a new set of challenges for these parties. Both remained in power for at least twelve years—no small achievement for any political party—but their administrations were recurrently troubled by conflicts over the proper relationship between religion and state. In both countries, ongoing debates over secularism and religious influence on politics led to acrimonious legal fights and regular mass mobilization by religious and secularist forces. However, the extent to which the PAN and the AKP were able to weather these conflicts was notably different.

In Mexico, PAN governments led by Vicente Fox and Felipe Calderón found it difficult to meet the expectations of their most religious followers. Despite the party's long-standing commitment to Catholic principles and their candidates' promises to defend Catholic values, PAN national governments were repeatedly outmaneuvered by secularist competitors in key conflicts over abortion and same-sex marriage. Under the PAN's watch, and despite its objections, Mexican courts and subnational governments expanded reproductive rights and extended legal recognition to same-sex couples.[1] The PAN fought back in multiple arenas, including the courts and national and regional legislatures, but lost more often than it won and emerged bruised by these conflicts. Ultimately, its insistence on fighting these issues hindered its ability to broaden its coalition, while its inability to deliver on them eroded its appeal to conservative Catholics. In 2012 the party was dealt a striking defeat when its candidate came in third in the presidential election.

In Turkey, the AKP administrations of Recep Tayyip Erdoğan and Abdullah Gül also faced difficulties in implementing a religious agenda but were better able to weather the crises and to sometimes turn them to their advantage. Symbolically important efforts to lift the ban on the use of headscarves in universities and state bureaucracies met with substantial backlash from civil society and painful defeats in the courts.[2] Unlike the PAN, however, the AKP was able to achieve victories, perhaps most notably in expanding religious education.[3] As Erdoğan and the AKP entrenched themselves in power, they faced growing accusations of authoritarianism and a growing level of polarization and discontent among secular youth that boiled over in the Gezi Park protest movement.[4] Perhaps the most dramatic challenge came from an unexpected direction, as Erdoğan and the AKP came into an increasingly acrimonious conflict with erstwhile religious allies in the Gülen movement, culminating in the dramatic 2016 coup attempt and the subsequent purging of Gülenists from courts, universities, police, and military forces. Through it all, the AKP was able to maintain a degree of electoral appeal that ensured its supremacy in the national legislature and executive branches.

In this chapter I examine the contrasting approaches to religious mobilization that the PAN and the AKP used after they came to power. I consider the specific challenges faced by religious parties as they navigate the transition from opposition to government and examine how these are shaped by religious community structures and political institutions. Consistently with the central arguments of this book, I find that the ability of political parties to leverage the power of the state to enhance partisan religious mobilization depends on the capacity and autonomy of religious authorities and on the institutions that govern religion-state relations.

Religious Mobilization and Incumbency

The postelectoral experiences of the PAN and the AKP reflect the distinctive challenges faced by religious parties that capture power in secular states. Winning elections is the raison d'être of political parties, but for organizations that have spent decades in opposition, the transition from critical outsiders to empowered insiders—from words to deeds—is rife with potential pitfalls. This shift is all the more perilous for religious parties for reasons that can be clearly derived from the three dimensions of religious mobilization. Religious parties rely on religious identities, doctrinally informed policy proposals, and/or links to sectarian associations to mobilize supporters, and each of these dimensions can generate specific complications for organizations that manage to become ruling parties.

Appeals to religious identity by government leaders can elicit far stronger reactions than similar actions by opposition figures. The sovereign nation-state has a powerful symbolic status, and rhetoric and gestures by officehold-ers that signal an allegiance to religious powers can provoke visceral responses from those not habituated to these actions. The boundary between accept-able and unacceptable displays is largely determined by informal practices and expectations: in one country, the public presence of a head of state at a religious service is a powerful symbolic moment, while in another it may just be another Sunday or Friday.[5] When religious parties come to power, both supporters and opponents anticipate novel symbolic gestures. Power-ful supporters may perceive failure to deliver them as betrayal, but correctly calibrating these appeals to signal continuing religious identity without pro-voking a powerful backlash and alienating less devout constituencies can be a difficult task.

Religious doctrine can have a similar, double-edged quality. Parties that rely on doctrine to mobilize voters often present it as the bedrock of their platforms, a guarantee that their policies are founded on deep, abiding com-mitments rather than the personal interests of party leaders or transient po-litical fashions. While the implications of most religious doctrines for pub-lic policy are ambiguous and rarely central to campaigns, particular points typically serve as rallying cries. In many Catholic countries, opposition to abortion and same-sex marriage has come to function in this way—that is, as a necessary marker of religious orientation for political parties.[6] Yet for that very reason opposition to these policies can rapidly become an equally compelling cause for otherwise-divided secularist groups. As a result, reforms in these areas may be particularly hard-fought, and if religious parties fail to deliver on them, they endanger their appeal to religious constituents.

Finally, strong religious associations, those most capable of mobilizing voters, have the resources and autonomy to demand a seat at the policy-making table and a share of political power. These benefits may be secured formally—for example, in the form of cabinet appointments—or informally, through reliable access to decision makers in the government.[7] Yet the pres-ence or visible influence of their representatives in government may lead to conflicts with party insiders jealous of their prerogatives and be unpopular with less devout segments of the electorate, particularly when these groups are seen as holding disproportionate power or advocating radical positions.

However, denying these individuals and organizations access to political spoils and policy-making influence can provoke hostility and divide the party's supporters.

Religious parties' ability to manage these challenges can have a profound impact on their ability to govern effectively after winning elections and thus to ultimately secure reelection. Being able to deliver policy objectives, satisfy supporters, pick winnable battles, and manage the fallout from inevitable scandals and failed reform efforts is central to converting a momentary electoral victory into an effective and long-lasting government. A party's ability to do so depends at least in part on factors outside its control, such as a favorable macroeconomic context, and on idiosyncratic factors, such as the skill and charisma of its leaders. However, parties are also powerfully enabled and constrained by the same two factors that shaped their evolution outside government: the structure of the religious communities they represent and the political institutions that shape religion-state relations.

Community Structures and Political Institutions

The structure and capacity of religious communities directly affect the ability of the governing party to set the agenda for religious political engagement. When the leadership of religious communities is autonomous and well coordinated and has direct access to substantial resources (e.g., the Catholic Church), the governing party may find it difficult to dictate the manner and timing of religious political mobilization, which will instead be driven by the preferences, goals, and reactions of the clerical leadership and its lay supporters. This matters relatively little when the interests of politicians and religious leaders overlap, though even in these cases religious initiatives may push the government to go further than it otherwise would in promoting particular reforms. It matters very much, however, when their interests do not overlap, particularly when unexpected shocks drive a wedge between them.

A sensitive news story that triggers mass protests—such as a young rape victim being forced to bear a child to term against her will—may prompt different reactions from politicians and religious leaders. The former, with an eye on electoral results, may be tempted to make concessions to appease the public, while the latter, more concerned with slippery slopes, are more likely to take a stand and demand doctrinal consistency.[8] The incentives may also line up the other way. Corruption scandals—such as flagrant nepotism in administrative hiring by a popular mayor—may provoke defensive reactions from fellow politicians, while religious leaders may be tempted to distance themselves from their ally to preserve the moral high ground.[9] The autonomy of religious leadership means that political leaders have relatively little influence on how broader religious communities respond to these types of unexpected challenges.

In contrast, when religious communities are fragmented, the government is better equipped to dictate which points will be conceded and which will be defended. Religious leaders may be more hesitant to call for mobilization against a reproductive health law that falls short of their preferences if they are uncertain about the stances of other religious leaders and fear being singled out and marginalized, or even punished, for taking a stance against the government. Similarly, even when corruption scandals come to light, state leaders may be able to call on a religious ally to stand next to a political leader accused of misuse of power by offering political access and positive coverage on state media that may enhance the status and influence of that particular leader. Thus, religious leaders who are divided can be played off against each other to neutralize the negative effects of criticism by any particular religious figure. Attempts to implement these kinds of policies when clerics present a united front are both costlier and less likely to yield political gains.

Ultimately, the ability of governing parties to shape, guide, and manage religious mobilization is most directly affected by the institutional means at their disposal. Indeed, the most important difference between a party in opposition and one in government lies in the latter's access to the apparatus of the state. Capturing the state virtually always brings with it vastly expanded opportunities for patronage as well as coercive capacity, since even those of small, weak states far exceed those available to all but the most robust non-state organizations. Yet the significance of electoral victory differs across contexts. A state flush with cash from a booming economy offers more opportunities for both innovative policy and traditional patronage than one strangled by economic crisis. More broadly, the formal and informal constraints on the ruling party and overall differences in state capacity play a critical role in determining what the range of options available to the ruling party really is.[10]

Beyond these general differences, particular states have distinctive arrays of tools with which to manage religious affairs and shape religious mobilization. As discussed in Chapter 1, there is growing awareness of the diversity of institutional arrangements that characterize religion-state relations. Recent scholarship distinguishes between policies that provide support for religion, restrict religion, or legislate specific religious precepts, as well as policies aimed at religious majorities, minorities, or all religious groups.[11] Aided by these measures, scholars have developed more finely crafted categories of religion-state relations. Secular states, for example, can now be subdivided into those with, for instance, assertive secularism, passive secularism, or benevolent secularism,[12] depending on the particularities of their institutional arrangements.

As discussed in Chapter 2, twentieth-century Mexico and Turkey could both be described as assertive secular states. Both had policies and institutions in place intended to restrict the autonomous influence of religion on public and political life. However, attention to the differences in their institutions demonstrates that assertive secularism has very different forms, depending on whether these are designed primarily to exclude or to direct religion. In the exclusive variant, religion is locked out of public affairs and political discourse and relegated, by law, to the private sphere. During much of the twentieth century Mexico epitomized this kind of exclusionary secularism: the state denied legal status to the Catholic Church and strictly limited its ability to participate in any political affairs, dealing with its representatives, when it did so at all, through informal channels. In contrast, the directive variant of assertive secularism, exemplified by Turkey during the same time period, possesses robust institutional means by which the state can control and guide religious affairs. The Diyanet state bureaucracy, which hires and fires all of Turkey's imams and muezzins and manages their performance with the explicit intent of rendering religion less dangerous to the state, epitomizes the institutions that characterize this directive variant of assertive secularism.

The victory of religious parties in long-secular states has profoundly different consequences depending on the political institutions they encounter when reaching office. When these institutions are capable of intervening effectively in religious affairs, as in Turkey, they can be redeployed to facilitate and guide religious mobilization in ways consistent with the party's political agenda. In contrast, religious parties coming to power in exclusive environments, as in Mexico, find that they have inherited remarkably few tools with which to shape religious political engagement and thus must continue to rely on their limited partisan means or less reliable, informal channels for bargaining with religious authorities.

Divergence of the PAN and the AKP

The victories of the PAN in Mexico and the AKP in Turkey placed them in very different situations. In Mexico, the PAN governments of Vicente Fox (2000–2006) and Felipe Calderón (2006–2012) faced a well-organized Catholic leadership and soon discovered that Mexico's state lacked the tools necessary to either guide or restrain religious political engagement. The PAN's victory resulted in heightened expectations among devout voters but also in a wave of anticipatory secularist mobilization to expand reproductive rights and to secure legal status for same-sex couples, which in turn led to Catholic countermobilization by lay groups with clerical support. The PAN found itself unprepared and ill-equipped to deal with the resulting political crises, adopting reactive and often ineffective stances that solidified its reputation for conservatism while simultaneously frustrating many of its devout supporters.

In contrast, the AKP in Turkey found itself nominally atop a state apparatus designed to manage and guide Turkey's increasingly empowered but organizationally fractious Sunni Muslim community. In an ironic twist, the secularist institutions designed by Kemalist officials to control Islam offered a unique means for directing religious affairs, as long as the government was able to overcome resistance from elsewhere in the state. The first challenges faced by the AKP administration thus centered on gaining effective control over state institutions that were often staffed by committed secularists. The AKP's ability to work with the Gülen movement, which had invested heavily in education and in placing its supporters in various state bureaucracies, proved vital to this task. The outcome was not foreordained, and the AKP faced resistance and setbacks both within the state and in civil society. The headscarf affair proved a particularly vexing area for the implementation of religiously oriented reforms, but the presence of a substantial, state-supported religious education sector created a fertile arena for the AKP government to deliver favorable policies. Yet when the alliance between the AKP and the Gülen movement fell apart and conflict erupted, the government was able to rely on its control over the Diyanet to direct religious mobilization against its former allies.

The similarities and differences between these two cases thus highlight the recurrent challenges faced by religious parties that come to power in secular states as well as the specific ways in which distinctive religious community structures and political institutions can shape their ability to address them.

Mexico

Religious political mobilization in Mexico under the PAN was characterized by a combination of continuity and change. The PAN remained committed to selective mobilization strategies based on limited appeals to religious identity and discreet associational linkages, pointing out to anyone who cared to ask that the party had no ties to the Catholic hierarchy or any other religious community. Moreover, its official platforms did not focus on distinctively religious themes, emphasizing instead issues such as economic growth, crime reduction, and good governance.[13] Nevertheless, there was also substantial change in the form of an escalating religious-secularist conflict around reproductive rights and the status of same-sex couples. These issues, which had previously been marginal and virtually invisible in the electoral arena, became regular topics of public political contention, with mass demonstrations in favor and against policies in these areas.[14] The PAN's national leaders did not choose to make opposition to abortion and same-sex marriage central to the party's electoral campaign strategies but could not prevent them from becoming highly salient aspects of national politics.

The disjuncture between the limited religious mobilization efforts of the PAN and the simultaneous exacerbation of religious-secular cleavages around reproductive and same-sex rights reflected the structural and institutional context faced by the PAN as it captured Mexico's presidency: an autonomous and well-coordinated Catholic Church and a state designed to exclude rather than manage religion.

Structural and Institutional Context

In the first decade of the twenty-first century, the multiplicity of lay associations limited the benefits and increased the risks of assertive religious mobilization by political parties, even as they encouraged nonpartisan forms of religious activism. Lay groups have not ceased to play a vital role in Mexican civil society, but the ability of any one association to act as a credible, autonomous resource for Catholic political mobilization at a national level has been dampened by fractionalization influenced by an increasingly well-coordinated hierarchy. Catholic Action, although a shadow of its former self, remains an active player, as do progressive Catholic institutions that resist the conservative turn of the church and, perhaps most prominently, reactionary groups that embrace and promote it. These groups advocate often incompatible readings of Catholic doctrine and its implication for Mexican politics, and many of them often adopt confrontational styles that make them as much a liability as an asset for political parties seeking to remain in government. The result is a pluralistic and contentious lay environment in which maintaining robust, public ties to any given lay organization entails substantial risks for national political parties.[15]

A clear example of the risks of coordinating too closely with lay associations is provided by the Comité Nacional ProVida (Pro-Life National Committee). The group was founded as an antiabortion organization by lay Catholics in 1978, initially to resist an effort by the Mexican Communist Party to legalize abortion in Mexico but more broadly to challenge the liberalization of reproductive rights.[16] It gradually emerged as an influential player in national politics, and it has featured prominently in critical debates surrounding abortion in Mexico. Its lay members have served as useful allies for the Catholic hierarchy because of their ability to engage in campaigns and forms of political speech beyond those available to the clergy. Given this pedigree, it is therefore unsurprising that the group has at times sought to work with the PAN in encouraging religious mobilization.[17] Yet the outspokenness of ProVida and the stridency of its campaigns have sometimes been costly to the PAN, mobilizing its opponents, alienating moderates, and forcing the party to take controversial positions at inopportune times.[18] Moreover, efforts by PAN members to provide financial support for the group triggered a political scandal.[19] Ultimately, the group's narrow focus on abortion, its limited mobilization capacity, and its tendency to alienate secularists and progressives substantially limit its value as a political ally.

In contrast to the narrowness and stridency of politically active lay associations, the CEM maintains a carefully centralized pattern of communication with the Mexican laity, the Mexican state, and the public at large by relying on tools ranging from informal coordination with elected officials to direct communiqués to the public at large. There are still, as there have always been, significant differences of opinion among bishops, including on issues of direct political import, such as the relative importance of addressing inequality or defending indigenous rights. Yet the CEM's permanent organization has generally allowed bishops to present a united front even in divisive times. In this way, it has managed to make its voice heard in policy debates about contentious topics, such as abortion,[20] birth control,[21] and gay marriage,[22] but also emphasized its commitment to social justice and inclusion.[23] In all of these cases the CEM has retained the ability to frame its statements as manifestations of a single, coherent, and official Catholic position. It has also managed to reaffirm its independence from political authority, criticizing the administration's policies and consistently asserting its above-partisan status.

During the twelve years of PAN government, the CEM continued to articulate a narrative within which its efforts to guide public discourse could be understood and seen as distinct from any partisan project. These framing projects have been particularly important for the hierarchy insofar as they allowed bishops to affirm their status as arbiters of the social and political significance of Catholicism in Mexico. Thus, in 2010, when the bicentennial of Mexican independence and the centennial of the revolution opened up an opportunity for bishops to articulate their vision for the country, the CEM put forth a comprehensive discussion of Mexican history in which Catholic identity and doctrine are assigned a central and constructive role.[24] The value that the Catholic hierarchy placed on its autonomy, even when a party friendly to religion presided over the state, is both reflected and reinforced by its emphasis on religious freedom as a banner for legal reform. Religious freedom became the dominant theme used by the CEM and its allies to describe its desired relationship to political authorities in Mexico.[25] Bishops have presented it as an effort to consolidate the autonomy of religion in relation to the state, secure the place of faith in the public sphere, and establish grounds for voluntary cooperation between secular and religious authorities.[26] Concretely, the search for religious freedom entailed lifting restrictions on media ownership, as well as remaining restrictions on religious education, and political participation. Thus, while lay associations focused on particular policy issues, such as abortion, the CEM pursued a broader project aimed at securing its long-term status in Mexican society in a way that transcended particular partisan or policy junctures.

If the structural environment encountered by the PAN was not conducive to party-led religious mobilization, neither did the Mexican state provide substantial mechanisms with which to carry it out. The political institutions inherited by the PAN were not well suited for using state power to promote partisan religious mobilization. Mexico's mixed electoral system, originally intended to encourage divisions among the opposition and thus sustain a dominant party system,[27] resulted in a moderately permissive electoral environment in which it was difficult for any party to secure an electoral majority. Indeed, the PAN was never able to obtain a majority of seats in the national congress. The Mexican presidency, long seen as a source of virtually absolute authority, proved far less powerful when it lacked the support of a dominant political party. Without control of either the Chamber of Deputies or the Senate, the PAN found it very difficult to engage in substantial reforms except when it could craft coalitions with its opponents. Mexico's federal structure added another layer of complications, as opposition-led states, most specifically the PRD-dominated Distrito Federal, were able to push agendas that struck directly against the religiously oriented policies of the PAN.

The limitations of leading an isolated executive branch proved frustrating for the PAN and its religious supporters. There were few mechanisms for promoting a religious agenda from the executive without substantial support in the legislature and only informal channels for collaboration between secular and religious authorities. The use of federal funds to promote sectarian agendas was carefully monitored by secularist opponents, who were quick to use courts to challenge any erosion in the legal barriers between religion and state. Appointing religiously friendly figures to positions of authority in the administration offered one avenue for appeasing the PAN's religious supporters. However, these appointments were largely the prerogative of the president himself, and Fox, who had not emerged from the religious wing of the PAN, proved idiosyncratic in his appointments. In this context, those who hoped for a sudden softening of Mexican secularism and the rapid implementation of key policy preferences found that they lacked the means to make meaningful changes.

Religious Mobilization during the PAN Administrations

Despite the shock that Fox's election represented for a party that had spent sixty years in opposition, his administration was characterized by continuity of religious mobilization. The PAN, both in government and during electoral campaigns, largely refrained from mobilizing supporters by means of religious doctrine or by forming substantial ties to religious associations. Instead, religion was mobilized primarily through personalized appeals to religious identity and discreet cooperation with the Catholic hierarchy and conservative Catholic associations. Thus, after the election, President Fox behaved much as candidate Fox had done: he combined symbolic allusions to his personal Catholicism with a governing style that revealed limited influence from Catholic doctrines and associations.

The contrast between symbolic gestures and concrete policy changes was dramatic. Among the former are the numerous examples of appeals to Catholic identity, presented as manifestations of personal religiosity, that characterized the Fox presidency. Many of these events scandalized his secularist critics, who repeatedly condemned them as efforts to subvert the separation between church and state. Thus, in the morning before being sworn in as Mexico's president, Fox visited, kneeled, and prayed at the Basílica de Guadalupe and left to cheers by a large crowd.[28] In 2002 Fox seized on Pope John Paul II's visit to Mexico to promote the canonization of a Mexican saint and produced an emblematic image when he kissed the pope's ring.[29] When John Paul II died in 2005, Fox attended a ceremony in the Vatican, after which he gave a press conference in which he emphasized the central role of the Catholic Church in Mexico and the constructive and positive relations between it and the state during his administration.[30] And as his term in office came to an end, Fox publicly announced his intention to visit the Basílica de Guadalupe once again to thank the Virgin for the opportunity to govern the country.[31]

Combined with his campaign promises to defend life and expand religious freedom, these gestures motivated a great deal of concern, particularly among secularist opponents of the PAN, who feared that the party would use its victory to fundamentally undermine the secular state and open the gates to religious influence in a wide range of policy areas.[32] Yet they contrasted sharply with the general absence of substantial policy shifts. The Fox administration entered office with the promise of making significant changes to the laws governing religious institutions, particularly those relating to continuing restrictions on education and media ownership, but these largely failed to materialize, much to the chagrin of some of his devout supporters.

One limited exception came in the form of political appointments, as Fox nominated some individuals with long-standing links to Catholic associations to significant cabinet posts. The most prominent was Carlos Abascal, who was initially secretary of labor and then secretary of the interior. He was a leading member of lay Catholic associations such as IMDOSOC and the Unión Social de Empresarios Mexicanos (USEM; Social Union of Mexican Businessmen). In addition to these associational linkages, Abascal consistently exhibited the strong influence of Catholic social thought.[33] Another was Ana Teresa Aranda, who was appointed secretary of social development and had been a leader of the Asociación Nacional Cívica Femenina (Ancifem; Feminine Civic National Association), a conservative group emblematic of the Catholic reaction to the left-leaning movements and government policies during the 1970s.[34] These were exceptions, however, more notable for their contrast with the independent technocrats and politicians who made up a large section of Fox's cabinet. Moreover, as noted previously, their ability to actually shape policies was sharply limited.

However, these appointments were countered by the selection of Julio Frenk as secretary of health. Frenk was a progressive and not a member of the PAN, and his appointment proved to be a particular blow to conservative Catholics.[35] Reproductive rights had become a salient issue during the 1990s as PAN-governed states attempted to pass restrictive legislation, successfully in Chihuahua 1994 and unsuccessfully in Baja California and Guanajuato in 1999.[36] However, the case of Paulina, a thirteen-year-old rape victim who was effectively denied access to an abortion by PAN officials in Baja California in 1999 brought nationwide attention to the issue.[37] As the ensuing scandal brewed in the shadow of the 2000 election, Paulina became a cause célèbre for women's rights advocates and others skeptical of the PAN. In this context, Fox appointed Frenk at least in part to defuse concerns about the PAN's sectarianism. The secretary engaged in a lengthy consultation with a broad range of civil-society organizations and in 2004 decided to include emergency contraception among public health services. The result was a major schism within the Fox administration, in which conservative ministers from the PAN publicly condemned Frenk's policy. Members of the Catholic hierarchy and lay Catholic activists, notably including ProVida, loudly protested what they interpreted as state-sanctioned abortion. As the controversy grew, these groups put pressure on Fox to dismiss Frenk and simmered down only after the president personally endorsed his secretary's policy.[38]

The end of Fox's term and the election of Felipe Calderón appeared to offer a new opening for the implementation of a distinctively Catholic agenda more in line with the historic roots of the PAN. Before becoming president, Calderón was vice president of the Christian Democratic International and a strong supporter of the role of ideology within the PAN. Indeed, unlike the neo-Panista Fox, Calderón was a quintessential party insider. Son of distinguished party leader, archivist, and activist Luis Calderón Vega, he became an active member at the age of seventeen. He rose rapidly through its ranks, first as youth wing secretary, then general secretary, and finally as president of the party. This long, partisan career aligned him with the more ideological wing of the party and distinguished him from personalist candidates such as Manuel Clouthier and Fox. Indeed, Calderón's campaign actually included fewer striking symbolic gestures than those of his more personalist predecessors, who had been more invested in credibly demonstrating their personal religiosity.[39]

Despite their differences, Calderón faced constraints similar to those encountered by Fox and proved equally ineffective at implementing a recognizably Catholic set of policies at the national level. While President Calderón publicly and repeatedly asserted his support for core Catholic positions on abortion and same-sex marriage, his government was frequently outmaneuvered on these fronts by its secularist adversaries. The battle of abortion was in many ways expected, so when Mexico City's progressive government decriminalized first-trimester abortion in 2007, the event provoked a widespread reaction. The Catholic hierarchy and conservative Catholic groups such as ProVida expressed dismay and organized mass marches and other forms of protest. The administration of President Calderón challenged the constitutionality of the policy in the Supreme Court, but its challenge failed in 2008. The PAN found greater success at the subnational level: In 2008 fourteen Mexican states effectively banned abortion within their jurisdictions. The PAN was a key player in these legal reforms, though it was opportunistically joined by PRI representatives.[40] By the end of Calderón's term the number of states with constitutional amendments protecting fetal life had increased to seventeen.[41]

In contrast to the conflict over abortion, Mexico City's legalization of same-sex unions in 2006 caught the government by surprise, which was compounded by the full legalization of same-sex marriage in 2009.[42] In both cases, the legal change was carried out by the PRD-dominated city legislature, where it was opposed by PAN delegates.[43] The national PAN government also resisted these proposals, but, as was the case with abortion, they lost the battle in the courts. Making matters worse for the PAN, the Supreme Court required all states to recognize the validity of marriages performed in Mexico City, effectively legalizing same-sex marriage across the national territory in 2010.[44] The inability of the Calderón government to successfully challenge these changes, despite substantial popular opposition to same-sex marriage and the strenuous objections of the Catholic Church, was characteristic of the situation in which the PAN found itself. Difficult conflicts over key policy issues strained alliances with religious associations and undermined appeals to religious identity.

These struggles dulled the appeal of the PAN to many conservative Catholics, but it was the escalating security crisis triggered by Calderón's campaign against drug cartels that ultimately sealed the fate of his administration. As violence reached unprecedented levels and the murder rate skyrocketed, doubling between 2006 and 2011,[45] the crisis drove a further wedge between the PAN and many Catholic voters. In this context, the CEM made several pronouncements regarding Mexico's escalating security crisis. These often echoed the administration's claims that the wave of crime and violence sweeping contemporary Mexico was due in large part to prior patterns of official indifference and collaboration with criminal organizations.[46] However, they also pointed to structural causes for violence, particularly in the free-market economic model and its inability to improve conditions concerning inequality or substantially improve the lot of vulnerable populations.[47] While avoiding detailed policy proposals, the CEM advocated a more robust degree of government involvement to ensure a more equitable distribution of wealth, as well as the articulation of robust social policies to reduce the burdens of poverty. These were a clear rebuke of the pro-market policies implemented by the administrations of Fox and Calderón. Indeed, by the final years of the Calderón government, the Catholic hierarchy had become openly critical of his administration.[48]

With the PAN seemingly headed for electoral defeat in 2012, party members opted not to select Calderón's chosen successor, Finance Minister Ernesto Cordero, instead favoring Josefina Vázquez Mota, who would have made history as Mexico's first female head of state. Vázquez Mota, facing an uphill struggle against a resurgent PRI, made a last-ditch effort to turn a potential liability—her gender, in a country where politics had always been dominated by males—into a strength by presenting herself as a mother in touch with the needs of everyday Mexicans. As part of this effort, she engaged in a controversial effort to reinvigorate religious mobilization, raising funds from Catholic business associations and telling voters, on the day of the election, "We all should get up early. First to mass, and then to vote. I ask you to go to 8am mass and then to vote."[49] Nevertheless, the Catholic hierarchy was cautious about its endorsements, issuing voting guidelines that emphasized the importance of voting in favor of candidates who were committed to protecting life from the moment of conception, a statement aimed at distancing voters from the left rather than necessarily driving them to the PAN.[50] Despite her efforts, Vázquez Mota came in third place in the election, pointing to the limits of religious mobilization and bringing an end to the PAN's period in power.

In summary, the PAN administrations led by Fox and Calderón found themselves unable to leverage their position in government to shape and guide partisan religious mobilization. Faced with a well-coordinated clerical hierarchy, fragmented lay associations, and a set of political institutions designed to exclude religion from the political arena, they were often on the back foot, reacting to changes on the ground rather than setting the terms of religious mobilization. As a result, the party's religious mobilization efforts thus took on an ambivalent character. PAN candidates sought to appeal to religious voters in a country where these constitute a substantial majority of the electorate without alienating the equally large majority that has deeply assimilated the importance of the secular state. It was ultimately unable to do either. The discontent expressed by the Catholic hierarchy and its allies in civil society regarding the unwillingness of PAN governments to forcefully promote policies more closely aligned with its doctrinal preferences, as well as its willingness to distance itself from its increasingly unpopular governments, highlighted the limitations inherent in the PAN's limited religious mobilization strategy.

Turkey

Regularly described as an "earthquake" and a "tsunami,"[51] the 2002 election dramatically altered the political landscape of Turkey by endowing a party that had an "Islamist pedigree" with an overwhelming majority in the national legislature.[52] Despite facing a committed opposition that challenged it consistently at the ballot box, in civil society, and within the very state apparatus that the party sought to govern, the AKP would go on to become the most electorally successful party in Turkish history, winning the next five general elections and securing an outright majority of legislative seats in four of them. During its long tenure in government, the AKP underwent substantial transformations. Its first six years in power were characterized by notable achievements, as the AKP implemented democratizing reforms aimed at meeting criteria for EU membership and presided over a period of economic expansion and prosperity.[53] Indeed, the AKP seemed to deliver on the promise of having "Muslim Democrats" in office[54]—for example, by substantially expanding the rights of Christians and other religious minorities.[55] Yet by the end of that decade, concerns about abuse of power and a growing intolerance of opposition had notably tarnished the AKP's image, and after 2013 the AKP presided over a period of escalating social confrontation and growing authoritarianism.[56]

Religion is at the heart of the AKP, but its precise role is difficult to ascertain, as is the part it played in the unraveling of Turkish democracy. During its early years in government, the AKP placed an onus on reconciling the religious beliefs of its supporters with liberal principles—for example, by framing the headscarf debate in terms of religious freedom and challenging secularist tutelary institutions by appealing to democratic norms.[57] Skeptics warned that despite these gestures the AKP was excessively reliant on sectarian appeals and on ties to religious associations that posed a threat to the secular Turkish state.[58] These critiques gained greater currency as the AKP government began to distance itself from liberal norms and to engage in more aggressive efforts to defang its opponents in the bureaucracy and the military. However, concerns of a sudden Islamist turn that would see Erdoğan use his growing powers to impose rigid religious laws on secular Turks were overstated; despite is creeping authoritarianism, Turkey did not become a new Islamic Republic. As they accumulated power, Erdoğan and his party consistently rejected Islamist labels and generally avoided doctrinally based policy proposals, even as they relied on increasingly explicit appeals to religious identity, expanded religious education and bureaucracies, and cultivated ties to a broad array of religious communities and associations.

To understand the ways in which religious mobilization has developed under AKP rule, one must consider the institutional and structural context that drove its initial success, as well as how these changed during its long tenure in office.

Structural and Institutional Context

The religious community structures that facilitated the rise of the AKP continued to expand once the party came to power. The religious associations that had empowered the RP in the 1980s and 1990s remained highly active, even if many of them suffered during the 1998–1999 military intervention that brought down Erbakan's government and the subsequent period of repression.[59] From Islamic business groups to Muslim women's associations, a broad array of local and national organizations engaged in formally nonpolitical work remained inextricably interwoven with the fabric of social and political life across much of Turkey.[60]

Even as the AKP maintained strong ties to diverse religious associations, the growing influence of the most prominent of these, the Gülen movement, sowed the seed of future confrontation. The Gülen movement worked closely with the AKP in its early years, but the two groups maintained distinct ideological positions even during their periods of most substantial cooperation.[61] Since the 1990s, this influential transnational organization, built around the teachings and personality of Fethullah Gülen, secured a substantial presence in Turkey's public sphere. At its height, it included a robust network of media outlets, including the major daily newspaper *Zaman*, the Samanyolu television channel, and the Burc radio station. The growth and diversification of these media outlets effectively endowed the AKP with a friendly voice in an arena that had once been largely dominated by secularist forces.[62] The Gülen movement invested even more substantially in education, establishing a vast network of hundreds of schools, dormitories, and academies in Turkey and beyond.[63] Moreover, the group engaged in a laborious effort to engage in sustained academic dialogues within and beyond Turkey, publishing numerous journals and hosting a wide array of conferences.[64] The salience of the Gülen movement was magnified by its direct engagement with audiences outside Turkey and its lively participation in transnational debates on religion and democracy. As a result, its members were in a position to articulate the vision and defend the record of its allies in the AKP in arenas where the party would otherwise have had difficulty making its case.

Arguably the most notorious aspect of the Gülen movement was the ability of its members to gain positions of influence within the once staunchly secularist bastions of the Turkish state. Despite his opposition to political Islamism, Fethullah Gülen encouraged his supporters to seek positions within the state to further the group's mission of bringing about social, moral, and political change. This strategy triggered a scandal in 1997 when recordings of Gülen telling supporters to wait until they were securely in power before openly advocating their agenda came to light.[65] The recordings appeared at the height of anti-Islamist campaigns following the toppling of Erbakan, and the response of the secularist establishment was swift: many of the educational institutions associated with Gülen were closed and the liberty of many of its members curtailed.[66] Fethullah Gülen, arguing he had been misconstrued and was facing political persecution, fled to self-imposed exile in Pennsylvania, from where he continued to lead the transnational movement.[67] Despite the exile of their leader and the effort to limit their political efficacy, the educated and discreet Gülenists continued to carry out their activism in civil society and to find positions in state bureaucracies. The movement reaffirmed its public arguments about the compatibility of Islam and democracy, appealing to human rights and religious liberty as the cornerstones of its position. Its members thus became obvious allies for the reformists who were organizing the AKP and who faced many of the same constraints and endorsed compatible strategies.

While the Gülen movement extended its influence, other religious associations also continued to flourish and the Sunni community in Turkey remained deeply pluralistic.[68] This diversity was visible in the broad range of opinions expressed in its media outlets,[69] as well as in the diversity of its local and transnational associations.[70] More conservative groups, such as the MG and the Suleymancı movements, remained significant players with a substantial transnational resource base and distinctive preferences in public policy. In addition, the continuing expansion of conservative business associations had a distinctive impact on the country's religious associational life. Turkey's GDP grew at a rapid pace during the first twelve years of the AKP's tenure, driven by the continuing expansion of Anatolian capital and halted only briefly by the 2009 global crisis. This facilitated the consolidation of MÜSIAD, the conservative business association, and the wide array of associated local businesses groups, many of which directly or indirectly contributed cadres and resources to the governing party organization.[71] The growth of pious, business-oriented groups rewarded appeal to sectarian identity but put pressure on the party to abstain from explicit endorsements of religious doctrine in favor of a more pragmatic approach to governance.[72]

The enduring diversity of Turkey's religious associational arena also sustained potential competitors for devout voters, providing a lifeline for small organizations. Specifically, MG remained committed to its own electoral vehicles, keeping the SP afloat even as it consistently failed to secure parliamentary representation. The persistent inability of the SP to secure seats in the legislature, despite being led by Erbakan and many of the cadres who had guided the RP to power in the 1990s, would have been striking, if not for the obvious role played by Turkey's electoral institutions.

Political institutions played a shifting but consistently important role in the evolution of religious mobilization in Turkey under the AKP. The ability of the AKP to secure sizable majorities in the legislature, which allowed it to control the policy agenda and voided any need for coalition building with other parties, was substantially enhanced by Turkey's electoral institutions. Specifically, the high vote threshold, which required that parties secure at least 10 percent of the national vote to gain representation, locked out religious competitors such as the SP as well as center-right parties such as the DYP and ANAP, which might have competed for the votes of Turkey's rising middle class.[73] The effect was most significant at the crucial founding moment: the magnitude of the AKP's initial victory in 2002 was greatly enhanced by the 10 percent threshold, which allowed it to capture two-thirds (66.4 percent) of the parliament with only one-third (34 percent) of the votes. In the highly divided electoral field, the only other party to cross the threshold was the venerable CHP, whose poor electoral performance in the 1990s had prevented it from becoming mired in the scandals of that decade. In 2002 its 19.4 percent of votes yielded almost a third of the legislative seats, making it the standard-bearer for the opposition to the AKP. The striking level of disproportionality of this election was not matched in subsequent elections, but that generally reflected the ability of the AKP to grow its share of the electorate rather than the ability of opposition parties to surpass the threshold. Electoral institutions effectively guaranteed the AKP a solid legislative majority as long as it could command the allegiance of somewhere near half the electorate.

Despite its durable, dominant position in the legislature, the early AKP government was only nominally in charge of much of the state apparatus, and the possibility of facing a judicial or military coup was consistently present for its leadership and supporters. Because of the constitutional status of secularism, the AKP faced the possibility that overt religious mobilization would trigger the closure of the party, as it nearly did in 2008.[74] This threat was particularly acute while the bureaucracy, the courts, and the military remained openly hostile to any attempt to implement an assertively religious policy agenda and suspicious enough of the AKP's motives to treat even minor reforms as major threats. Moreover, the AKP was bound by the severely restrictive quality of Turkey's political party law, which established the organizational format for all parties. This law banned political organizations from extending to the village or neighborhood level, although all major parties got around this by maintaining informal representatives.[75] Partnerships with religious civil-society organizations allowed the AKP to sidestep both the prohibition on overt religious appeals and the restrictions on local organization and thus became a critical and distinctive part of its strategy for mobilizing religious voters at the local level.[76]

In this context, the capacity of the Turkish state to intervene in religious affairs and shape religious mobilization was not fully available to the AKP despite its legislative supermajority, and the struggle for control of the state apparatus was predictably central to the evolution of religious mobilization in Turkey.

Some parts of the bureaucracy were useful from the beginning, while others were won only gradually, through a virtual war of attrition against secularists. The Diyanet offered a particularly important means for promoting the party's vision of a devout society without relying on its party apparatus to do so, and as a result it experienced a remarkable enhancement of its budget and personnel.[77] Education policy, particularly the defense and enhancement of Imam Hatip schools, also offered an opportunity for delivering policy goods to conservative and devout constituencies. As intrastate conflicts began to tilt in favor of the AKP, thanks in part to its Gülenist allies, the party found itself less constrained in its ability to deploy the powers of the state to further its partisan mobilization efforts. The result was a notable change in the intensity, but not in the fundamental character, of the AKP's religious mobilization.

Religious Mobilization under the AKP

The AKP entered government with a style of religious mobilization that differed significantly from that of its MG predecessors and more closely resembled that of Turkey's traditional conservative parties. However, even during its early years, there were aspects of this approach that distinguished it from other center-right parties, most notably its distinctive deployment of religious identity and the complexity of its ties to religious associations. As structural and institutional conditions shifted, these elements became increasingly salient. While the AKP did not suddenly become an assertive religious mobilizer, its growing control over the state apparatus empowered its appeals to religious identity. At the same time, this created tensions between the party and its most important associational ally.

Even though many of its leaders had been prominent figures in Erbakan's RP, the AKP opted not to mobilize religion by articulating exclusive sectarian appeals and abandoned most of its predecessor's doctrinal positions.[78] These breaks with the past were clearly signaled to the public through a wide array of symbols and rhetoric. While MG parties used labels as a way to reference religious concepts, the new party's acronym, pronounced "ak" for short, translates to "clean" and signals an effort by the party to distance itself from corruption.[79] Its party banner no longer featured the Islamic crescent used by the RP and its successors, the FP and the SP, but rather a light bulb. While cleanliness and light are certainly not lacking in religious connotations, these labels and symbols stood for a rupture with the MG tradition, which emphasized continuity by relying on terms from its own religiously infused canon. Moreover, AKP leaders emphatically rejected the Islamist label, preferring to present the party as an organization of "conservative democrats" whose personal values were informed by religion,[80] much like the Republican Party in the United States.[81] Erdoğan and his affiliates drew a distinction between Islam as a source of public policy, which they rejected, and religion as a source of norms and values that give meaning to the life of individual Muslims, which they espoused.[82] Concretely, notions of a distinctively Islamic "third way" and an interest-free economy, or the more general resistance to liberal market economics, which were prominent during the MSP and RP eras, were notably absent from the AKP's rhetorical repertoire.[83] The shift was perhaps most dramatic when comparing the AKP's attitude toward the EU, which the RP considered highly suspect but which the new party went out of its way to embrace during its early years in government.[84] Rather than subjection to the whims of a "Christian club," as Erbakan had described it,[85] the AKP embraced the EU and saw in the Copenhagen membership criteria an opportunity to weaken the strictures imposed on political mobilization by the architects of the Constitution of 1982.[86]

Bearing in mind the dramatic changes in Turkey's economic, social, and political environment, religious mobilization under the AKP bore a remarkable resemblance to the style of Özal's ANAP in the 1980s and, to a lesser extent, to Süleyman Demirel's AP in the 1960s and Menderes's DP in the 1950s.[87] In contrast to its efforts to distance itself from the MG lineage, this was a legacy that the AKP opted to embrace.[88] Indeed, many AKP members came from the ANAP, including prominent figures such as Cemil Çiçek, who had been a minister of state but left ANAP amid the internal crises of the 1990s and became speaker of parliament under Erdoğan. Like these other hegemonic center-right parties, the AKP relied primarily on ties to religious associations rather than appeals to religious identity or the inclusion of religious doctrine in policy programs to mobilize religious voters. Also like its center-right predecessors, the AKP justified its efforts to curb Turkey's assertive secularism not in the language of religious obligation, as was sometimes the case with the RP, but rather in terms of human rights, democracy, and religious freedom.[89] The AKP made only two distinctively religious proposals during its 2002 campaign: loosening restrictions on the headscarf and enhancing religious education, and equating the status of Imam Hatip schools with those of secular schools.[90] Both proposals, provocative though they were in the Turkish context, were defensible within a human rights and religious freedom framework, particularly when combined with reforms aimed at improving relations with Turkey's Christian minority.[91]

Nevertheless, even during its early years in power the AKP's religious mobilization strategy had elements that built on its more explicitly religious lineage. First, while the party's cautious treatment of religious identity formally resembled that of its center-right predecessors, the historical ties between the AKP's leaders and the MG endowed their actions with religious meanings. In some ways, figures such as Erdoğan could scarcely avoid making appeals to religious identity, since their careers and personal lives were replete with broadly recognized references to the struggle between devout Muslims and the secular state. Erdoğan and the AKP implicitly and explicitly invoked a discourse that presented them as devout Muslims oppressed by a secularist elite, in ways that emphasized their outsider status and reinforced their popular credentials.[92] From the time Erdoğan spent in prison for reciting a poem to the uproar caused when the wives of Erdoğan and Gül appeared in public wearing headscarves, the AKP's religious credentials were woven into the party's identity. Consequently, to argue that the party did not engage in substantial appeals to religious identity would be disingenuous. Rather, because of its history, the AKP was able to send clear signals using discreet appeals to religious identity that did not automatically discredit it among liberal supporters. The revaluation of the Ottoman past or the emphasis placed by the AKP on the family, for example, took on religious meanings even when they were formally framed in secular-nationalist terms,[93] as did its support for Islamic-style architecture or its efforts to advertise Ramadan in Istanbul.[94]

Second, the ties that linked the party to the broader religious community were more robust than those of its center-right predecessors. The rapidity with which the ANAP's relationship with religious orders dissipated following the death of Özal in 1993 revealed the contingent nature of the ties between this highly personalist organization and its religious supporters. Similarly, while Demirel had cultivated the explicit support of many Nurcu communities in the 1960s, the DYP faced few internal constraints when it moved away from religious appeals in the 1990s. In contrast, the AKP maintained far more coherent and reliable connections to religious groups, forming partnerships with Islamic charities and voluntary associations to provide social services,[95] partnering with Muslim women's rights groups to frame gender issues,[96] and endorsing private religious education,[97] among others. From the beginning, these partnerships operated in a wide array of contexts and ranged from neighborhood mosque communities to transnational movements. The most prominent was the Gülen movement, and ties between the two were a subject of significant speculation in both media and the academy from the beginning of the AKP's time in office.[98]

These features were complemented by the Turkish state's robust institutional mechanisms for managing religion in ways that further enhanced the ability of the AKP government to manage religious mobilization and to navigate potentially sensitive areas. Under the AKP, the Diyanet experienced a "golden age" characterized by rapidly expanding budgets and influence.[99] Crucially, the AKP government favored programs that extended the reach of the Diyanet beyond the mosques and into schools, prisons, and media, allowing it to deploy favorable, and increasingly partisan, messages across multiple arenas of public discourse.[100]

This combination of associational linkages and bureaucratic capacity proved quite effective for mobilizing religion while simultaneously engaging with liberal audiences. In addressing issues of women's rights, for example, the government variously provided support for Muslim women's organizations, engaged in academic dialogues with liberal feminist groups, and issued conservative statements through the Diyanet.[101] At the same time, the AKP recruited women candidates from religious civil-society organizations for prominent positions and relied on women's auxiliaries as critical emissaries for reaching out to female voters at election time. While the party was not able to get its way in all areas—the headscarf became a particularly vexing issue—or prevent conflicts over issues such as reproductive rights, by deploying this broad array of policies and avenues of influence, it has largely been able to manage and meet the expectations of its conservative and religious constituents, respond to secularist critiques, and present itself as an avatar for its vision of women's rights.[102]

The ability of Erdoğan and the AKP to navigate these treacherous waters and appeal to religious identity without automatically alienating apolitical moderates and liberals was an important component of the party's electoral success. The party gradually came to concentrate more political power than any other party has held since the inauguration of multiparty elections in 1946. Following its dominant performance in 2002, the party expanded its vote share to 46 percent in the 2007 elections, marking the first time a governing party did so since the CHP in 1977. That same year the party was also able to capture the presidency, removing one important secularist constraint. Subsequent electoral victories in 2011 and 2015 took place in a climate of growing polarization and concern over the AKP's ability to operate with fewer and fewer political checks on its power. In the context of the government's increasingly hostile attitude toward independent media and its willingness to use regulatory powers against opposition groups and state resources to finance its campaigns, the electoral hegemony of the AKP convinced many observers that Turkey has become an electoral or competitive authoritarian regime.[103]

A critical part of this process was the dismantlement of secularist tutelary institutions that had formally and informally constrained the AKP during its first years in power, and here too religious mobilization played a notable role. The party faced a particularly trying period in 2007–2008, when the military attempted to derail Abdullah Gül's ascension to the presidency and the party barely survived a closure case against it in the Constitutional Court. In response to these challenges, the AKP relied on its Gülenist allies in the judiciary to launch investigations into alleged coup plots by members of the military, most notably the Ergenekon and Sledgehammer cases,[104] which brought hundreds of officers, including on-duty and high-ranking ones, to court and profoundly undermined the ability of the armed forces to intervene in political affairs. In addition, in 2010 the government won a constitutional referendum that included the substantial reorganization of the judicial branch, this time with the explicit support of Fethullah Gülen, who campaigned in its favor.[105] The AKP thus faced down challenges from both the judiciary and the military, effectively reducing the autonomy and political influence of these important constraints on its mandate.[106]

The collapse of these secularist tutelary institutions raised concerns that the AKP's limited approach to religious mobilization would give way to a full embrace of assertive religious mobilization.[107] In a limited sense, this has been the case: Erdoğan, whose persona came to dominate the government and the party,[108] appealed to religious identity in increasingly explicit ways—for example, when he invoked his desire to raise a "devout generation" of Turkish youth or spoke out against alcohol use or cohabitation by unmarried couples.[109] These statements were not consistently accompanied by legal reforms, and when they were, reforms were typically framed in ambiguous terms: legislators often defended them in secular terms, while statements by the Diyanet endowed them with religious legitimacy. Yet the credibility of the AKP's appeals to religious identity was not dulled by the absence of dramatic legal changes. The consistent reliance on religious symbols and language, even when it fell far short of full-throated calls for the implementation of Sharia, created an environment in which religious supporters could feel that the AKP embraced their worldviews.

This persistent reliance on appeals to religious identity also had a cost, as it contributed to the growing disenchantment of the AKP's liberal backers and the sense of frustration and discontent among secular, and not only ideologically secularist, youth. The Gezi Park protests of 2013 marked the final collapse of the increasingly tense relationship between these groups and the AKP. Nominally a local conflict over the fate of a public park, the protest soon escalated into a massive movement that spread across the country. Specific symbolic features of the protest—from its rejection of the neo-Ottoman remaking of the city to its calls for a new vision of the nation and democratic participation—were direct challenges to the religious mobilization strategies used by Erdoğan and the AKP.[110] Yet while the Gezi protests posed a significant challenge to the AKP, the government was gradually able to reframe the protests as a violent uprising by a secularist minority backed by sinister international forces aiming to destabilize Turkey.[111] Erdoğan and his administration relied on their growing control over the media and deployed their distinctive arsenal of religious mobilization, including countermobilization on the basis of religious identity, to weather the storm and reassert their electoral dominance.[112]

Reliance on associational ties also proved to be a double-edged sword as conflict brewed between the AKP and the Gülen movement. In many ways, the very success of their joint struggle against the secularist establishment made it increasingly difficult for the two to manage their divergent positions on matters ranging from foreign policy to the distribution of electoral spoils.[113] Fethullah Gülen's preference for elite-oriented reform and distrust of Erdoğan's majoritarian populism had been a potential source of conflict from the beginning. Moreover, Gülen and his supporters were far more committed to building and sustaining ties with Europe and the United States, which were profoundly important for the group's transnational operations, while the AKP had proved willing to distance itself from its Western allies once these signaled their unwillingness to make meaningful concessions.[114] The 2010 Mavi Marmara incident, in which a flotilla of Turkish activists sought to break the Israeli blockade of Gaza and was subsequently attacked by Israeli forces, triggered the first public conflict between the two allies, with the AKP supporting the activists while Gülen spoke out against their breach of Israeli law.[115] This was only a mild skirmish. Over the next three years, the AKP and Gülenists exchanged an escalating series of blows, with the Gülenists relying on their positions in the police and the judiciary to launch overt and covert investigations against key figures in the AKP administration, while the government went after the movement's resources by closing down its profitable university preparatory classes.[116] By the time the Gezi Park protests began, Gülen-affiliated media refused to cover the conflict in the way that the AKP administration demanded, and the government treated its reporter and outlets with open hostility.[117]

The dispute between the two erstwhile allies flared into an open conflict that vividly illustrates both the limits and the power of religious mobilization.

In December 2013 Gülenists sought to strike a direct blow against the AKP by exposing corruption in the administration. The anticorruption unit of the Istanbul police detained dozens of prominent figures tied to the AKP, including the sons of three ministers, on live television,[118] accusing them of orchestrating a scheme to bypass American sanctions on Iran through covert gold-for-oil trading.[119] Erdoğan and his administration condemned the raids as part of a conspiracy to overthrow the government at the behest of Gülen, whom they portrayed as the leader of a parallel state beholden to transnational interests. The government dismissed thousands of suspected Gülen sympathizers in the police and the judiciary and seized major media properties linked to the movement. By 2015 the movement was being accused of terrorism and being referred to as FETÖ, the Fethullah Gülen Terror Organization.[120]

In July 2016 an attempted coup shocked the country. The scope of the coup and the identity of its leaders were initially unclear, but their forces were able to seize control of key objectives in Ankara and Istanbul and to launch attacks on the parliament building and the National Intelligence Agency.[121] The government called for popular mobilization against the coup, using both mass and social media and, most strikingly, the network of more than eighty thousand mosques controlled by the Diyanet.[122] Mosque loudspeakers across the country repeatedly issued the call to prayer and called on citizens to defend the government.[123] The crowds that faced down the putschist soldiers on bridges and squares included a sizable number of people in religious garb, suggesting that this effort played a prominent role in the anticoup mobilization.[124] As the key role of Gülenist officers in the coup became clear, Erdoğan's administration blamed the event squarely on FETÖ, completing the conversion of the Gülen movement from close ally to existential threat. In the aftermath of the coup, the AKP launched a massive purge of military, police, and members of the bureaucracy, as well as a dizzying array of government critics and opponents, justified as an effort to root out Gülenist influence. These purges dramatically accelerated the concentration of power in Erdoğan's hands and furthered the country's slide into electoral authoritarianism.[125]

In summary, the distinctive style of religious mobilization pursued by the AKP has reflected the structural and institutional conditions the party has faced and in turn altered these conditions. Endowed with a legislative supermajority by the country's idiosyncratic electoral system, the AKP nevertheless faced a state apparatus largely staffed by staunch secularists and designed to control religious political engagement. To gain greater control over the state and its resources, the AKP drew effectively on its repertoire of religious mobilization and its expanding influence within the bureaucracy.

Its ability to appeal to religious identity without delivering major religious policy reforms allowed it to cement a broad electoral base that entrenched it in power, while its alliances with well-endowed religious groups in civil society proved crucial in overcoming its opponents within the state. Yet these successes bred new challenges. The AKP's ongoing reliance on appeals to religious identity deepened the polarization of the country along religious-secular lines, contributing to the outbreak of mass protests. Similarly, its reliance on religious partners with their own policy agendas began to fray as common enemies were overcome and disagreements escalated into conflict. Thus, while the AKP proved remarkably adept at mobilizing religion to achieve its political ends, it paid a significant price for doing so.

Conclusion

The leaders of Mexico's PAN and Turkey's AKP came to power after careers spent in opposition, and both faced the challenge of converting organizations built as challengers into parties capable of governing. In both cases, parties' historic ties to religion were an important feature of this transition. The modern Mexican and Turkish states were designed as bastions of assertive secularism, built to contain the religious impulses of the societies they governed. In both countries, displays of religious piety by political leaders provoked strong sentiments, secularist elites prepared themselves to resist the implementation of doctrinal policies, and religious associations expected to wield political influence in exchange for their political support.

Yet these similarities belied critical differences. In Mexico, the PAN faced a Catholic community effectively presided over by an autonomous and cohesive set of religious authorities—the Catholic bishops organized around the CEM—and a fragmented set of lay associations oriented toward specific causes, exemplified by ProVida. In Turkey, the AKP was connected to a wide array of lay associations with varying degrees of capacity and cohesiveness, ranging from local Islamic business associations to the transnational Gülen movement, none of which could claim the ability to speak for the broader community of believers. Moreover, the Turkish state possessed substantial mechanisms with which to guide and shape religious mobilization, most notably the Diyanet, which managed the country's mosques and employed its imams. In contrast, the Mexican state had extended legal recognition to the Catholic Church only in 1992, and its laws were designed to exclude, rather than manage, religious communities.

As a result, the two religious parties handled secular power in very different ways. The PAN administrations of Fox and Calderón found it exceed-ingly difficult to maintain control over the religious agenda and found themselves dragged into conflicts over abortion and same-sex marriage that alienated liberals and moderates while failing to appease conservative supporters. When hard times arrived—particularly as the security situation degenerated amid Calderón's war against drug cartels—religious leaders did not mobilize in substantial ways to defend the PAN administration, and its candidates' efforts to regain their support by adopting more explicitly religious rhetoric fell on deaf ears. The AKP, in contrast, was largely able to contain expectations and retain its appeal to a broad swath of the electorate, including religious conservatives. It relied on liberal arguments to pass reforms that reduced the undemocratic power of secularist tutelary institutions and on its religious allies in civil society to take control over key bureaucracies. When potentially difficult issues arose, such as education or gender policies, it used the state's bureaucratic capacity to deliver reforms and handle the political fallout at relatively little cost. As Erdoğan's grip on power tightened, his administration faced down major challenges in the form of the Gezi Park youth protests and the coup attempt by its erstwhile allies in the Gülen movement. In both cases, it was able to rely on religious mobilization to confront and outlast its challengers.

Conclusion

Lessons from Mexico and Turkey

In the twenty-first century, a remarkably varied cast of religious actors can be found playing major roles in political contests around the world. Evangelical activists in the United States, Hindu nationalists in India, Pentecostal preachers in Brazil, and Shia militias in Iraq—these and myriad others occupy prominent places in the politics of their respective countries. As a result, where scholars once announced the inevitable decline of religion, many now speak of a global religious resurgence.[1] Yet, widespread as it appears to be, resurgence is not universal, and it takes different forms in different contexts. In this book, I therefore focus on the particular dynamics of religious engagement in the electoral arena—that is, how and under what conditions political parties mobilize religion.

I develop a flexible yet rigorous concept of religious parties that can travel across traditions and propose two major factors that shape religious political mobilization in a broad range of contexts: political institutions and religious community structures. The cross-national statistical analysis in Chapter 1 demonstrates the diversity of religious parties in Catholic- and Sunni-majority countries and highlights how adopting different standards for considering parties as religious can dramatically alter assessments of their abundance and distribution. It also shows that both structures and institutions can play an important role in shaping religious political mobilization. The case studies of Mexico and Turkey, countries with historically secularist regimes in which contentious democratization processes led to religious parties winning dramatic electoral victories, identify the mechanisms by which evolving structures and institutions shaped the strategies used by religious parties and how coming to power necessitated altering their approaches to religious political mobilization. These investigations yield a number of lessons regarding the causes and consequences of religious political mobilization, with implications that extend far beyond Mexico and Turkey.

First, religious political mobilization is highly adaptable and can endure and even flourish in inhospitable environments. To banish religion from the electoral arena without abolishing elections altogether is almost always a quixotic project. The structural foundations of mobilization are variable but resilient, and political institutions are more likely to redirect religious political mobilization than to prevent it.

Second, both democratization and economic development, once considered drivers of religious decline, can also enable religious political engagement. In practice, their effects are often complex: they can erode certain forms of religious influence while simultaneously endowing religious communities with substantial mobilizing resources and creating institutional openings for effective political engagement.

Third, autonomous and well-coordinated clerical authorities can serve as important obstacles to assertive religious political mobilization, while co-opted or fragmented clerical authorities often pave the way for religious appeals by ambitious political entrepreneurs. This does not mean that strong clerical leaders necessarily oppose political engagement but rather that they are often wary of losing or diluting their moral authority. State-led attacks on clerical hierarchies aimed at preventing assertive religious mobilization are likely to be counterproductive in an electoral setting.

Fourth, institutions designed to constrain religious political mobilization can be turned into instruments for its furtherance if and when religious parties come to power. Secularist regimes that actively intervene in religious communities rely on mechanisms such as ministries of religious affairs that are often well suited for state-led religious mobilization. In other words, the tools designed to contain and domesticate religious partisanship can be redeployed to further deepen it.

These lessons, drawn from the Mexican and Turkish cases, can inform our expectations about the likely development of religious political parties in a broad range of countries. They travel most easily to other Catholic- and Sunni-majority contexts, such as the cases included in the quantitative analysis in the first chapter. In this Conclusion, however, I go further afield to consider how they may inform our understanding of religious political mobilization by parties associated with other traditions: Pentecostal Protestantism in Brazil, Hinduism in India, Evangelicalism in the United States, and Shia Islam in Iraq. These discussions are only preliminary sketches that draw connections to ongoing scholarly conversations about the features of religious political engagement in those contexts. Its goal is to enable discussions that bridge traditional divides based on religious tradition and geographic region and build toward a general theory of religious political mobilization.

Variety and Adaptability of Religious Parties

The first lesson is that religious parties take many forms because religion is mobilized in different ways. The concept of religious political parties developed here is based on the notion of "family resemblance," in which parties are considered religious insofar as they appeal to religious identity, articulate doctrinally informed platforms, and/or maintain ties to religious associations. These dimensions of religious mobilization necessarily take different forms in different religious contexts, if only because the sets of symbols, associations, and doctrines in each tradition are different. Depending on whether one requires mobilization along some or all dimensions and how central this mobilization is required to be, this approach can yield a very broad and inclusive definition of religious parties or a very narrow and exclusive one. It thus leaves significant room for judgment in measurement, but as long as these judgments are made transparently and convincingly, I consider this to be an advantage, given the uncertainty and complexity of the topic.

The case studies of Mexico and Turkey demonstrate the usefulness of the approach: rather than become bogged down in debates over whether or not the PAN and the AKP are truly religious parties—depending, for example, on the sincerity or intensity of their leaders' beliefs—they proceed by examining how these organizations mobilized religion in practice, finding that they did so in different ways and with different intensities at different times.

In Mexico, the founders of the PAN did not imagine it as a religious party and rejected the religious mobilization strategies pursued by the assertive Sinarquista movement and its partisan offshoots. However, by the 1950s the PAN had become increasingly reliant on religious mobilization as its secular resources were co-opted by the hegemonic ruling party (the PRI). Over the next four decades, a series of intraparty struggles impeded attempts to endow the PAN with an explicit religious identity, eroded the role of doctrinal references in its platforms, and loosened its ties to lay religious associations. Then, as Mexico's elections became more competitive in the 1980s and 1990s, its candidates developed new ways to appeal to religious identity while keeping Catholic doctrines and associations largely on the sidelines. Once in power, the party was repeatedly drawn into debates over the role of religious doctrine in shaping policies around abortion and same-sex marriage.

In Turkey, the inauguration of multiparty competition in the late 1940s led to the deployment of limited religious mobilization by centrist conservative parties, the DP and the AP. Two decades later, the MG movement pioneered assertive religious mobilization through dedicated partisan vehicles, the MNP and the MSP. In the 1980s a new party, the ANAP, successfully combined links to religious associations and limited appeals to sectarian identity to dominate the electoral arena, while in the 1990s assertive religious mobilization became the basis for the largest party in the legislature, the RP. The AKP, which combined a style of mobilization reminiscent of that of conservatives in the 1980s with the religious reputation and associational linkages forged by assertive religious mobilizers during the 1990s, succeeded spectacularly, dominating electoral competition during the first two decades of the new millennium.

In both Mexico and Turkey, the observed variety of religious mobilization reflected efforts by parties to adapt to the challenges posed by secularist regimes amid complex democratization processes. Facing a hegemonic ruling party (in Mexico) or secularist military interventions (in Turkey), parties nevertheless found ways to draw support from religious communities and channel it into the electoral arena. Their adaptability and persistence show that religious parties are capable of flourishing in very hostile political environments.

This should come as no surprise to observers of Middle Eastern and North African politics, where political organizations such as Egypt's Muslim Brotherhood, Morocco's Justice and Development Party, and Yemen's Reform Party relied in part on religious mobilization to compete in, and even win, elections under extremely challenging conditions.[2] Less widely recognized is the remarkable record of Catholic parties in Latin America, which were often able to compete in authoritarian elections and were frequently the first to succeed following transitions from authoritarian rule, in part because of their ability to mobilize religious identities and associational ties.[3] To be sure, Sunni and Catholic parties typically adopted radically different approaches to religious mobilization, as shown in Chapter 1: assertive religious mobilization has been far more common among Sunni organizations, while Catholic ones have typically mobilized religion in far more limited ways. These differences reflect the very different structural and institutional contexts in which they operated but also highlight the versatility of religious political mobilization.

The same procedure can be applied to understand shifting patterns of religious political mobilization by organizations ranging from Hindu nationalists in India to Evangelical churches in Brazil. Like Mexico and Turkey, India has a historically secularist regime, although not an assertively secularist one.[4] Moreover, it has also witnessed the increasingly successful mobilization of religious (Hindu) identity, doctrine, and associations in the electoral arena, prompting a vigorous debate about the place of religion in politics.[5] Since its formation in 1980, the Bharatiya Janata Party (BJP; Indian People's Party) has gradually become India's most successful party, first leading a government in 1996 and then capturing an absolute majority of parliamentary seats in 2014 and again in 2019—a rare feat in India's often fractionalized electoral environment. Since its inception, the BJP has mobilized religion along multiple dimensions, most notably by articulating a powerful vision of Hindu identity and by leveraging its ties to major religious associations, particularly the Rashtriya Swayamsevak Sangh (RSS; National Volunteer Association).[6] In this sense, it is a classic example of an assertive religious party. Yet the BJP has mobilized religion in different ways at different times. For example, in the 1980s the party attempted to distance itself from the RSS and went as far as to recruit Muslim candidates, while in the 1990s it adopted a much more assertive religious strategy by supporting the RSS campaign to topple the Babri Mosque and replace it with the Temple of Ram.[7] Over the next two decades, the party reduced the salience of its doctrinal points while retaining its emphasis on appealing to Hindu identity in a bid to expand its geographic scope and defuse accusations of radicalism.[8] In light of the arguments presented in this book, these changes highlight the adaptability of religious parties and offer an opportunity to consider how and when parties engage in different forms of religious mobilization.

An even more dramatic example of the variability of religious political engagement can be observed in Brazil, where the spread of Protestantism, and more specifically of Pentecostal churches whose members Brazilians refer to as *evangélicos* (Evangelicals), has transformed the religious landscape and generated potential opportunities for new forms of religious mobilization.[9] In Brazil, prominent Evangelical communities, such as the Assemblies of God and the Universal Church of the Kingdom of God (UCKG), developed a distinctive mode of political engagement that entailed sponsoring political candidates while largely sidestepping party organizations.[10] Evangelical clerical leaders have typically opted to sponsor specific politicians who are members of their churches rather than ally with political parties, plausibly as a way of maintaining greater control over religious mobilization and exercising influence across a broad range of the political spectrum.[11] This is a striking adaptation to the reality of Brazil's weak and fractionalized party system and highlights how flexible religious political mobilization can be. The framework developed in this book allows us to think systematically about how the prevalence of this practice is shaping particular parties in Brazil, specifically by considering the extent to which particular organizations and their candidates rely on appeals to religious identity, doctrine, and associations to mobilize voters.

Ambiguities of Democratization and Development

A second lesson to be drawn from the cases of Mexico and Turkey is that political and economic development can often enable, rather than limit, religious political mobilization. In both countries, the expansion of religious parties coincided with periods of democratization and economic growth. This stands in stark contrast to the expectations of secularization theory, which argues that the influence of religion on political affairs would diminish in direct proportion to the strength of modern economic and political systems.[12] However, this does not mean that religious political mobilization consistently contributes to democratization and economic development: in Mexico, PAN governments preserved democratic institutions but presided over a turbulent period marked by economic instability and growing insecurity, while in Turkey, the AKP's administration enabled economic growth but took a markedly autocratic turn as the party consolidated its grip on power. Democratization and economic growth are often good for religious mobilizers, but the inverse is not necessarily the case.

The classic secularist notion that economic and political development inevitably results in the decline and privatization of religion has been challenged by compelling evidence from a dizzying array of cases across virtually all religious traditions and world regions.[13] Yet secularization is not dead: cross-national studies often find a significant negative correlation between development and various forms of religious influence.[14] The theory and evidence presented in this book contribute to our understanding of the ambiguous effects of economic growth and democratization on religious political engagement. These processes can erode established religious mores and institutions, but they simultaneously reshape political opportunities in ways that can also enable new forms of religious political engagement.

Democratization and economic development transformed the lives of enormous numbers of Mexicans and Turks in ways that sometimes eroded traditional religious power structures. For example, women in Mexico, empowered by economic participation and democratic rights, increasingly challenged traditional views of womanhood espoused by the Catholic Church.[15] In Turkey, the youth that led the Gezi protest movement drew on global struggles for democratic participation, environmental rights, and economic justice to challenge conservative political projects favored by nationalist religious leaders.[16] Yet economic growth and democratic institutions have also created spaces and resources that enable religious political mobilization. In both countries, a growing private sector fueled conservative business associations that played a critical role in supporting the rise of religious parties, and explicitly religious associations benefited from the loosening of authoritarian constraints on civil society. These empowering effects of democratic reform and economic growth competed with, and often overwhelmed, their better-known secularizing effects. Similar processes can be observed far beyond Mexico and Turkey.

In the United States, robust democratic institutions and an expanding private sector contributed to the rise of the religious right in the final three decades of the twentieth century.[17] Despite their contemporary prominence, Evangelical Christians have not been consistently active in America's electoral politics, and they began to coordinate around their current conservative political agenda explicitly grounded in religious doctrine only in the 1970s.[18] The ability of Evangelical Christian activists, often marginal to national politics, to organize networks and put effective pressure on political elites is in many ways a testament to the quality and openness of the country's democratic participatory mechanisms. Moreover, the resources that sustained conservative religious activism were the fruit of a lively economic arena that, despite significant downturns and growing inequality, nevertheless endowed a broad range of actors with sufficient resources to participate effectively in the democratic process. The increasing influence of Evangelical voices within the Republican Party converted that organization into a substantially religious organization—that is, one in which religious identity, doctrine, and associational ties play an important, though not necessarily dominant, role in mobilizing voters and recruiting cadres.[19] While the consequences of growing religious political mobilization for the health of American democracy (and religion) are widely contested,[20] the fact that inclusive political and economic institutions made it possible merits greater recognition than it often receives in public discourse.

A similar process took place in India, where economic development and democratic institutions were central to the emergence of effective religious political mobilization. India's BJP benefited from the growing competitiveness that accompanied the decline of India's once-hegemonic Congress Party, which was in part a consequence of Congress's autocratic experiment during the Emergency (1975–1977).[21] Moreover, the ability of Hindu nationalist political entrepreneurs to organize sectarian groups to challenge the Congress-dominated establishment was conditional on the resilience of that country's democracy, which, despite its uneven quality, prevented Indira Gandhi and her son, Rajiv, from tightening their grip on power despite scoring major electoral successes in the 1980s. In terms of economic growth, as in Turkey and Mexico, the gradual emergence and consolidation of an urban middle class during the 1980s created much of the conservative constituency that the BJP subsequently mobilized through appeals to religious identity, doctrine, and associational linkages.[22]

In Brazil, Evangelical churches also drew on the resources and opportunities created by democratization and an expanding economy to more effectively mobilize voters in favor of selected candidates. The transition to democracy in the 1980s allowed church leaders to engage in the potentially risky business of religious political mobilization, launching the Evangelical caucus in 1986 and securing a growing share of the legislature in each subsequent election. Brazil's highly fractured party system resulted in very competitive elections in which Evangelical bloc voting could yield substantial political influence. Moreover, an expanding economy allowed Evangelical communities' most successful leaders to accumulate enormous fortunes, as exemplified by Bishop Edir Macedo, head of the UCKG, whose billionaire status both reflects and extends his enormous network of influence. The media and financial resources that Evangelical churches are able to provide for their candidates are a vital complement to their ability to mobilize voters through direct appeals.

Clerical Constraints

The third lesson is that religious authorities can be unexpected allies for secularists concerned by the assertive mobilization of religion in the electoral arena. Robust and autonomous clerical organizations often resist efforts by lay activists to mobilize confessional communities, particularly when these efforts threaten to infringe on clerics' status as standard-bearers for their faith and undermine their moral authority. In contrast, when religious authorities are divided, these collective costs may be outweighed by the individual advantage garnered by religious leaders who ally with political entrepreneurs to mobilize religion. The degree of coordination that characterizes a religious community's clerical body thus emerges as a key factor in whether religious authorities are likely to resist lay efforts to mobilize religion. In addition, the relative resources of clerical hierarchies and lay activists are also important, as not all clerical authorities are in a position to raise the cost of unapproved religious mobilization.

This argument challenges an older and still widely held view of religious politics that sees clerical hierarchies as the primary advocates of religious mobilization. Since at least the French Revolution, secular-religious political conflict has been understood typically as a struggle between state officials and clerical hierarchies, in which the capacity of the clerical hierarchies determines the substantive importance of religious politics. The classic notion of a church-state cleavage, central to seminal sociological models of party development in Europe,[23] is often modeled as resulting from a conflict between bishops and bureaucrats that percolates down to the population at large. In that view, the stronger the clerical authorities, the more religious a country's politics are likely to be.

In contrast, evidence from Mexico and Turkey favors a more complex assessment, one in which clerical authorities are at least as likely to oppose as to support religious political mobilization, particularly when it takes an assertive form. In Mexico, Catholic bishops were critical in tempering the assertive political mobilization of the Sinarquista movement in the 1940s but supported the PAN's struggle against electoral fraud in the 1980s and 1990s. In Turkey, religious leaders were divided in their support for assertive religious parties, with prominent Nakşibendi sheikhs sponsoring their formation while the Nurcu leadership remained far more skeptical. The Gülen movement was a vital ally to the AKP in the 2000s until it became its most notorious foe in the 2010s.

Beyond this overall diversity, there were clear differences in the relationship between political parties and religious authorities in the two countries. In Mexico, the powerful influence wielded by Catholic bishops was more often a constraint on an overtly religious politics, even as it enabled limited religious mobilization. While individual bishops sometimes favored assertive religious politics, as a collective they were usually hostile to overt Catholic partisanship.

In Turkey, members of the fractured set of religious leaders were more likely to provide the impetus for religious mobilization at key junctures and were seldom in a position to effectively constrain the partisan mobilization of religion. This reflects the very different positions of religious authorities in each country and more broadly in contemporary Catholicism and Sunni Islam. It is worth remembering, however, that the capacity and autonomy of religious leaders in a given tradition can vary significantly over time. Indeed, both Mexico and Turkey have witnessed major changes in clerical capacity, from troughs in the aftermath of assertive secularist reforms to peaks toward the end of the century. Moreover, religious authorities of the same tradition in different countries, or even within the same country,[24] differ in their effective resources, degrees of coordination, and even their desired ends.

This argument can be extended to other traditions, with the caveat that these extensions should be sensitive to the variety of existing religious community structures. The organization of many Protestant denominations formally resembles that of Sunni Islam: decentralized and with an emphasis on personal relations with the divine rather than those mediated by a clerical hierarchy. This may account, at least in part, for their rapid growth in Latin America and other developing areas, as entrepreneurial members can set up churches without having to pass complex training processes or requiring the approval of a centralized hierarchy.[25] However, like their Sunni counterparts, Protestant communities empirically demonstrate a wide range of organizational capacity and hierarchy. Many Pentecostal and Evangelical churches are weakly organized and possess limited means to block the mobilization of their symbols and doctrines by competing groups, suggesting that they would be ineffectual at setting the terms of religious political engagement. In environments in which members of these fragmented communities constitute a plurality or majority of voters, it appears likely that political parties will be able to mobilize religion assertively and effectively. However, some Evangelical churches, such as Brazil's UCKG, are highly organized and resource rich. Operating as a disciplined hierarchical organization in a country characterized by an increasingly diverse religious environment and a highly fractionalized political party system, the UCKG has responded to perceived threats from the political arena by engaging in direct political mobilization that minimizes delegation to party organizations while allowing the church leadership to make its voice heard, generating a great deal of electoral clout despite its minority status.[26] The result has been Brazil's highly distinctive pattern of religious mobilization: church-sponsored politicians who rely on clerical authorities rather than party organizations to mobilize voters and who advocate church policy preference in a narrow range of issue areas while working within parties across the political spectrum.

India emerges as an interesting case in this context as well, as Hinduism does not possess a clear clerical hierarchy that can potentially limit assertive religious mobilization. Indian politicians of various ideological stripes have argued that Hinduism is inherently tolerant and adaptable and can thus serve as the basis for a religiously plural society.[27] Yet the absence of clerical veto players has enabled political activists to autonomously generate highly divisive doctrinal policy proposals and use them to mobilize voters on the basis of markedly sectarian political projects. Among the most striking examples is the demand for the demolition of the Babri Mosque and its replacement by a Temple of Ram in Ayodhya. This campaign, developed and launched by Hindu nationalist activists linked to the RSS and its affiliates but seized on by BJP leaders and candidates, proved to be a critical moment in the transformation of the BJP from a marginal party to a major contender in national politics.[28] The ability of the RSS and the BJP to set the terms of debate regarding the political implications of Hinduism, particularly around a profoundly divisive and politically incendiary point, is remarkable when considered in comparative perspective.

Post-2003 Iraq may serve as an example of the opposite dynamic, one in which a clerical hierarchy attempts to contain assertive religious mobilization that threatens to undermine its leadership. Iraq, where politics has come to be dominated by severe sectarian cleavages, in many ways constitutes a least-likely case for this type of clerical constraint. In the aftermath of American intervention, with political institutions largely undefined, the manner in which the Shia majority would engage in politics emerged as a crucial question. The prospect of competitive multiparty elections created substantial opportunities for Shia political entrepreneurs to engage in assertive religious mobilization, often by sponsoring or working with sectarian militias.[29] In this extremely volatile scenario, lower-ranking clerics such as Moqtada al-Sadr adopted hypersectarian strategies that emphasized direct religious confrontation as a means of assuring political influence.[30] In contrast, Grand Ayatollah Ali al-Sistani, the leading Shia cleric in Iraq, was regularly identified as a constraint on these hyperassertive forms of political mobilization.[31] This is not to say that al-Sistani opposed religious influence in politics or eschewed partisan alliances—he called for a Supreme Court composed of religious scholars and was widely seen as supporting both a political party and a militia[32]—but rather that he preferred mechanisms of political influence that allowed him to remain above the partisan fray and did not make clerical influence contingent on electoral results.

Double-Edged Secularist Institutions

The fourth lesson pertains to the way in which political institutions can shape, contain, or redirect religious political mobilization. The growing prominence of religious politics in the twenty-first century has prompted many scholars, policy makers, and activists to worry about its potential to undermine established secular institutions and norms, particularly those considered central to the proper functioning of democracy.[33] Alternatively, others have found institutional arrangements that can channel the constructive energy of religion to deepen and reinforce processes of democratization.[34] As the cases of Mexico and Turkey show, religious mobilization and democratization can go hand in hand, but the decline of liberal rights in Erdoğan's Turkey dramatically demonstrates that religious mobilization can also contribute to the decline of democracy. Among political scientists, the question of which institutional arrangements are best equipped to manage rising religious political mobilization has become a pressing one.[35]

Can religious political mobilization be effectively restrained by secularist institutions? The architects of the modern Mexican and Turkish states certainly believed so: they considered it crucial that a modern, national state be able to intervene in religious affairs to protect secular politics from religious intrusion. The notion that state authorities should act as bulwarks against reaction by both guiding and regulating religious practice was a core tenet of the secularist, modernizing elites who dominated both countries in the 1920s and 1930s. The results, however, were ultimately very different.

In Mexico, the project of interventionist secularism was effectively abandoned in the 1940s, leaving in its place a highly exclusive regime with enormous nominal power but little real capacity for involvement in religious affairs. Religion-state relations were instead governed through informal negotiations between party officials and the Catholic Church. In contrast, in Turkey the vast regulatory apparatus centered on the Directorate of Religious Affairs, the Diyanet, became a powerful instrument with which the state could guide and regulate official Sunni Islam, even as the autonomous networks headed by formally banned religious brotherhoods and movements grew during the second half of the twentieth century.

Despite the similar visions and motivations of their founding architects, both countries were therefore ultimately left with very different forms of assertive secularism: one based on exclusion and the other on control. Ultimately, neither version was able to prevent the rise and eventual success of political parties that mobilized religion to compete in elections. However, they created very different opportunities for the subsequent governments led by these parties. In Mexico, the PAN's federal governments had few tools with which to shape or satisfy the expectations of religious constituents, forcing it to engage in disadvantageous policy debates and rendering it vulnerable to critiques from religious authorities and lay movements. In contrast, the AKP was able to use the dominant position of the Turkish state in regard to religion to set the terms of policy debates, advance religious agendas through multiple channels, and appease religious supporters even when it faced legal and political setbacks.

These insights shed light on the growing scholarship on the varieties of state secularism and regulation of religion.[36] First, it underscores the notion that categories such as assertive secularism, while useful, necessarily obscure a great deal of variation. Second, and perhaps more important, it points out that secularist institutions do not consistently constitute an effective bulwark against religious political mobilization. Instead, they are more likely to channel religious engagement in particular directions—for example, toward informal bargaining with heads of state in Mexico and toward control of bureaucratic offices in Turkey. Even institutions designed to resist religious influence tend to redirect it rather than prevent it.

The varieties of assertive secularism developed in Mexico and Turkey are often contrasted with the separationist model developed in the United States, which bans the use of state power to either establish religion or to impede its free exercise.[37] In the late twentieth century, courts rather than politicians have generally safeguarded this separation, which ultimately rests on their interpretation of the First Amendment of the American Constitution. Yet while the U.S. model is often praised for its ability to protect religious liberty while tempering religious passions and preventing violent conflicts over religion, its impact on religious political mobilization is more ambiguous. American politicians have often demonstrated a degree of public religiosity that would have shocked most Mexicans and Turks. Moreover, since the late 1970s the growing influence of the Religious Right within the Republican Party has contributed to the politicization of religion.[38] Reliance on courts to draw the terms of separation has resulted in high levels of religious mobilization around court appointments, as religious activists have come to see control of the courts—particularly the Supreme Court—as the cornerstone of effective policy influence.[39] Rather than contain religious politics and thus reduce the salience of religious conflict, the separation model has increasingly made American courts an effective symbol around which to coordinate religious political mobilization.

India offers another interesting contrast that highlights the way in which secularist institutions tend to become engines of religious engagement. Its model of secularism is distinctive, as it is based neither on secularist supremacy, as Turkey and Mexico are, nor on strict separation, as the United States is. Instead, India has attempted to maintain a framework based on "principled distance" and "equal treatment" for all religions, in which the state itself engages with all religious communities in a way that respects their differences and is free from favoritism.[40] In practice, maintaining this stance has proven difficult, and critics point to numerous instances when practice does not live up to principle.[41] The criticisms have come from all sides. Muslim activists note that the state has often adopted laws that effectively impose Hindu doctrines on non-Hindu citizens, such as banning cow slaughter.[42] Hindu nationalists point to the unwillingness of the secular state to impose a unified civil code on the Muslim minority, despite having done so for the Hindu majority.[43] The rise of the BJP has been driven in part by these perceptions of secular dysfunction, as its candidates and supporters effectively argue that Congress administrations had manipulated secularism in pursuit of political advantage. Critics of the BJP, of course, do the same. In light of the developments in Mexico and Turkey, the fact that Indian institutions, which in practice set out a substantial but ill-defined scope for state intervention in religious affairs, have been reappropriated by Hindu nationalists is not a surprise. As in Mexico, Turkey, and the United States, the increasingly pressing question is whether, and to what extent, this transformation will ultimately undermine or reinforce democratic politics.

Conclusion

Around the world, democracy is being transformed by the mobilization of religion by political parties. Parties mobilize religion in myriad ways, coordinating and appealing to voters by means that are quite legible to national publics but not necessarily to those unfamiliar with local idioms, beliefs, or networks of influence. To grasp how religious mobilization is transforming global democratic practice, scholarship on religious politics must be able to find a way across barriers to systematic comparison across religious traditions. Moreover, it should engage in sustained dialogue with other areas of scholarship that aim to understand political change. In this book, I seek to contribute to this effort by setting up an analytical framework that can be used to study religious parties in diverse settings and by putting forth a set of causal arguments that draw on and contribute to established accounts of political party development, electoral institutions, social movements, and democratization, among others.

It is my hope that this book contributes to broadening and deepening ongoing debates about the role of religion in democratic politics. Religious political mobilization is a complex and widespread phenomenon that frequently arouses passionate responses from both supporters and opponents. The four lessons presented here are intended to enable, rather than conclude, constructive conversations over the politicization of religion. Whether political parties recognize themselves, or are recognized by others, as "religious parties" should matter less than the ways in which they mobilize religion in practice. The debate over labels, while useful to partisan actors, should not guide scholarship or policy.

Religious politics is not inherently reactionary and will not inevitably disappear, swept away by the rise of democracies and markets. These modern forces largely account for much of the power with which religion entered the political arena in the late twentieth century and continues to shape it in the twenty-first. The advocates and opponents of religious political mobilization are not necessarily those one might expect. Religious communities character-ized by decentralization and doctrinal flexibility are often ripe for religious mobilization by political entrepreneurs, while rigid, unrepresentative clerical hierarchies may resist their efforts. Finally, political institutions are powerful and play a prominent role in shaping religious mobilization but do not always work as their architects intended. The rules built to protect secularism can be turned into a means for its dismantlement.

Appendix 1

Religious Political Parties by Country

Country	Party name	Religious tradition	Highest religious mobilization threshold
Algeria	Green Algeria Alliance	Sunni	3
	Islamic Salvation Front	Sunni	3
	Justice and Development Party	Sunni	3
	Movement for National Reform	Sunni	3
	Movement of Society for Peace	Sunni	3
	National Liberation Front	Sunni	1
	Renaissance	Sunni	3
Argentina	Movement for Dignity and Independence	Catholic	1
Bangladesh	Bangladesh Islamic Assembly	Sunni	3
	Bangladesh Nationalist Party	Sunni	2
	Islamic Bloc	Sunni	3
	Islamic Unity Front	Sunni	3
	Jatiya Party	Sunni	1
Brazil	Christian Democratic Party	Catholic	1
	Christian Labor Party	Catholic	1
	Christian Social Democratic Party	Catholic	1
	Social Christian Party	Catholic	1
Chile	Christian Democracy	Catholic	2
	Independent Democratic Union	Catholic	2
	Independent Regionalist Party	Catholic	1
Colombia	Conservative Party	Catholic	2

(*continued*)

Country	Party name	Religious tradition	Highest religious mobilization threshold
Croatia	Croatian Christian Democratic Union	Catholic	3
	Croatian Democratic Union	Catholic	2
	Croatian Peasant Party	Catholic	2
Dominican Republic	Social Christian Reformist Party	Catholic	1
Ecuador	Conservative Party	Catholic	1
	People's Democracy—Christian Democratic Union	Catholic	1
	Social Christian Movement	Catholic	1
	Social Christian Party	Catholic	1
Egypt	Building and Development Party	Sunni	3
	Center Party	Sunni	3
	Freedom and Justice Party	Sunni	3
	Muslim Brotherhood	Sunni	3
	Party of the Light	Sunni	3
El Salvador	Authentic Christian Democratic Movement	Catholic	2
	Christian Democratic Party	Catholic	2
	Democratic Change	Catholic	1
	Social Christian Renewal Party	Catholic	2
Guatemala	Guatemalan Christian Democracy	Catholic	2
Hungary	Christian Democratic People's Party	Catholic	3
	Federation of Young Democrats–Hungarian Civic Alliance	Catholic	2
	Hungarian Democratic Forum	Catholic	2
	Hungarian Justice and Life Party	Catholic	1
	Independent Smallholders, Agrarian Workers and Civics Party	Catholic	2
	Movement for a Better Hungary	Catholic	1
Indonesia	Crescent Star Party	Sunni	3
	Justice and Unity Party	Sunni	3
	National Awakening Party	Sunni	3
	Party of Functional Groups	Sunni	1
	Prosperous Justice Party	Sunni	3
	National Mandate Party	Sunni	3
	United Development Party	Sunni	3

Country	Party name	Religious tradition	Highest religious mobilization threshold
Italy	Christian Democracy	Catholic	2
	Christian Democratic Center	Catholic	2
	Daisy	Catholic	1
	Forward Italy	Catholic	1
	Italian People's Party	Catholic	1
	Northern League	Catholic	1
	People of Freedom	Catholic	1
	Union of Democrats for Europe	Catholic	1
	United Christian Democrats	Catholic	2
Jordan	Islamic Action Front	Sunni	3
Kuwait	Islamic Constitutional Movement	Sunni	3
	Islamic Heritage	Sunni	3
	Islamic Salafi Association	Sunni	3
	Islamist Independents	Sunni	3
Malaysia	Pan-Malaysian Islamic Party	Sunni	3
	People's Justice Party	Sunni	1
	Spirit of 46	Sunni	2
	United Malays National Organization	Sunni	2
Mali	National Congress for Democratic Initiative	Sunni	1
	Patriotic Movement for Renewal	Sunni	1
Mexico	National Action Party	Catholic	2
Morocco	Democratic and Constitutional Popular Movement	Sunni	3
	Independence Party	Sunni	1
	Justice and Development Party	Sunni	3
Pakistan	Assembly of Islamic Clerics	Sunni	3
	Assembly of Pakistani Clerics	Sunni	3
	Islamic Democratic Alliance	Sunni	2
	Pakistan Muslim League-F	Sunni	2
	Pakistan Muslim League-J	Sunni	1
	Pakistan Muslim League-N	Sunni	2
	Pakistan Muslim League-Q	Sunni	1
	United Council of Action	Sunni	3
Peru	National Renovation	Catholic	2
	National Unity	Catholic	1
	Popular Christian Party	Catholic	1
Philippines	Lakas Christian Muslim Democrats	Catholic	1

(*continued*)

Country	Party name	Religious tradition	Highest religious mobilization threshold
Poland	Catholic Electoral Action	Catholic	3
	Christian Democracy	Catholic	3
	Law and Justice	Catholic	2
	League of Polish Families	Catholic	3
	Movement for the Reconstruction of Poland	Catholic	1
	Peasant's Agreement	Catholic	2
	Polish People's Party	Catholic	2
	Self-Defense of the Republic of Poland	Catholic	2
	Solidarity Electoral Action	Catholic	2
Slovakia	Christian Democratic Movement	Catholic	2
	Ordinary People and Independent Personalities	Catholic	1
	Slovak Democratic and Christian Union	Catholic	1
Slovenia	New Slovenia	Catholic	2
	Slovene Christian Democrats	Catholic	3
	Slovenian Democratic Party	Catholic	2
	Slovenian People's Party	Catholic	2
Spain	Convergence and Union	Catholic	1
	Popular Party	Catholic	1
Tunisia	Renaissance	Sunni	3
Turkey	Justice and Development Party	Sunni	3
	Motherland Party	Sunni	2
	Nationalist Movement Party	Sunni	2
	True Path Party	Sunni	1
	Virtue Party	Sunni	3
	Welfare Party	Sunni	3
Venezuela	Social Christian Copei Party	Catholic	1
Yemen	General People's Congress	Sunni	2
	Yemeni Congregation for Reform	Sunni	3

Appendix 2

Coding Protocol for Religious Parties

1. Party name: Full party name in English.

2. Party name in original language: No special characters or accents; follow the conventional transliteration.

3. Acronym: Based on the name in original language.

4. Website: Full web address.

5. Country: Country in which the party operates.

6. Electoral performance since 1990: List of every election year since 1990 in which the party obtained more than 1 percent of seats in the national legislature, along with its share of legislative seats in that election (only lower house if bicameral).

7. Total religious mobilization score: Sum of identity, doctrine, and association scores.

8. Identity: Does the party appeal to voters on the basis of their membership in a religious community? Assign one of three possible scores: *0*, *1*, or *2*.

- *0:* The party does not appeal to religious identity. There are no references to religion in party name, no religious symbols are used in party propaganda, and party leaders do not engage in prominent displays of personal religiosity. There are no reports that the party has a particular appeal to religious voters.
- *1:* The party is associated with a religious tradition, but this is not the central element in its appeal to voters. These appeals may take the form of references to religion in party name (e.g., "Christian" or "Islamic"), religious symbols in party banners (e.g., crosses or crescents), or distinctively religious statements or behaviors associated with party leaders or candidates (e.g., news reports of prominent appearances at religious services not usually attended by political leaders). Religious voters are known to at least somewhat favor party.

- *2:* The party explicitly and consistently defines itself as a religious party, and religion is central to the party's identity. Religion is referenced in party name and/or propaganda. Party leaders and candidates consistently appeal to religion through their statements and behavior. The party is widely reported to draw its support primarily from religious voters.

9. Identity explanation: Brief explanation of the assigned identity score.

10. Identity sources: List of sources used to determine identity score.

11. Doctrine: Do the party's manifestos, platforms, statements of doctrine, or other formal statements refer to religious doctrines or principles? Does the party appeal to religious voters by promising to implement specific, religion-based policies? Assign one of three possible scores: *0, 1,* or *2.*

- *0:* The party's manifestos, platforms, statements of doctrine, or propaganda do not contain references to religious principles or doctrines. Its policies have no identifiable religious elements.
- *1:* The party's formal documents make some references to recognizable religious principles or doctrines (e.g., Catholic Social Doctrine, Sharia), but these references play a limited role in the overall documents (e.g., restricted to opening statements). These references may be indirect (e.g., by referencing prominent religious thinkers rather than spelling out their ideas) or not explicitly presented as religious (e.g., references to the sanctity of life since conception). At least some experts link party policy preferences to religious principles.
- *2:* The party's formal documents repeatedly and consistently reference religious principles or doctrines, and these play a central role across the documents. Not every element must be religious (e.g., economic policies need not be justified in religious terms), but they must do more than provide a general preface and must be referenced in multiple sections. Most experts agree that religion played a major role in the development of the party's positions.

12. Doctrine explanation: Brief explanation of the assigned doctrine score.

13. Doctrine sources: List of sources used to determine doctrine score.

14. Associations: Does the party have known ties to religious organizations in civil society, such as religious leaders, charities, social movements, or social service providers? Do these groups help it reach out to voters, recruit candidates, or select its leaders? Assign one of three possible scores: *0, 1,* or *2.*

- *0:* There is no evidence of active cooperation between the party and religious associations in civil society.
- *1:* The party has some ties to religious organizations, as documented by primary sources or experts, but these are not central to the party's voter mobilization or leadership recruitment strategies. Ties may have been more important in the past and retain only a secondary role. Religious organizations are only some of the associations linked to the party and do not have a preeminent status among them.

- *2:* Religious associations are central to the functioning of the party. The party may be an offshoot of a larger religious movement or organization that provides its leaders, shapes its programs, and defines its voter base. If the party leadership is formally independent, it nevertheless relies on a religious movement or organization to carry out voter outreach and recruit candidates.

15. Associations explanation: Brief explanation of the assigned associations score.

16. Associations sources: List of sources used to determine associations score.

Notes

INTRODUCTION

1. Román 2000: 2.
2. *BBC News* 2002.
3. Weber 1993; Huntington 1992.
4. Tibi 2002; Kepel 2002.
5. Casanova 1994; Philpott 2004.
6. Weber 1993: 246–274; Huntington 1992.
7. Philpott 2004, 2007; Fish, Jensenius, and Michel 2010; Toft, Philpott, and Shah 2011; Gleditsch and Rudolfsen 2016.
8. Mitchell 1969.
9. Sullivan and Abed-Kotob 1999: 72.
10. For a notable exception, see Toft, Philpott, and Shah 2011.
11. Kalyvas and van Kersbergen 2010; Mainwaring and Scully 2003.
12. Schwedler 2006; Kurzman and Naqvi 2010; Kurzman and Türkoğlu 2015.
13. See, e.g., Kalyvas 2000.
14. Kalyvas 2000; Tepe 2008; Altınordu 2010; Driessen 2014; Buckley 2017.
15. Casanova 2001; Kalyvas 2003.
16. Bellin 2008: 316.
17. But see Sigmund 2003 and Manuel, Reardon, and Wilcox 2006 for notable exceptions.
18. Gill 1998; Trejo 2009.
19. Pierson 2004.
20. Downs 1957.
21. A party whose candidates are religious or that draws votes from religious constituencies without relying on religion to do so, perhaps because it operates in a society

in which the overwhelming majority of potential candidates and voters is religious, is not for this reason a religious party.

22. Yavuz 2003: 222–225.

23. Loaeza 1999; Greene 2007.

24. J. White 2002; Clark 2004; Wiktorowicz 2001; Gumuscu and Sert 2009.

25. Goertz 2006: 41; see also Wittgenstein 1953.

26. Kalyvas 2000; Mantilla 2012, 2016a.

27. The terms "clergy" and "laity" are used throughout this book as shorthand for specialized religious leaders and nonspecialized religious activists, respectively. As discussed later, while Sunni Islam formally lacks a clergy in the doctrinal Roman Catholic sense, it possesses a variety of specialized religious leaders.

28. Mantilla 2019; Esposito and Voll 1996: 4.

29. Duverger 1954; Sartori 1976; Taagepera and Shugart 1989; Cox 1997.

30. Lust-Okar and Jamal 2002; Lust-Okar 2006; Blaydes 2010; Masoud 2014.

31. These are all the Catholic- and Sunni-majority countries included in the World Values Survey. I used these data to perform reliability tests on religious mobilization coding decisions.

32. Tarrow 2010.

33. See, e.g., Collier and Collier 1991.

34. Fearon 2003.

CHAPTER 1

1. Akdoğan 2003.

2. Fuentes Díaz 1972; Loaeza 1999. The PAN eventually became an observing member of the Christian Democrat Organization of America in 1994 and a full member in 1998.

3. See, e.g., Calfano and Djupe 2009.

4. Ghannouchi 2016; Malka 2019.

5. Duverger 1954.

6. Casanova 2001.

7. Kalyvas 1996.

8. Warner 2000.

9. Grzymala-Busse 2015.

10. See, e.g., Esposito and Voll 1996; and Eickelman and Piscatori 1996.

11. Kurzman and Naqvi 2010.

12. Salih and El-Tom 2009.

13. Tibi 2008.

14. Leiken and Brooke 2007; Ghannouchi 2016.

15. Kurzman and Naqvi 2010; Kurzman and Türkoğlu 2015; Masoud 2014.

16. Schwedler 2011; Pahwa 2017.

17. Schwedler 2006.

18. Kurzman and Naqvi 2010; Kalyvas and van Kersbergen 2010; Mainwaring and Scully 2003.

19. Brocker and Künkler 2013: 172.

20. Ozzano 2013: 810.

21. Kalyvas 2003: 293.
22. Layman 2001; Smidt, Kellstedt, and Guth 2017.
23. Menchik 2016.
24. Anderson 1983; Menchik 2014.
25. Machiavelli notes this in his discussion of Roman religion, and Thucydides notes it in his account of the Peloponnesian War, to name but a pair of well-known examples.
26. Christian Democracy is explicitly ecumenical, and some parties associated with it have been led by Protestant communities. Nevertheless, in countries with large Catholic majorities, this ecumenism, while symbolically important and critical in regard to sustaining the distance between the party and the Catholic hierarchy, is far less important in signaling a religious identity to voters.
27. Sigmund 2003.
28. Mainwaring and Scully 2003; Van Hecke and Gerard 2004; Kalyvas and van Kersbergen 2003.
29. The term "Muslim Democracy" is a scholarly construct designed to note similarities between Christian Democracy and some religious parties in Muslim-majority contexts (Nasr 2005).
30. Tepe 2008.
31. Kurzman and Naqvi 2010.
32. Tepe 2009.
33. Sigmund 2003.
34. Gunther and Diamond 2003: 182.
35. Eickelman and Piscatori 1996; Kalyvas 1996; Wickham 2002.
36. Wickham 2002, 2015
37. Clark 2004; see also J. White 2002.
38. Wittgenstein 1953: 250.
39. Cizre 2002.
40. Iveković 2002.
41. Pupcenoks 2012.
42. Menchik 2016.
43. The protocol used by research assistants is available in Appendix 2.
44. These are all the Catholic- and Sunni-majority countries for which the World Values Survey (WVS) has data between 1990 and 2015. WVS data were used as a robustness check to evaluate coding decisions by examining whether parties coded as religious were also more likely to receive support from religious voters. See WVS website, at http://www.worldvaluessurvey.org.
45. I counted each party by the highest proportion of seats captured.
46. However, the data capture only parties that have won seats in a national legislature. There may be additional political parties that seek to mobilize religion but fail to secure legislative seats.
47. Lipset 1960; Norris and Inglehart 2004.
48. Casanova 1994.
49. D. Smith 1970: 124.
50. See, e.g., Finke and Stark 2005.
51. Finke and Stark 1998; Stark 1999.

52. Layman 2001; Campbell, Green, and Layman 2011; Putnam and Campbell 2012.

53. Göle 2000; Gumuscu and Sert 2009.

54. Lewis 2002.

55. Huntington 1992.

56. Toft, Philpott, and Shah 2011.

57. Finke and Stark 1998; Gill 1998, 2008; Trejo 2009.

58. Gill 2008.

59. Trejo 2009.

60. Lipset and Rokkan 1967.

61. Iannaccone, Finke, and Stark 1997.

62. Toft, Philpott, and Shah 2011.

63. Wickham 2002; Singerman 2004; Masoud 2014.

64. Hibbard 2010; Bose 2018; Lord 2018.

65. Wittenberg 2006; Mainwaring 2003; Almeida 2014; Mantilla 2018.

66. See, e.g., Hout and Fisher 2002; and Djupe, Neiheisel, and Sokhey 2018.

67. See, e.g., Norris and Inglehart 2004.

68. Clark 2004; Gumuscu 2010.

69. De Leon, Desai, and Tuğal 2009; Disch 2011.

70. Kalyvas 2003.

71. Putnam and Campbell 2012; Djupe, Neiheisel, and Conger 2018.

72. Grzymala-Busse 2015, 2016.

73. Kalyvas 1996; A. Smith 2016.

74. Grzymala-Busse 2015; Hagopian 2008.

75. Mantilla 2012.

76. Altınordu 2010; Rosenblum 2003.

77. Wiktorowicz 2001; J. White 2002.

78. Schwedler 2011: 354.

79. Schedler 2002.

80. Mainwaring 2003; Masoud 2014; Mantilla 2016b.

81. J. Fox 2008, 2015.

82. Casanova 1994; Stepan 2001: 216.

83. J. Fox 2008, 2015; Monsma and Soper 2008; Stepan 2011; Buckley 2016; Buckley and Mantilla 2013.

84. Kuru 2008.

85. Bhargava 1998.

86. Buckley 2015.

87. Cox 1997; Taagepera and Shugart 1989.

88. I use WVS data as a robustness check on religious party coding decisions by assessing whether parties coded as religious were more likely to have the support of religious voters. I also use WVS data to measure popular religiosity, one of the key independent variables in the statistical analysis.

89. J. Fox 2008, 2015.

90. Data are from Bormann and Golder 2013, expanded to include nondemocracies based on data from the Inter-Parliamentary Union's PARLINE database, at http://archive.ipu.org/parline/parlinesearch.asp.

91. Taagepera and Shugart 1989; Ordeshook and Shvetsova 1994; Cox 1998.

92. To describe levels of religious pluralism, I construct a measure labeled effective number of religions (ENR), such that ENR = $1/\Sigma(p_i^2)$, where p is the proportion of the population that adheres to each religion according to the WRD (https://worldreligion database.org). The WRD estimates the proportion of adherents for each tradition (e.g., Islam, Christianity) and subtradition (e.g., Sunni, Catholic) in every country in the world at five-year intervals. ENR is calculated at the subtradition level. A simple linear interpolation is used to generate estimates for missing years. I made minor corrections for obvious measurement discrepancies between years.

93. Finke and Stark 2005; Huntington 1991; Toft, Philpott, and Shah 2011.

94. Relying on logistic regressions rather than probit ones does not affect the direction of coefficients but alters the levels of significance.

CHAPTER 2

1. Gerring 2007: 133.
2. See, e.g., Kalyvas 2000.
3. Schwedler 2011.
4. Falletti and Lynch 2009; Zaks 2017.
5. George and Bennett 2005.
6. George and Bennett 2005.
7. Falleti and Lynch 2009; Gerring 2007.
8. Pierson 2004; Hall 2016.
9. George and Bennett 2005: 67–72.
10. Collier 2011: 824.
11. George and Bennett 2005: 207.
12. Zaks 2017.
13. Pierson 2004; Grzymala-Busse 2010.
14. Greene 2007.
15. Gurses 2014.
16. Barkey 2008.
17. Colomer 2004.
18. Karpat 1972; Deringil 1993.
19. Di Tella 1994.
20. Buzpinar 1996; Deringil 1991.
21. Roeder 1973.
22. Raat 1973.
23. Super 2000.
24. Masters 2013.
25. R. Rojas 2001.
26. O'Dogherty Madrazo 2001.
27. Mango 2002.
28. Kuru 2009: 11.
29. Lord 2018: 90–91.
30. P. White 2000.
31. Zürcher 2004: 179.

32. Lewis 1952.
33. Emrence 2000.
34. García Ugarte 1995.
35. Bailey 1974; J. Meyer 1973–1975.
36. Karpat 1959.
37. Guerra Manzo 2007; J. Meyer 2003.
38. Langston 2017.
39. Data come from the World Bank's World Development Indicators, available at https://databank.worldbank.org/reports.aspx?source=world-development-indicators.
40. See, e.g., Fearon 2003.
41. Trejo 2009.
42. Kılınç 2019.
43. Lord 2018: 128.
44. Lord 2018: 134–150.
45. Gill 2008.
46. Trejo 2009.
47. Özkul 2015.
48. Lapidus 1997.
49. Greene 2007; Ahmad 1993.
50. Önis 2008.
51. Gerhards and Hans 2011; Arikan 2017.
52. Kılınç 2019.
53. Kuru 2005.
54. Greene 2007; Magaloni 2006.
55. Kuru 2007, 2009.
56. Eligür 2010: 85–135.
57. J. Fox 2017.
58. Grim and Finke 2006.
59. Lord 2018: xiii.
60. Lord 2018: 80; Gözaydın 2009.
61. Sarkissian 2015.

CHAPTER 3

1. Pérez Franco 1999.
2. Loaeza 1999.
3. Pérez Franco 1999.
4. Mabry 1973: 29–30.
5. Aguilar and Zermeño 1992a: 23.
6. Wiechers 1988.
7. Serrano Álvarez 1992: 299–302.
8. Andes 2012.
9. Camp 1997.
10. Loaeza 1985: 161.
11. Eckstein 1975.
12. J. Meyer 1973–1975.

13. Espinosa 2003.
14. Calderón Vega 1962; Mabry 1973: 23–24.
15. Pérez Franco 1999.
16. Castellanos Hernández 1996: 121–124.
17. Posusney 2002.
18. Garrido 1982: 339.
19. Castellanos Hernández 1996: 132–142.
20. Loaeza 1999: 213.
21. Calderón Vega 1967; Shirk 2005.
22. Pérez Franco 1999.
23. Loaeza 1996: 430–432.
24. González Luna 1999; Calderón Vega 1967: 33, 101.
25. Mabry 1973: 37–41.
26. Partido Acción Nacional 1990: 19.
27. Martínez Valle 2000: 99.
28. Loaeza 1999: 225.
29. Mabry 1973: 43.
30. Pérez Franco 1999.
31. Fuentes Díaz 1972: 44–49.
32. *La Nación* 1958.
33. Partido Acción Nacional 1990: 19–20.
34. Gómez Morin 1961; Loyola Pérez 2000: 279–284.
35. Vives Segl 2000: 262.
36. Romero Silva 1993: 228–233.
37. Mabry 1973: 64.
38. J. Meyer 2003.
39. Wiechers 1988.
40. Serrano Álvarez 1992: 271–273.
41. Argudín 1992.
42. Blancarte 1992: 227–229.
43. Himes 2006: 21.
44. Hale 2015, 2018.
45. Norget 1997.
46. Blancarte 1992: 212–215.
47. Hale 2015.
48. Camp 1997: 236–237.
49. Blancarte 1992; Godínez Valencia 2011.
50. Blancarte 1992: 333.
51. Loaeza 1999: 352–354.
52. Camp 1997: 238.
53. Blancarte 1992: 290–293, 350–353; Tangerman 1995.
54. Loaeza 1985; Camp 1997.
55. Turner 1967: 602.
56. Castellanos Hernández 1996: 142–152.
57. Martínez Valle 2000: 64.
58. Wuhs 2008: 151.

59. Serrano Álvarez 1992.
60. Mabry 1974: 222.
61. Rodríguez Lapuente 1989.
62. Loaeza 1999: 263–277; Martínez Valle 2000: 61–65.
63. Lujambio 1994.
64. Christlieb 2001: 57–58.
65. Calderón Vega 1965.
66. Cited in Fuentes Díaz 1972: 62.
67. Turner 1967; Blancarte 1992: 8.
68. Mabry 1974: 229.
69. González Hinojosa et al. 1991: 11.
70. Calderón Vega 1978: 98.
71. Pérez Franco 2007.
72. Arriola 1977; Greene 2007.
73. Partido Acción Nacional 1990: 20 (translated by the author).
74. Martínez Valle 2000: 77.
75. González Hinojosa 1991: 37.
76. Martínez Valle 2000: 82–83; Reveles Vázquez 2002: 114–115.
77. Arriola 1977: 552.
78. Shirk 2005.
79. Castillo Peraza 1990; Loaeza 1996: 334; Camp 1997.
80. Philpott 2004.
81. Gill 2008: 157.
82. Hale 2015.
83. John Paul II 1979.
84. Camp 1997: 31; Loaeza 1989: 223–224.
85. Camp 1994; Loaeza 1999: 349–354.
86. Dresser 2003.
87. Camp 1997: 205.
88. Camp 1997: 230.
89. Camp 1997: 229–233; Hernández Vicencio 2014: 145.
90. Beer 2017: 49
91. Beer 2017: 50–51.
92. Carrillo Nieto 2010.
93. Loaeza 1999: 484; Blancarte 1993: 784.
94. García Ugarte 1993: 105–106; Camp 1997: 230.
95. Blancarte 2004.
96. García Ugarte 1992: 241; Loaeza 1996; Camp 1997: 238.
97. Camp 1997: 205–207.
98. Loaeza 1996: 117.
99. Floyd 1996.
100. Harvey 1998.
101. Camp 1997.
102. Méndez de Hoyos 2006: 34.
103. Cornelius 1988.
104. Middlebrook 1988; Méndez de Hoyos 2006.

105. Díaz-Cayero and Magaloni 2001: 276.

106. Martínez Valle 2000: 252–253.

107. Díaz-Cayero and Magaloni 2001.

108. Magaloni 2006; Greene 2007.

109. Langston 2008.

110. Aguilar and Zermeño 1992a: 25.

111. Beer 2017.

112. Aguilar and Zermeño 1992a: 282–287.

113. Gómez Tagle 1984: 84–86.

114. Aguilar and Zermeño 1992a: 293.

115. Aguilar and Zermeño 1992a: 26.

116. Loaeza 1999; Pérez Franco 2007.

117. Greene 2007.

118. Loaeza 1989.

119. Cited in Loaeza 1999: 392.

120. Blancarte 1992.

121. Loaeza 1996: 114.

122. Pérez Franco 2007; Loaeza 1999: 448.

123. Magaloni 2006.

124. Langston 2017.

125. Camp 1997: 205.

126. Langston 2008: 473.

127. Arriola 1994: 113–158.

128. Rodríguez Lapuente 1989: 457; Blancarte 1991: 163.

129. Loaeza 1999: 530.

130. Magaloni and Moreno 2003: 265–267; Camp 1994.

131. Magaloni 2006; Greene 2007; Shirk 2000; Camp 1997.

132. Loaeza 2006: 10–12.

133. Reveles Vázquez 2002: 367.

134. Blancarte 2006: 433.

135. Conferencia del Episcopado Mexicano 2000.

136. Blancarte 2004: 238–240.

137. Conferencia del Episcopado Mexicano 2000: 107–109.

138. Blancarte 2004: 254.

CHAPTER 4

1. Arslanbenzer 2015.

2. Yavuz 2003: 208.

3. J. White 2002: 180–186.

4. Mardin 1973.

5. Compare, e.g., Ahmad 1993 and Yavuz 2003.

6. For a comparison of these terms, see Kuru 2008 and Kuru and Stepan 2012.

7. Karpat 1959.

8. Reed 1954; Brockett 2009.

9. Karpat 1959: 287.

10. Ulutas 2010: 392.
11. Keyman 2007: 222.
12. Lord 2018: 92–97.
13. Ulutas 2010: 392.
14. Ulutas 2010: 393.
15. Lord 2018: 97.
16. Lord 2018: 101.
17. Bianchi 1984: 113.
18. Bianchi 1984: 114.
19. Reed 1954: 277–278.
20. Bianchi 1984: 158–164.
21. Yavuz 2003: 133–150.
22. Mardin 1989; Yavuz 2003: 151–178.
23. Reed 1954: 275.
24. Mardin 1989.
25. Yavuz 2003: 139–140, 155–157.
26. Yavuz 2003: 156.
27. Sunar and Toprak 1983; Mardin 2003.
28. Karpat 1959: 284.
29. Ahmad 1977: 367; Yavuz 2003: 62.
30. Ahmad 1977: 6–7.
31. Zürcher 2005: 179.
32. Kadioğlu 1996.
33. Hale 1980: 402.
34. Ayata 1996: 44.
35. Karpat 1959: 152.
36. Karpat 1959: 162.
37. Ahmad 1993: 108–109.
38. Zürcher 2004: 215.
39. Reed 1954: 271.
40. Karpat 1959: 220.
41. Karpat 1959: 235.
42. Zürcher 2004: 223.
43. Ahmad 1977: 365.
44. Ulutas 2010: 394–395.
45. Mardin 1989; Yavuz 2003: 156.
46. Lewis 1952; Brockett 2006.
47. Ahmad 1977: 47.
48. Brockett 2009.
49. Ahmad 1977: 368.
50. Ahmad 1988: 756.
51. Yavuz 2003: 62.
52. Gözaydın 2008: 223.
53. Yavuz 2003: 145.
54. Yavuz 2003: 62.
55. Ahmad 1977: 138–140.

56. Weiker 1963: 9.
57. Ahmad 1977: 61.
58. Weiker 1963.
59. Zürcher 2005: 247–248.
60. Zürcher 2005: 245.
61. Mardin 1973.
62. Yavuz 2003: 174.
63. Mardin 1989; Ahmad 1991.
64. Yavuz 2003: 172.
65. Yavuz 2003: 173.
66. Hendrick 2011.
67. Yavuz 2003: 207.
68. Yavuz 2003: 141.
69. Yavuz 2003: 142.
70. Ulutas 2010: 397.
71. Yavuz 2003: 146–147.
72. Ulutas 2010: 397.
73. Lord 2018: 102–106.
74. Weiker 1963.
75. Hale 1980: 410.
76. Sakallioğlu 1997.
77. Nye 1977: 212–213.
78. Ahmad 1977; Szyliowicz 1962: 430.
79. Weiker 1963.
80. Sherwood 1967: 60.
81. Yavuz 2003: 65.
82. Ayata 1996: 44.
83. Sayari 1976: 190; Sherwood 1967: 61.
84. Salt 1995: 15.
85. Ahmad 1977: 242.
86. Göle 1997: 55.
87. Lerner 1958: 405.
88. Ahmad 1977.
89. Yavuz 1997.
90. Öniş 1997: 757.
91. Yeşilada 2002: 65.
92. Yildiz 2003.
93. Toprak 1984: 124.
94. Ahmad 1977.
95. Yeşilada 2002: 65–67; Lord 2018: 106–107.
96. Yavuz 2003.
97. Ayata 1996.
98. Sayari 2010.
99. Mardin 1978; Tachau and Heper 1983.
100. Gunter 1989: 69.
101. Ahmad 1988: 750; Lombardi 1997: 208; Tachau and Heper 1983: 25.

102. Heper 2013: 144–147.
103. J. White 2002.
104. Lombardi 1997; K. Yilmaz 2009: 123–125.
105. Hosgör 2011.
106. Kuru 2005.
107. Eligür 2010: 85–96.
108. Yavuz 1997; Narli 1999: 40–41.
109. Cizre and Yeldan 2000; Demir, Acar, and Toprak 2004; Öniş and Türem 2002.
110. Kuran 1995; Demiralp 2009.
111. Hosgör 2011: 343–344.
112. Kuru 2005; Maigre 2007.
113. Yavuz 2003: 228.
114. Demir, Acar, and Toprak 2004: 170.
115. Göle 2000; Keyman 2007; Gumuscu and Sert 2009.
116. Gulalp 2001: 439.
117. Keyman and Koyuncu 2005: 112; Gürakar 2016.
118. Eligür 2010: 93.
119. Lord 2018: 107–108; Sarfati 2017.
120. Gunter 1989; Lombardi 1997.
121. Taagepera 2007; Shugart 2011.
122. Heper and Çinar 1996: 491–492.
123. Ahmad 1988: 767; Salt 1995: 17; Eligür 2010: 118–124.
124. Sayari 2008.
125. Yavuz 2003; Eligür 2010: 93.
126. Yavuz 1997: 67.
127. Yavuz 1997: 71.
128. Ahmad 1988: 751.
129. Karabelias 1999: 137.
130. Ahmad 1988: 768.
131. Yıldız 2003: 195.
132. Yavuz 1997: 70; Eligür 2010: 198.
133. Eligür 2010: 144; M. Yilmaz 2012: 368–369.
134. Akinci 1999; Eligür 2010: 164.
135. J. White 2002.
136. Heper and Çinar 1996.
137. Lombardi 1997: 194.
138. Yıldız 2003: 195.
139. M. Yilmaz 2012: 370.
140. Yavuz 1997: 73–74; Eligür 2010: 189.
141. Mecham 2004: 342.
142. J. H. Meyer 1998: 491–492.
143. Gulalp 1999: 38.
144. Robins 1997: 90–93.
145. Çevik 1996.
146. Küçük 2002: 244.

147. Toprak 2005: 175.
148. Mecham 2004: 344; Yavuz 2003: 242.
149. Akinci 1999.
150. *Hürriyet Daily News* 2001; J. H. Meyer 1998.
151. Yavuz 1997: 74.
152. Yavuz 2003: 275–276.
153. Eligür 2010: 220–229.
154. Kogacioglu 2004: 448.
155. Yavuz 2003: 246.
156. Mecham 2004; Özel 2003.
157. Atacan 2005: 194.
158. Yeşilada 2002: 65.
159. Daği 2005; I. Yilmaz 2005: 405–406.
160. Toprak 2005: 177; Mecham 2004: 348.
161. Yeşilada 2002.
162. J. White 2002: 180–182.
163. K. Yilmaz 2009.

CHAPTER 5

1. Beer 2017; Beer and Cruz-Aceves 2018.
2. Kaya 2015: 55–56.
3. Lüküslü 2016.
4. Göle 2013.
5. Kuru 2009.
6. Blofield 2008.
7. Warner 2000; Grzymala-Busse 2015.
8. Blofield 2008.
9. Hagopian 2008.
10. Buckley and Mantilla 2013.
11. J. Fox 2008, 2015, 2019; Grim and Finke 2010; Sarkissian 2015.
12. Kuru 2008; Buckley 2016.
13. Shirk 2005; Camp 2008.
14. Amuchástegui et al. 2010; Beer 2017; Beer and Aceves 2018.
15. De la Torre Castellanos and Gutiérrez Zúñiga 2008.
16. Hernández Vicencio 2011: 373n10; Beer 2017: 50.
17. Kulczycki 2007: 58–59.
18. Taracena 2002.
19. Hofbauer Balmori 2017.
20. Maier 2010.
21. González López 2011.
22. Bustillos 2011.
23. Hagopian 2008: 164.
24. Conferencia del Episcopado Mexicano 2010a.
25. Blancarte 2008.
26. Conferencia del Episcopado Mexicano 2010b: 27.

27. Magaloni and Moreno 2003.
28. Loaeza 2006: 11.
29. Beatty 2006.
30. Herrera Beltran 2005.
31. Ruíz 2006.
32. Hernández Vicencio 2014: 149.
33. Pérez Franco 2007: 16; Blancarte 2008: 79.
34. Blancarte 2008: 71–75.
35. Amuchástegui et al. 2010.
36. Beer 2017: 52–53.
37. Taracena 2002; Lamas 2012.
38. Amuchástegui et al. 2010.
39. Blancarte 2008: 96–98.
40. Amuchástegui et al. 2010.
41. Beer 2017.
42. Beer and Cruz-Aceves 2018.
43. Hernández Vicencio 2011.
44. Bustillos 2011.
45. Shirk and Wallman 2015.
46. Conferencia del Episcopado Mexicano 2010b: 8.
47. Conferencia del Episcopado Mexicano 2010b: 12–14.
48. Hernández Vicencio 2014: 151.
49. Hernández Navarro 2012.
50. Conferencia del Episcopado Mexicano 2012.
51. Sayarı 2007: 197; Özel 2003.
52. Sayarı 2007: 197.
53. Öniş 2015: 23.
54. Nasr 2005: 13; Yilmaz and Bashirov 2018: 1816.
55. Kılınç 2019: 7.
56. Taspinar 2014; Esen and Gumuscu 2016; Karaveli 2016; Somer 2016.
57. Daği 2008; Kılınç 2019: 21.
58. Tepe 2005.
59. J. White 2002.
60. Ocaklı 2017.
61. Yavuz 2003; Gözaydın 2009; Taş 2018.
62. Yavuz 2006; Yavuz and Koç 2016: 137.
63. Yavuz 2009; Gözaydın 2009; Agai 2007: 160–162; Maigre 2007: 40–41.
64. Bilici 2006: 15–16.
65. Yavuz and Koç 2016: 138.
66. Bilici 2006: 12.
67. Yavuz and Koç 2016: 138.
68. Taş 2018: 397.
69. Somer 2011.
70. Kuru 2005.
71. Ocakli 2016: 736–739.
72. Gumuscu and Sert 2009: 963–974.

73. Önis and Keyman 2003.
74. Taş 2015: 780.
75. Özbudun 2006: 550.
76. Sarkissian and Özler 2013.
77. Öztürk 2016; Lord 2018: 111–115.
78. Çavdar 2006; Cizre 2008; Hale and Özbudun 2009; Keyman and Öniş 2007; Yavuz 2009.
79. Yavuz 2006.
80. Çavdar 2006: 479; Turunc 2007.
81. Insel 2003.
82. Gumuscu and Sert 2009: 958.
83. Hale 2005: 297.
84. Yavuz 2006.
85. Daği 2005: 9.
86. Önis 2006; Kılınç 2019.
87. Aral 2001.
88. Daği 2008: 27.
89. Kuru 2005; Çavdar 2006; Daği 2008; Cindoglu and Zencirci 2008.
90. Kaya 2015: 55.
91. Barras 2009; Kılınç 2019.
92. Kaya 2015: 54.
93. Saraçoğlu and Demirkol 2015; Yilmaz and Bashirov 2018: 1822.
94. Shukri and Hossain 2017.
95. Bugra and Candas 2011.
96. Coşar and Yeğenoğlu 2011.
97. Kaya 2015.
98. Park 2008.
99. Lord 2018: 111–113.
100. Lord 2018: 114–117.
101. Coşar and Yeğenoğlu 2011: 563–565.
102. Ayata and Tütüncü 2008.
103. Esen and Gumuscu 2016; Yilmaz and Bashirov 2018.
104. Esen and Gumuscu 2016: 1585; Taş 2018: 397–398.
105. Taş 2018: 398.
106. Abramowitz and Barkey 2009; Cizre 2011; Polat 2011.
107. Atacan 2005; Özbudun 2006; Taniyici 2003.
108. Yilmaz and Bashirov 2018.
109. *Hürriyet Daily News* 2012; Özbudun 2014: 157.
110. Göle 2013; Moudouros 2014; Önis 2015.
111. Özbudun 2014: 158.
112. Bashirov and Lancaster 2018: 218.
113. Yavuz 2018.
114. Yavuz and Koç 2016: 139.
115. Taş 2018: 398.
116. Yavuz and Koç 2016: 139–140.
117. Yeşil 2018: 248.

118. Yavuz and Koç 2016: 140.
119. Taş 2018: 400.
120. Taş 2018: 401.
121. Altınordu 2017.
122. Öztürk 2016: 626–630.
123. Yavuz and Koç 2016: 142; Esen and Gumuscu 2017: 65–66.
124. Esen and Gumuscu 2017: 65.
125. Yilmaz and Bashirov 2018.

CONCLUSION

1. Toft, Philpott, and Shah 2011.
2. See, e.g., Wickham 2015; Wegner 2011; and Schwedler 2006.
3. Mainwaring and Scully 2003; Mantilla 2018.
4. Bhargava 1998.
5. Madan 1987; Bose 2018.
6. Bose 2018; Hansen 1999.
7. Hansen 1999: 157–158.
8. Bose 2018: 155–159.
9. Mariano and Oro 2011; Boas 2020.
10. Chesnut 2003; A. Smith 2019a.
11. Reich and dos Santos 2013.
12. D. Smith 1970; Casanova 1994.
13. Toft, Philpott, and Shah 2011.
14. Norris and Inglehart 2004; Bruce 2011.
15. Loaeza 2009.
16. Göle 2013.
17. Wilcox and Robinson 2018.
18. Wald and Calhoun-Brown 2014. For discussions of earlier periods of evangelical activism, see Kruse 2015 and Compton 2014.
19. Patrikios 2008.
20. Djupe, Neiheisel, and Sokhey 2018; Campbell et al. 2018.
21. Hibbard 2010; Bose 2018: 124–126.
22. Hansen 1999: 188–196.
23. Lipset and Rokkan 1967.
24. Hale 2015, 2018.
25. Finke and Stark 2005.
26. A. Smith 2016, 2019b.
27. Bose 2018: 92–97.
28. Hansen 1999: 159–185.
29. Thurber 2014.
30. Godwin 2012.
31. Mowle 2006: 46.
32. Thurber 2014; S. Schmidt 2009: 131.
33. Hibbard 2010; Bose 2018.
34. Driessen 2014; Buckley 2017.

35. Toft, Philpott, and Shah 2011; Tamadonfar and Jelen 2013.

36. Kuru 2008; J. Fox 2008, 2015; Driessen 2010; Buckley and Mantilla 2013; Sarkissian 2015.

37. Gill 2008.

38. Putnam and Campbell 2012; Patrikios 2008.

39. Blum and Wilcox 2013.

40. Bhargava 1998: 105–109.

41. Madan 1987.

42. Bose 2018: 96–98.

43. Bose 2018: 86–89.

References

Abramowitz, M., and H. J. Barkey. 2009. "Turkey's Transformers: The AKP Sees Big." *Foreign Affairs* 88:118–128.

Agai, B. 2007. "Islam and Education in Secular Turkey: State Policies and the Emergence of the Ferhullah Gülen Group." In *Schooling Islam: The Culture and Politics of Modern Muslim Education*, edited by R. W. Hefner and M. Q. Zaman, 149–171. Princeton, NJ: Princeton University Press.

Aguilar, R., and G. Zermeño. 1992a. "Ensayo introductorio: La iglesia y el sinarquismo en México." In *Religión, política y sociedad: El sinarquismo y la iglesia en México (nueve ensayos)*, edited by R. Aguilar and G. Zermeño, 17–30. Mexico City: Universidad Iberoamericana.

———. 1992b. "Religión y política en el caso de la militancia del Partido Demócrata Mexicano (PDM): Una aproximación." In *Religión, política y sociedad: El sinarquismo y la iglesia en México (nueve ensayos)*, edited by R. Aguilar and G. Zermeño, 273–303. Mexico City: Universidad Iberoamericana.

Ahmad, F. 1977. *The Turkish Experiment in Democracy, 1950–1975*. London: Hurst.

———. 1988. "Islamic Reassertion in Turkey." *Third World Quarterly* 10:750–769.

———. 1991. "Politics and Islam in Modern Turkey." *Middle Eastern Studies* 27 (1): 3–21.

———. 1993. *The Making of Modern Turkey*. New York: Routledge.

Akdoğan, Y. 2003. *Muhafazakar Demokrasi*. Ankara: AK Parti Yayınları.

Akinci, U. 1999. "The Welfare Party's Municipal Track Record: Evaluating Islamist Municipal Activism in Turkey." *Middle East Journal* 53:75–94.

Almeida, P. 2014. *Mobilizing Democracy: Globalization and Citizen Protest*. Baltimore: Johns Hopkins University Press.

Altınordu, A. 2010. "The Politicization of Religion: Political Catholicism and Political Islam in Comparative Perspective." *Politics and Society* 38:517–551.

————. 2017. "A Midsummer Night's Coup: Performance and Power in Turkey's July 15 Coup Attempt." *Qualitative Sociology* 40 (2): 139–164.

Amuchástegui, A., G. Cruz, E. Aldaz, and M. C. Mejía. 2010. "Politics, Religion and Gender Equality in Contemporary Mexico: Women's Sexuality and Reproductive Rights in a Contested Secular State." *Third World Quarterly* 31 (6): 989–1005.

Anderson, B. 1983. *Imagined Communities*. London: Verso.

Andes, S. J. 2012. "A Catholic Alternative to Revolution: The Survival of Social Catholicism in Postrevolutionary Mexico." *The Americas* 68 (4): 529–562.

Aral, B. 2001. "Dispensing with Tradition? Turkish Politics and International Society during the Özal Decade, 1983–93." *Middle Eastern Studies* 37 (1): 72–88.

Argudín, M. L. 1992. "Una sociedad autárquica, utopía sinarquista (1946–1960)." In *Religión, política y sociedad: El sinarquismo y la iglesia en México (nueve ensayos)*, edited by R. Aguilar and G. Zermeño, 17–30. Mexico City: Universidad Iberoamericana.

Arikan, H. 2017. *Turkey and the EU: An Awkward Candidate for EU Membership?* New York: Routledge.

Arriola, C. 1977. "La crisis del Partido Acción Nacional (1975–1976)." *Foro Internacional* 17:542–556.

————. 1994. *Ensayos sobre el PAN*. Mexico City: Editorial Porrúa.

Arslanbenzer, H. 2015. "Necmettin Erbakan: Engineering Genius and Politician." *Daily Sabah*, June 12. https://www.dailysabah.com/portrait/2015/06/12/necmettin-erbakan-engineering-genius-and-politician.

Atacan, F. 2005. "Explaining Religious Politics at the Crossroad: AKP-SP." *Turkish Studies* 6:187–199.

Ayata, A. G., and F. Tütüncü. 2008. "Party Politics of the AKP (2002–2007) and the Predicaments of Women at the Intersection of the Westernist, Islamist and Feminist Discourses in Turkey." *British Journal of Middle Eastern Studies* 35 (3): 363–384.

Ayata, S. 1996. "Patronage, Party, and State: The Politicization of Islam in Turkey." *Middle East Journal* 50:40–56.

Bailey, D. C. 1974. *¡Viva Cristo Rey! The Cristero Rebellion and the Church-State Conflict in Mexico*. Austin: University of Texas Press.

Barkey, K. 2008. *Empire of Difference: The Ottomans in Comparative Perspective*. Cambridge: Cambridge University Press.

Bashirov, G., and C. Lancaster. 2018. "End of Moderation: The Radicalization of AKP in Turkey." *Democratization* 25 (7): 1210–1230.

BBC News. 2002. "Turkey's Charismatic Pro-Islamic Leader." November 4. http://news.bbc.co.uk/2/hi/europe/2270642.stm.

Beatty, A. 2006. "The Pope in Mexico: Syncretism in Public Ritual." *American Anthropologist* 108 (2): 324–335.

Beer, C. 2017. "Making Abortion Laws in Mexico: Salience and Autonomy in the Policymaking Process." *Comparative Politics* 50 (1): 41–59.

Beer, C., and V. D. Cruz-Aceves. 2018. "Extending Rights to Marginalized Minorities: Same-Sex Relationship Recognition in Mexico and the United States." *State Politics and Policy Quarterly* 18 (1): 3–26.

Bellin, E. 2008. "Faith in Politics: New Trends in the Study of Religion and Politics." *World Politics* 60:315–347.

Bhargava, R. 1998. "What Is Secularism For?" In *Secularism and Its Critics*, edited by R. Bhargava, 487–550. New Delhi: Oxford University Press.

Bianchi, R. 1984. *Interest Groups and Political Development in Turkey*. Princeton, NJ: Princeton University Press.

Bilici, M. 2006. "The Fethullah Gülen Movement and Its Politics of Representation in Turkey." *Muslim World* 96:1–20.

Blancarte, R. 1991. *El poder, salinismo e Iglesia católica: ¿Una nueva convivencia?* Mexico City: Grijalbo.

———. 1992. *Historia de la Iglesia católica en México*. Mexico City: Fondo de Cultura Económica.

———. 1993. "Recent Changes in Church-State Relations in Mexico: An Historical Approach." *Journal of Church and State* 35 (4): 781–805.

———. 2004. *Entre la fe y el poder: Política y religión en México*. Mexico City: Grijalbo.

———. 2006. "Religion, Church, and State in Contemporary Mexico." In *Changing Structure of Mexico: Political, Social, and Economic Prospects*, edited by L. Randall, 424–437. Armonk, NY: M. E. Sharpe.

———. 2008. *Sexo, religión, y democracia*. Mexico City: Editorial Planeta.

Blaydes, L. 2010. *Elections and Distributive Politics in Mubarak's Egypt*. Cambridge: Cambridge University Press.

Blofield, M. 2006. *The Politics of Moral Sin: Abortion and Divorce in Spain, Chile and Argentina*. New York: Routledge.

———. 2008. "Women's Choices in Comparative Perspective: Abortion Policies in Late-Developing Catholic Countries." *Comparative Politics* 40 (4): 399–419.

Blum, R., and C. Wilcox. 2013. "A Tangled Web: Religion and the Regime in the United States." In *Religion and Regimes: Support, Separation, and Opposition*, edited by M. Tamadonfar and T. Jelen, 1–24. Lanham, MD: Lexington.

Boas, T. 2020. "The Electoral Representation of Evangelicals in Latin America." In *Oxford Encyclopedia of Latin American Politics*, edited by R. Stahler-Sholk and H. Vanden. New York: Oxford University Press. https://doi.org/10.1093/acrefore/9780190228637.013.1748.

Bormann, N. C., and M. Golder. 2013. "Democratic Electoral Systems around the World, 1946–2011." *Electoral Studies* 32 (2): 360–369.

Bose, S. 2018. *Secular States, Religious Politics: India, Turkey, and the Future of Secularism*. Cambridge: Cambridge University Press.

Brocker, M., and M. Künkler. 2013. "Religious Parties: Revisiting the Inclusion-Moderation Hypothesis." *Party Politics* 19 (2): 171–186.

Brockett, G. D. 2006. "Revisiting the Turkish Revolution, 1923–1938: Secular Reform and Religious 'Reaction.'" *History Compass* 4 (6): 1060–1072.

———. 2009. "Provincial Newspapers as a Historical Source: Büyük Cihad and the Great Struggle for the Muslim Turkish Nation (1951–53)." *International Journal of Middle East Studies* 41:437–455.

Bruce, S. 2011. *Secularization: In Defence of an Unfashionable Theory*. Oxford: Oxford University Press.

Buckley, D. T. 2015. "Beyond the Secularism Trap: Religion, Political Institutions and Democratic Commitments." *Comparative Politics* 47 (4): 439–458.

———. 2016. "Demanding the Divine? Explaining Cross-national Support for Clerical Control of Politics." *Comparative Political Studies* 49 (3): 357–390.

———. 2017. *Faithful to Secularism: The Religious Politics of Democracy in Ireland, Senegal, and the Philippines.* New York: Columbia University Press.

Buckley, D. T., and L. F. Mantilla. 2013. "God and Governance: Development, State Capacity, and the Regulation of Religion." *Journal for the Scientific Study of Religion* 52 (2): 328–348.

Bugra, A., and A. Candas. 2011. "Change and Continuity under an Eclectic Social Security Regime: The Case of Turkey." *Middle Eastern Studies* 47 (3): 515–528.

Bustillos, J. 2011. "Derechos humanos y protección constitucional: Breve estudio sobre el matrimonio entre personas del mismo sexo en México y en perspectiva comparada." *Boletín Mexicano de Derecho Comparado* 132:1017–1045.

Buzpinar, Ş. T. 1996. "Opposition to the Ottoman Caliphate in the Early Years of Abdülhamid II: 1877–1882." *Die Welt des Islams* 36:59–89.

Calderón Vega, L. 1962. *Cuba 88: Memoria de la UNEC.* Mexico City: FIMEX.

———. 1965. *Memorias del PAN (1962–1964).* Mexico City: EPESSA.

———. 1967. *Memorias del PAN (1939–1946).* Mexico City: EPESSA.

———. 1978. *Memorias del PAN: Tomo III.* Mexico City: EPESSA.

Calfano, B. R., and P. A. Djupe. 2009. "God Talk: Religious Cues and Electoral Support." *Political Research Quarterly* 62 (2): 329–339.

Calvo, E., and T. Hellwig. 2011. "Centripetal and Centrifugal Incentives under Different Electoral Systems." *American Journal of Political Science* 55:27–41.

Camp, R. A. 1994. "The Cross in the Polling Booth: Religion, Politics, and the Laity in Mexico." *Latin American Research Review* 29 (3): 69–100.

———. 1997. *Crossing Swords: Politics and Religion in Mexico.* Oxford: Oxford University Press.

———. 2008. "Exercising Political Influence, Religion, Democracy and the Mexican 2006 Presidential Race." *Journal of Church and State* 50:49–72.

Campbell, D. E., J. C. Green, and G. C. Layman. 2011. "The Party Faithful: Partisan Images, Candidate Religion, and the Electoral Impact of Party Identification." *American Journal of Political Science* 55 (1): 42–58.

Campbell, D. E., G. C. Layman, J. C. Green, and N. G. Sumaktoyo. 2018. "Putting Politics First: The Impact of Politics on American Religious and Secular Orientations." *American Journal of Political Science* 62 (3): 551–565.

Carrillo Nieto, J. J. 2010. "La transformación del proyecto constitucional mexicano en el neoliberalismo." *Política y Cultura* 33:107–132.

Casanova, J. 1994. *Public Religions in the Modern World.* Chicago: University of Chicago Press.

———. 2001. "Civil Society and Religion: Retrospective Reflections on Catholicism and Prospective Reflections on Islam." *Social Research* 68:1041–1082.

Castellanos Hernández, E. 1996. *Formas de gobierno y sistemas electorales en México: Tomo II.* Mexico City: Centro de Investigación Científica "Ing. Jorge L. Tamayo," A.C.

Castillo Peraza, C. 1990. *El PAN nuestro.* Mexico City: Producción Editorial Dante.

Çavdar, G. 2006. "Islamist New Thinking in Turkey: A Model for Political Learning?" *Political Science Quarterly* 121:477–497.

Center for Systemic Peace. 2018. "Polity Vd: Polity-Case Format, 1800–2018." http://www.systemicpeace.org/inscrdata.html.

Çevik, I. 1996. "Erbakan Returns to a Country Angered by Moammar Gaddafi." *Hürriyet Daily News*, October 9.

Chesnut, R. A. 2003. "A Preferential Option for the Spirit: The Catholic Charismatic Renewal in Latin America's New Religious Economy." *Latin American Politics and Society* 45:55–85.

Christlieb Ibarrola, A. 2001. *Ideas fuerza mística de Acción Nacional*. Mexico City: EPESSA.

Cindoglu, D., and G. Zencirci. 2008. "The Headscarf in Turkey in the Public and State Spheres." *Middle Eastern Studies* 44 (5): 791–806.

Cizre, Ü. 2002. "From Ruler to Pariah: The Life and Times of the True Path Party." *Turkish Studies* 3 (1): 82–101.

———. 2008. "Introduction: The Justice and Development Party: Making Choices, Revisions and Reversals Interactively." In *Secular and Islamic Politics in Turkey: The Making of the Justice and Development Party*, edited by Ü. Cizre, 1–14. New York: Routledge.

———. 2011. "Disentangling the Threads of Civil-Military Relations in Turkey: Promises and Perils." *Mediterranean Quarterly* 22:57–75.

Cizre, Ü., and E. Yeldan. 2000. "Politics, Society and Financial Liberalization: Turkey in the 1990s." *Development and Change* 31 (2): 481–508.

Clark, J. A. 2004. *Islam, Charity, and Activism: Middle Class Networks and Social Welfare in Egypt, Jordan, and Yemen*. Bloomington: Indiana University Press.

Collier, D. 2011. "Understanding Process Tracing." *PS: Political Science and Politics* 44:823–830.

Collier, R. B., and D. Collier. 1991. *Shaping the Political Arena: Critical Junctures, the Labor Movement, and Regime Dynamics in Latin America*. Notre Dame, IN: Notre Dame University Press.

Colomer, J. M. 2004. "Voting Rights and Political Instability in Latin America." *Latin American Politics and Society* 46:29–58.

Compton, J. W. 2014. *The Evangelical Origins of the Living Constitution*. Cambridge, MA: Harvard University Press.

Conferencia del Episcopado Mexicano. 2000. "Del Encuentro con Jesucristo a la Solidaridad con Todos: El Encuentro con Jesucristo, camino de conversión, comunión, solidaridad y misión en México en el umbral del tercer milenio." https://diocesisdetuxpan.files.wordpress.com/2013/01/del-encuentro-con-jesucristo-a-la-solidaridad-con-todos.pdf.

———. 2010a. "Conmemorar nuestra historia desde la fe, para comprometernos hoy con nuestra patria." http://es.catholic.net/catholic_db/archivosWord_db/carta_pastoral_bicentenario.pdf.

———. 2010b. *Que en Cristo nuestra paz México tenga vida digna: Exhortación pastoral del Episcopado mexicano sobre la misión de la iglesia en la construcción de la paz, para la vida digna del pueblo de México*. Mexico City: Conferencia del Episcopado Mexicano. http://www.cristoresucitadocancun.org/documents/documento_final_press.pdf.

———. 2012. "La democracia en México ha de consolidarse en la paz, el desarrollo, la participación y la solidaridad." https://issuu.com/cepastoralprofetica/docs/elecciones2012-120412132141-phpapp01.

Cornelius, W. A. 1988. *Carlos Salinas and the Prospects for Political Change in Mexico.* San Diego, CA: Center for US-Mexican Studies.

Coşar, S., and M. Yeğenoğlu. 2011. "New Grounds for Patriarchy in Turkey? Gender Policy in the Age of AKP." *South European Society and Politics* 16 (4): 555–573.

Cox, G. W. 1997. *Making Votes Count: Strategic Coordination in the World's Electoral Systems.* Cambridge: Cambridge University Press.

Daği, I. 2005. "Transformation of Islamic Political Identity in Turkey: Rethinking the West and Westernization." *Turkish Studies* 6:1–16.

———. 2008. "Turkey's AKP in Power." *Journal of Democracy* 19:25–30.

De la Torre Castellanos, R. 2006. *La ecclesia nostra: El catolicismo desde la perspectiva de los laicos: El caso de Guadalajara.* Mexico City: Centro de Cultura Económica.

De la Torre Castellanos, R., and C. Gutiérrez Zúñiga. 2008. "Tendencias a la pluralidad y la diversificación del paisaje religioso en el México contemporáneo." *Sociedade e Estado* 23 (2): 381–424.

De Leon, C., M. Desai, and C. Tuğal. 2009. "Political Articulation: Parties and the Constitution of Cleavages in the United States, India, and Turkey." *Sociological Theory* 27:193–219.

Demir, Ö., M. Acar, and M. Toprak. 2004. "Anatolian Tigers or Islamic Capital: Prospects and Challenges." *Middle Eastern Studies* 40:166–188.

Demiralp, S. 2009. "The Rise of Islamic Capital and the Decline of Islamic Radicalism in Turkey." *Comparative Politics* 41:315–335.

Deringil, S. 1991. "Legitimacy Structures in the Ottoman State: The Reign of Abdulhamid II (1876–1909)." *International Journal of Middle East Studies* 23:345–359.

———. 1993. "The Invention of Tradition as Public Image in the Late Ottoman Empire, 1808–1908." *Comparative Studies in Society and History* 35:3–29.

Díaz-Cayero, A., and B. Magaloni. 2001. "Party Dominance and the Logic of Electoral Design in Mexico's Transition to Democracy." *Journal of Theoretical Politics* 13:271–293.

Disch, L. 2011. "Toward a Mobilization Conception of Democratic Representation." *American Political Science Review* 105:100–114.

Di Tella, T. S. 1994. *Política nacional y popular en Mexico, 1820–1847.* Mexico City: Fondo de Cultura Económica.

Djupe, P. A., J. R. Neiheisel, and K. H. Conger. 2018. "Are the Politics of the Christian Right Linked to State Rates of the Nonreligious? The Importance of Salient Controversy." *Political Research Quarterly* 71 (4): 910–922.

Djupe, P. A., J. R. Neiheisel, and A. E. Sokhey. 2018. "Reconsidering the Role of Politics in Leaving Religion: The Importance of Affiliation." *American Journal of Political Science* 62 (1): 161–175.

Downs, A. 1957. *An Economic Theory of Democracy.* New York: Harper.

Dresser, D. 2003. "Mexico: From PRI Dominance to Divided Democracy." In *Constructing Democratic Governance in Latin America*, edited by J. I. Dominguez and M. Shifter, 321–349. Baltimore: Johns Hopkins University Press.

Driessen, M. D. 2010. "Religion, State, and Democracy: Analyzing Two Dimensions of Church-State Arrangements." *Politics and Religion* 3 (1): 55–80.

———. 2014. *Religion and Democratization: Framing Religious and Political Identities in Muslim and Catholic Societies.* Oxford: Oxford University Press.

Duverger, M. 1954. *Political Parties: Their Organization and Activity in the Modern State.* Translated by B. North and R. North. London: Methuen.

Eckstein, S. 1975. "La ley ferrea de la oligarquia y las relaciones inter-organizacionales: Los nexus entre la Iglesia y el Estado en Mexico." *Revista Mexicana de Sociología* 37:327–348.

Eickelman, D. F., and J. Piscatori. 1996. *Muslim Politics.* Princeton, NJ: Princeton University Press.

Eligür, B. 2010. *The Mobilization of Political Islam in Turkey.* Cambridge, MA: Cambridge University Press.

Emrence, C. 2000. "Politics of Discontent in the Midst of the Great Depression: The Free Republican Party of Turkey (1930)." *New Perspectives on Turkey* 23:31–52.

Esen, B., and S. Gumuscu. 2016. "Rising Competitive Authoritarianism in Turkey." *Third World Quarterly* 37 (9): 1581–1606.

———. 2017. "Turkey: How the Coup Failed." *Journal of Democracy* 28 (1): 59–73.

Espinosa, D. 2003. "'Restoring Christian Social Order': The Mexican Catholic Youth Association (1913–1932)." *The Americas* 59:451–474.

Esposito, J. L., and J. O. Voll. 1996. *Islam and Democracy.* Oxford: Oxford University Press.

Falleti, T. G., and J. F. Lynch. 2009. "Context and Causal Mechanisms in Political Analysis." *Comparative Political Studies* 42:1143–1166.

Fearon, J. D. 2003. "Ethnic and Cultural Diversity by Country." *Journal of Economic Growth* 8:195–222.

Finke, R., and R. Stark. 1998. "Religious Choice and Competition." *American Sociological Review* 63 (5): 761–766.

———. 2005. *The Churching of America, 1776–2005: Winners and Losers in Our Religious Economy.* New Brunswick, NJ: Rutgers University Press.

Fish, M. S., F. R. Jensenius, and K. E. Michel. 2010. "Islam and Large-Scale Political Violence: Is There a Connection?" *Comparative Political Studies* 43 (11): 1327–1362.

Floyd, J. C. 1996. "A Theology of Insurrection? Religion and Politics in Mexico." *Journal of International Affairs* 50 (1): 142–165.

Fox, J. 2008. *A World Survey of Religion and the State.* Cambridge: Cambridge University Press.

———. 2015. *Political Secularism, Religion, and the State: A Time Series Analysis of Worldwide Data.* Cambridge: Cambridge University Press.

———. 2017. "Religion and State Codebook: Round 3." https://www.thearda.com/ras/downloads/Religion%20and%20State%20Codebook%20Round%203.4%20main.pdf.

———. 2019. "A World Survey of Secular-Religious Competition: State Religious Policy from 1990 to 2014." *Religion, State and Society* 47 (1): 10–29.

Fuentes Díaz, V. 1972. *La democracia cristiana en México: ¿Un intento fallido?* Mexico City: Editorial Altiplano.

García Ugarte, M. E. 1992. "Las posiciones políticas de la jerarquía católica, efectos en la cultura religiosa mexicana." In *Religiosidad y política en México*, edited by C. Martínez Assad, 230–250. Mexico City: Universidad Iberoamericana.

———. 1993. "El Estado y la Iglesia católica: Balance y perspectivas de una relación." *Revista Mexicana de Sociología* 55:225–242.

———. 1995. "Los católicos y el presidente Calles." *Revista Mexicana de Sociología* 57:131–155.

Garrido, L. J. 1982. *El Partido de la Revolución Institucionalizada (Medio siglo de poder político en México): La formación del nuevo estado (1928–1945)*. Mexico City: Siglo Veintiuno Editores.

George, A. L., and A. Bennett. 2005. *Case Studies and Theory Development in the Social Sciences*. Cambridge, MA: MIT University Press.

Gerhards, J., and S. Hans. 2011. "Why Not Turkey? Attitudes towards Turkish Membership in the EU among Citizens in 27 European Countries." *JCMS: Journal of Common Market Studies* 49 (4): 741–766.

Gerring, J. 2007. *Case Study Research: Principles and Practices*. Cambridge: Cambridge University Press.

Ghannouchi, R. 2016. "From Political Islam to Muslim Democracy: The Ennahda Party and the Future of Tunisia." *Foreign Affairs* 95:58–67.

Gill, A. 1998. *Rendering unto Caesar: The Catholic Church and the State in Latin America*. Chicago: University of Chicago Press.

———. 2008. *The Political Origins of Religious Freedom*. Cambridge: Cambridge University Press.

Gleditsch, N. P., and I. Rudolfsen. 2016. "Are Muslim Countries More Prone to Violence?" *Research and Politics* 3 (2): 1–9.

Godínez Valencia, V. 2011. "Élite episcopal y poder en la Iglesia católica en México." *Estudios Políticos* 22:27–40.

Godwin, M. J. 2012. "Political Inclusion in Unstable Contexts: Muqtada al-Sadr and Iraq's Sadrist Movement." *Contemporary Arab Affairs* 5 (3): 448–456.

Goertz, G. 2006. *Social Science Concepts: A User's Guide*. Princeton, NJ: Princeton University Press.

Göle, N. 1997. "Secularism and Islamism in Turkey: The Making of Elites and Counter-elites." *Middle East Journal* 51:46–58.

———. 2000. "Snapshots of Islamic Modernities." *Daedalus* 129:91–117.

———. 2013. "Gezi—Anatomy of a Public Square Movement." *Insight Turkey* 15 (3): 7–14.

Gómez Morin, M. 1961. "Correspondencia, Sección Partido Acción Nacional, subsección Correspondencia, serie Chihuahua, sub-serie Jovita Granados, 1955–1971." r.a. vol. 113, exp. 431, Centro Cultural Manuel Gómez Morin, Mexico City.

Gómez Tagle, S. 1984. "El Partido Demócrata Mexicano y su presencia en la sociedad." *Revista Mexicana de Sociología* 46:75–110.

González Hinojosa, M., J. Angel Conchello, A. Vicencio Tovar, and P. Emilio Madero. 1991. *Las bases de la modernidad: Colección informes de los presidentes de Acción Nacional 3 1970–1987*. Mexico City: EPESSA.

González López, G. 2011. "Las prácticas contraceptivas de las mujeres católicas en Xalapa, Veracruz (México)." *Revista Sociedad y Equidad* 2:86–102.

González Luna, E. 1999. *Humanismo político*. Mexico City: EPESSA.

Gözaydın, İ. B. 2008. "Diyanet and Politics." *Muslim World* 98:216–227.

————. 2009. "The Fethullah Gülen Movement and Politics in Turkey: A Chance for Democratization or a Trojan Horse?" *Democratization* 16:1214–1236.

Greene, K. F. 2007. *Why Dominant Parties Lose: Mexico's Democratization in Comparative Perspective*. Cambridge: Cambridge University Press.

Grim, B. J., and R. Finke. 2006. "International Religion Indexes: Government Regulation, Government Favoritism, and Social Regulation of Religion." *Interdisciplinary Journal of Research on Religion* 2. https://www.religjournal.com/articles/article_view.php?id=13.

————. 2010. *The Price of Freedom Denied: Religious Persecution and Conflict in the Twenty-First Century*. Cambridge: Cambridge University Press.

Grzymala-Busse, A. 2010. "Time Will Tell? Temporality and the Analysis of Causal Mechanisms and Processes." *Comparative Political Studies* 44:1267–1297.

————. 2015. *Nations under God: How Churches Use Moral Authority to Influence Policy*. Princeton, NJ: Princeton University Press.

————. 2016. "Weapons of the Meek: How Churches Influence Public Policy." *World Politics* 68 (1): 1–36.

Guerra Manzo, E. 2007. "La salvación de las almas: Estado e Iglesia en la pugna por las masas, 1920–1940." *Argumentos* 20:121–153.

Gulalp, H. 1999. "Political Islam in Turkey: The Rise and Fall of the Refah Party." *Muslim World* 89:22–41.

————. 2001. "Globalization and Political Islam: The Social Bases of Turkey's Welfare Party." *International Journal of Middle East Studies* 33:433–448.

Gumuscu, S. 2010. "Class, Status, and Party: The Changing Face of Political Islam in Turkey and Egypt." *Comparative Political Studies* 43 (7): 835–861.

Gumuscu, S., and D. Sert. 2009. "The Power of the Devout Bourgeoisie: The Case of the Justice and Development Party in Turkey." *Middle Eastern Studies* 45:953–968.

Gunter, M. M. 1989. "Political Instability in Turkey during the 1970s." *Conflict Quarterly* 9:63–77.

Gunther, R., and L. Diamond. 2003. "Species of Political Parties: A New Typology." *Party Politics* 9 (2): 167–199.

Gürakar, E. Ç. 2016. *Politics of Favoritism in Public Procurement in Turkey: Reconfigurations of Dependency Networks in the AKP Era*. New York: Springer.

Gurses, M. 2014. "Islamists, Democracy and Turkey: A Test of the Inclusion-Moderation Hypothesis." *Party Politics* 20 (4): 646–653.

Hagopian, F. 2008. "Latin American Catholicism in an Age of Religious and Political Pluralism: A Framework for Analysis." *Comparative Politics* 40:149–168.

Hale, C. W. 2015. "Religious Institutions and Civic Engagement: A Test of Religion's Impact on Political Activism in Mexico." *Comparative Politics* 47 (2): 211–230.

————. 2018. "Religious Institutions and Collective Action: The Catholic Church and Political Activism in Indigenous Chiapas and Yucatán." *Politics and Religion* 11 (1): 27–54.

Hale, W. 1980. "The Role of the Electoral System in Turkish Politics." *International Journal of Middle East Studies* 11:401–417.

————. 2005. "Christian Democracy and the AKP: Parallels and Contrasts." *Turkish Studies* 6:293–310.

Hale, W., and E. Özbudun. 2009. *Islamism, Democracy and Liberalism in Turkey: The Case of the AKP*. New York: Routledge.

Hall, P. A. 2016. "Politics as a Process Structured in Space and Time." In *Oxford Handbook of Historical Institutionalism*, edited by O. Fioretos, T. G. Falleti, and A. Sheingate, 31–51. Oxford: Oxford University Press.

Hansen, T. B. 1999. *The Saffron Wave: Democracy and Hindu Nationalism in Modern India*. Princeton, NJ: Princeton University Press.

Harvey, N. 1998. *The Chiapas Rebellion: The Struggle for Land and Democracy*. Durham, NC: Duke University Press.

Hendrick, J. D. 2011. "Neo-liberalism and Third Way Islamic Activism: Fethullah Gulen and Turkey's New Elite." In *The Sociology of Islam: Secularism, Economy and Politics*, edited by T. Keskin, 61–84. Reading, UK: Ithaca Press.

Heper, M. 2013. "Islam, Conservatism, and Democracy in Turkey: Comparing Turgut Özal and Recep Tayyip Erdoğan." *Insight Turkey* 15 (2): 141–156.

Heper, M., and M. Çinar. 1996. "Parliamentary Government with a Strong President: The Post-1989 Turkish Experience." *Political Science Quarterly* 111:483–503.

Hernández Navarro, L. 2012. "Presidential Nominee Resurrects a Holy Ghost of Mexico's Past." *The Guardian*, February 7. https://www.theguardian.com/commentisfree/2012/feb/07/presidential-nominee-mexico-josefina-vazquez-mota.

Hernández Vicencio, T. 2011. "El Partido Acción Nacional en la lucha por la no despenalización del aborto en el Distrito Federal." *Andamios: Revista de Investigación Social* 8:367–396.

————. 2014. "La Iglesia católica en la lucha por la contrarreforma religiosa en México." *Desacatos* 44:143–158.

Herrera Beltran, C. 2005. "Fox expresa pesar por la muerte del Papa." *La Jornada*, April 3. https://www.jornada.com.mx/2005/04/03/index.php?section=politica&article=018n1pol.

Hibbard, S. W. 2010. *Religious Politics and Secular States: Egypt, India, and the United States*. Baltimore: John Hopkins University Press.

Himes, K. R. 2006. "Vatican II and Contemporary Politics." In *The Catholic Church and the Nation-State: Comparative Perspectives*, edited by P. C. Manuel, L. C. Reardon, and C. Wilcox, 15–32. Washington, DC: Georgetown University Press.

Hofbauer Balmori, H. 2017. *El caso Provida: Los alcances del acceso a la información vs los límites de la rendición de cuentas*. Mexico City: Instituto de Investigaciones Jurídicas de la UNAM.

Hosgör, E. 2011. "Islamic Capital/Anatolian Tigers: Past and Present." *Middle Eastern Studies* 47:343–360.

Hout, M., and C. S. Fischer. 2002. "Why More Americans Have No Religious Preference: Politics and Generations." *American Sociological Review* 67 (2): 165–190.

Huntington, S. P. 1991. *The Third Wave: Democratization in the Late Twentieth Century*. Norman: University of Oklahoma Press.

————. 1992. "The Clash of Civilizations?" *Foreign Affairs* 72:22–49.

Hürriyet Daily News. 2001. "Susurluk Verdict: Guilty." February 13.

————. 2012. "Debate on Religion Takes Over Politics in Ankara." February 2. http://www.hurriyetdailynews.com/debate-on-religion-takes-over-politics-in-ankara.aspx?pageID=238&nID=12814&NewsCatID=338.

Iannaccone, L. R., R. Finke, and R. Stark. 1997. "Deregulating Religion: The Economics of Church and State." *Economic Inquiry* 35:350–364.

Insel, A. 2003. "The AKP and Normalizing Democracy in Turkey." *South Atlantic Quarterly* 102:293–308.

Iveković, I. 2002. "Nationalism and the Political Use and Abuse of Religion: The Politicization of Orthodoxy, Catholicism and Islam in Yugoslav Successor States." *Social Compass* 49 (4): 523–536.

John Paul II. 1979. "Address of His Holiness John Paul: Meeting with Diocesan Priests and Men Religious of Mexico." January 27. http://www.vatican.va/holy_father/john_paul_ii/speeches/1979/january/documents/hf_jp-ii_spe_19790127_messico-guadalupe-sac-relig_en.html.

Kadioğlu, A. 1996. "The Paradox of Turkish Nationalism and the Construction of Official Identity." *Middle Eastern Studies* 32:177–193.

Kalyvas, S. N. 1996. *The Rise of Christian Democracy in Europe.* Ithaca, NY: Cornell University Press.

————. 2000. "Commitment Problems in Emerging Democracies: The Case of Religious Parties." *Comparative Politics* 32:379–398.

————. 2003. "Unsecular Politics and Religious Mobilization." In *European Christian Democracy: Historical Legacies and Comparative Perspectives*, edited by T. Kselman and J. A. Buttigieg, 293–320. Notre Dame, IN: Notre Dame University Press.

Kalyvas, S. N., and K. van Kersbergen. 2010. "Christian Democracy." *Annual Review of Political Science* 13:183–209.

Karabelias, G. 1999. "The Evolution of Civil-Military Relations in Post-war Turkey, 1980–95." *Middle Eastern Studies* 35:130–151.

Karaveli, H. 2016. "Erdogan's Journey: Conservatism and Authoritarianism in Turkey." *Foreign Affairs* 95:121–136.

Karpat, K. 1959. *Turkey's Politics: The Transition to a Multi-party System.* Princeton, NJ: Princeton University Press.

————. 1972. "The Transformation of the Ottoman State." *International Journal of Middle East Studies* 3:243–281.

Kaya, A. 2015. "Islamisation of Turkey under the AKP Rule: Empowering Family, Faith and Charity." *South European Society and Politics* 20 (1): 47–69.

Kepel, Gilles. 2002. *Jihad: The Trail of Political Islam.* Cambridge, MA: Harvard University Press.

Keyman, E. F. 2007. "Modernity, Secularism and Islam: The Case of Turkey." *Theory, Culture and Society* 24:215–234.

Keyman, E. F., and B. Koyuncu. 2005. "Globalization, Alternative Modernities and the Political Economy of Turkey." *Review of International Political Economy* 12:105–128.

Keyman, E. F., and Z. Öniş. 2007. *Turkish Politics in a Changing World: Global Dynamics and Domestic Transformations.* Istanbul: Bilgi University Press.

Kılınç, Ramazan. 2019. *Alien Citizens: The State and Religious Minorities in Turkey and France.* Cambridge: Cambridge University Press.

Kogacioglu, D. 2004. "Progress, Unity, and Democracy: Dissolving Political Parties in Turkey." *Law and Society Review* 38:433–462.

Kruse, K. M. 2015. *One Nation under God: How Corporate America Invented Christian America*. New York: Basic Books.

Küçük, H. 2002. *The Role of the Bektāshīs in Turkey's National Struggle: A Historical and Critical Study*. Leiden, Netherlands: Brill.

Kulczycki, A. 2007. "The Abortion Debate in Mexico: Realities and Stalled Policy Reform." *Bulletin of Latin American Research* 26:50–68.

Kuran, T. 1995. "Islamic Economics and the Islamic Subeconomy." *Journal of Economic Perspectives* 9:155–173.

Kuru, A. T. 2005. "Globalization and Diversification of Islamic Movements: Three Turkish Cases." *Political Science Quarterly* 120:253–274.

———. 2008. "Changing Perspectives on Islamism and Secularism in Turkey: The Gülen Movement and the AK Party." In *Muslim World in Transition: Contributions of the Gülen Movement*, edited by I. Yilmaz, 140–151. London: Leeds Metropolitan University Press.

———. 2009. *Secularism and State Policies toward Religion: The United States, France, and Turkey*. Cambridge: Cambridge University Press.

Kuru, A. T., and A. Stepan, eds. 2012. *Democracy, Islam, and Secularism in Turkey*. New York: Columbia University Press.

Kurzman, C., and I. Naqvi. 2010. "Do Muslims Vote Islamic?" *Journal of Democracy* 21 (2): 50–63.

Kurzman, C., and D. Türkoğlu. 2015. "After the Arab Spring: Do Muslims Vote Islamic Now?" *Journal of Democracy* 26 (4): 100–109.

Langston, J. K. 2008. "Legislative Recruitment in Mexico." In *Pathways to Power: Political Recruitment and Candidate Selection in Latin America*, edited by P. M. Siavelis and S. Morgenstern, 143–163. University Park: Pennsylvania State University Press.

———. 2017. *Democratization and Authoritarian Party Survival: Mexico's PRI*. Oxford: Oxford University Press.

Lapidus, I. 1997. "Islamic Revival and Modernity: The Contemporary Movements and the Historical Paradigms." *Journal of the Economic and Social History of the Orient* 40:444–460.

Layman, G. 2001. *The Great Divide: Religious and Cultural Conflict in American Party Politics*. New York: Columbia University Press.

Leiken, R. S., and S. Brooke. 2007. "The Moderate Muslim Brotherhood." *Foreign Affairs* 86 (2): 107–121.

Lerner, D. 1958. *The Passing of Traditional Society: Modernizing the Middle East*. New York: Free Press.

Lewis, B. 1952. "Islamic Revival in Turkey." *International Affairs* 28:38–48.

———. 1968. *The Emergence of Modern Turkey*. Oxford: Oxford University Press.

———. 2002. *What Went Wrong? The Clash between Islam and Modernity in the Middle East*. Oxford: Oxford University Press.

Lipset, S. M. 1960. *Political Man: The Social Bases of Politics*. Garden City, NY: Anchor Books.

Lipset, S. M., and S. Rokkan. 1967. "Cleavage Structures, Party Systems, and Voter Alignments: An Introduction." In *Party Systems and Voter Alignments: Cross-national Perspectives*, edited by S. M. Lipset and S. Rokkan, 1–64. New York: Free Press.

Loaeza, S. 1985. "La iglesia y la democracia en México." *Revista Mexicana de Sociología* 47:161–168.

———. 1989. "Cambios en la cultura política mexicana: El surgimiento de una derecha moderna (1970–1988)." *Revista Mexicana de Sociología* 51:221–235.

———. 1996. "Las relaciones Estado-Iglesia católica en México, 1988–1994: Los costos de la institucionalización." *Foro Internacional* 36:107–132.

———. 1999. *El Partido Accion Nacional: La larga marcha, 1939–1994; Oposicion leal y partido de protesta*. Mexico City: Fondo de Cultura Economica.

———. 2006. "Vicente Fox's Presidential Style and the New Mexican Presidency." *Mexican Studies/Estudios Mexicanos* 22:3–32.

———. 2009. "Cambios en la cultura política mexicana: El surgimiento de una derecha moderna (1970–1988)." *Revista Mexicana de Opinión Pública* 6:91–102.

Lombardi, B. 1997. "Turkey: The Return of the Reluctant Generals?" *Political Science Quarterly* 112:191–215.

Lord, C. 2018. *Religious Politics in Turkey: From the Birth of the Republic to the AKP*. Cambridge: Cambridge University Press.

Loyola Pérez, A. A. 2000. *Memorias del PAN (1960–1962)*. Mexico City: EPESSA.

Lujambio, A. 1994. "El dilema de Christlieb Ibarrola: Cuatro cartas a Gustavo Díaz Ordaz." *Estudios* 38:49–75.

Lüküslü, D. 2016. "Creating a Pious Generation: Youth and Education Policies of the AKP in Turkey." *Southeast European and Black Sea Studies* 16 (4): 637–649.

Lust-Okar, E. 2006. "Elections under Authoritarianism: Preliminary Lessons from Jordan." *Democratization* 13 (3): 456–471.

Lust-Okar, E., and A. A. Jamal. 2002. "Rulers and Rules: Reassessing the Influence of Regime Type on Electoral Law Formation." *Comparative Political Studies* 35:337–366.

Mabry, D. J. 1973. *Mexico's Acción Nacional: A Catholic Alternative to Revolution*. Syracuse, NY: Syracuse University Press.

———. 1974. "Mexico's Party Deputy System: The First Decade." *Journal of Interamerican Studies and World Affairs* 16:221–233.

Madan, T. N. 1987. "Secularism in Its Place." *Journal of Asian Studies* 46 (4): 747–759.

Magaloni, B. 2006. *Voting for Autocracy: Hegemonic Party Survival and Its Demise in Mexico*. Cambridge: Cambridge University Press.

Magaloni, B., and A. Moreno. 2003. "Catching All Souls: The Partido Acción Nacional and the Politics of Religion in Mexico." In *Christian Democracy in Latin America: Electoral Competition and Regime Conflicts*, edited by M. Mainwaring and T. R. Scully, 247–280. Stanford, CA: Stanford University Press.

Maier, E. 2010. "El aborto y la disputa cultural contemporánea en México." *La Aljaba* 14:11–30.

Maigre, M. E. 2007. "The Influence of the Gülen Movement in the Emergence of a Turkish Cultural Third Way." In *Muslim World in Transition: Contributions of the Gülen Movement*, edited by I. Yilmaz, 33–45. London: Leeds Metropolitan University Press.

Mainwaring, S. 2003. "Party Objectives in Authoritarian Regimes with Elections or Fragile Democracies: A Dual Game." In *Christian Democracy in Latin America: Electoral Competition and Regime Conflicts*, edited by S. Mainwaring and T. R. Scully, 3–29. Stanford, CA: Stanford University Press.

Mainwaring, S., and T. R. Scully. 2003. "The Diversity of Christian Democracy in Latin America." In *Christian Democracy in Latin America: Electoral Competition and Regime Conflicts*, edited by S. Mainwaring and T. R. Scully, 30–63. Stanford, CA: Stanford University Press.

Malka, H. 2019. "Beyond Tunisia's Niqab Ban." Center for Strategic and International Studies, July 30. https://www.csis.org/analysis/beyond-tunisias-niqab-ban.

Mango, A. 2002. *Atatürk: The Biography of the Founder of Modern Turkey*. New York: Overlook Press.

Mantilla, L. F. 2012. "Scripture, Structure and the Formation of Catholic Parties: The Case of Venezuela." *Party Politics* 18 (3): 369–390.

———. 2016a. "Church-State Relations and the Decline of Catholic Parties in Latin America." *Journal of Religious and Political Practice* 2 (2): 231–248.

———. 2016b. "Democratization and the Secularization of Religious Parties: The Case of Mexico." *Democratization* 23 (4): 395–416.

———. 2018. "Faith and Experience: Authoritarian Politics and Catholic Parties in Latin America." *Party Politics* 24 (4): 370–381.

———. 2019. "Feed the Church, Starve the Party? Church-State Relations and Religious Political Mobilisation in 21 Catholic-Majority Countries." *Religion, State and Society* 47 (1): 87–103.

Manuel, P. C., L. C. Reardon, and C. Wilcox, eds. 2006. *The Catholic Church and the Nation-State: Comparative Perspectives*. Washington, DC: Georgetown University Press.

Mardin, Ş. 1973. "Center-Periphery Relations: A Key to Turkish Politics?" *Daedalus* 102:169–190.

———. 1978. "Youth and Violence in Turkey." *European Journal of Sociology* 19:229–254.

———. 1989. *Religion and Social Change in Modern Turkey: The Case of Bediüzzaman Said Nursi*. New York: SUNY Press.

———. 2003. *Laicism in Turkey*. Istanbul: Konrad Adenauer Foundation Press.

Mariano, R., and A. P. Oro. 2011. "The Reciprocal Instrumentalization of Religion and Politics in Brazil." *Annual Review of the Sociology of Religion* 2:245–266.

Martínez Valle, A. 2000. *El Partido Acción Nacional: Una historia política*. Mexico City: Editorial Porrúa.

Masoud, T. 2014. *Counting Islam: Religion, Class, and Elections in Egypt*. Cambridge: Cambridge University Press.

Masters, B. 2013. *The Arabs of the Ottoman Empire, 1516–1918: A Social and Cultural History*. Cambridge: Cambridge University Press.

Mecham, R. Q. 2004. "From the Ashes of Virtue, a Promise of Light: The Transformation of Political Islam in Turkey." *Third World Quarterly* 25:339–358.

Menchik, J. 2014. "Productive Intolerance: Godly Nationalism in Indonesia." *Comparative Studies in Society and History* 56 (3): 591–621.

———. 2016. *Islam and Democracy in Indonesia: Tolerance without Liberalism*. Cambridge: Cambridge University Press.

Méndez de Hoyos, I. 2006. *Transición a la democracia en México: Competencia partidista y reformas electorales, 1977–2003.* Mexico City: Fontamara.

Meyer, J. 1973–1975. *La Cristiada.* 3 vols. Mexico City: Siglo Veintiuno Editores.

———. 2003. *El sinarquismo, el cardenismo y la iglesia (1937–1947).* Mexico City: Tusquest Editores.

Meyer, J. H. 1998. "Politics as Usual: Ciller, Refah and Susurluk; Turkey's Troubled Democracy." *East European Quarterly* 32:489–503.

Middlebrook, K. J. 1988. "Review: Dilemmas of Change in Mexican Politics." *World Politics* 41:120–141.

Mitchell, R. P. 1969. *The Society of the Muslim Brothers.* Oxford: Oxford University Press.

Monsma, S. V., and J. C. Soper. 2008. *The Challenge of Pluralism: Church and State in Five Democracies.* Lanham, MD: Rowman and Littlefield.

Moudouros, N. 2014. "Rethinking Islamic Hegemony in Turkey through Gezi Park." *Journal of Balkan and Near Eastern Studies* 16 (2): 181–195.

Mowle, T. S. 2006. "Iraq's Militia Problem." *Survival* 48 (3): 41–58.

La Nación. 1958. "Discurso de Gutiérrez Vega." December 21, p. 897.

Narli, N. 1999. "The Rise of the Islamist Movement in Turkey." *Middle East Review of International Affairs* 3 (3): 38–48.

Nasr, V. 2005. "The Rise of 'Muslim Democracy.'" *Journal of Democracy* 16 (2): 13–27.

Norget, K. 1997. "The Politics of Liberation: The Popular Church, Indigenous Theology, and Grassroots Mobilization in Oaxaca, Mexico." *Latin American Perspectives* 24·96–127.

Norris, P., and R. Inglehart. 2004. *Sacred and Secular: Religion and Politics Worldwide.* Cambridge: Cambridge University Press.

Nye, R. P. 1977. "Civil-Military Confrontation in Turkey: The 1973 Presidential Election." *International Journal of Middle East Studies* 8:209–228.

Ocaklı, F. 2016. "Political Entrepreneurs, Clientelism, and Civil Society: Supply-Side Politics in Turkey." *Democratization* 23 (4): 723–746.

———. 2017. "Islamist Mobilisation in Secularist Strongholds: Institutional Change and Electoral Performance in Turkey." *South European Society and Politics* 22 (1): 61–80.

O'Dogherty Madrazo, L. 2001. "De urnas y sotanas: El Partido Católica Nacional en Jalisco." Mexico City: Universidad Nacional Autónoma de México.

Öniş, Z. 1997. "The Political Economy of Islamic Resurgence in Turkey: The Rise of the Welfare Party in Perspective." *Third World Quarterly* 18:743–766.

———. 2006. "The Political Economy of Islam and Democracy in Turkey: From the Welfare Party to the AKP." In *Democratization and Development: New Political Strategies for the Middle East,* edited by D. Jung, 103–128. New York: Palgrave Macmillan.

———. 2008. "Turkey-EU Relations: Beyond the Current Stalemate." *Insight Turkey* 10 (4): 35–50.

———. 2015. "Monopolising the Centre: The AKP and the Uncertain Path of Turkish Democracy." *International Spectator* 50 (2): 22–41.

Öniş, Z., and E. F. Keyman. 2003. "Turkey at the Polls: A New Path Emerges." *Journal of Democracy* 14 (2): 95–107.

Öniş, Z., and U. Türem. 2002. "Entrepreneurs, Democracy, and Citizenship in Turkey." *Comparative Politics* 34:439–456.

Ordeshook, P. C., and O. V. Shvetsova. 1994. "Ethnic Heterogeneity, District Magnitude, and the Number of Parties." *American Journal of Political Science* 38:100–123.

Özbudun, E. 2006. "From Political Islam to Conservative Democracy: The Case of the Justice and Development Party in Turkey." *South European Society and Politics* 11:543–557.

———. 2014. "AKP at the Crossroads: Erdoğan's Majoritarian Drift." *South European Society and Politics* 19 (2): 155–167.

Özel, S. 2003. "After the Tsunami." *Journal of Democracy* 14:80–94.

Özkul, D. 2015. "Alevi 'Openings' and Politicization of the 'Alevi Issue' during the AKP Rule." *Turkish Studies* 16 (1): 80–96.

Öztürk, A. E. 2016. "Turkey's Diyanet under AKP Rule: From Protector to Imposer of State Ideology?" *Southeast European and Black Sea Studies* 16 (4): 619–635.

Ozzano, L. 2013. "The Many Faces of the Political God: A Typology of Religiously Oriented Parties." *Democratization* 20 (5): 807–830.

Park, B. 2008. "The Fethullah Gulen Movement." *Middle East Review of International Affairs* 12:1–11.

Partido Acción Nacional. 1990. *Relaciones iglesia estado: Cambios necesarios; Tesis del Partido Acción Nacional.* Mexico City: EPESSA.

Patrikios, S. 2008. "American Republican Religion? Disentangling the Causal Link between Religion and Politics in the US." *Political Behavior* 30 (3): 367–389.

Pérez Franco, A. R. 1999. "Raíces históricas del Partido Acción Nacional." *Propuesta* 8 (4): 77–130.

———. 2007. *Quiénes son el PAN.* Mexico City: Editorial Porrúa.

Philpott, D. 2004. "The Catholic Wave." *Journal of Democracy* 15:32–46.

———. 2007. "Explaining the Political Ambivalence of Religion." *American Political Science Review* 101:505–525.

Pierson, P. 2004. *Politics in Time: History, Institutions, and Social Analysis.* Princeton, NJ: Princeton University Press.

Polat, N. 2011. "The Anti-coup Trials in Turkey: What Exactly Is Going On?" *Mediterranean Politics* 16:213–219.

Posusney, M. P. 2002. "Multi-party Elections in the Arab World: Institutional Engineering and Oppositional Strategies." *Studies in Comparative International Development* 36:34–62.

Pupcenoks, J. 2012. "Democratic Islamization in Pakistan and Turkey: Lessons for the Post–Arab Spring Muslim World." *Middle East Journal* 66 (2): 273–289.

Putnam, R. D., and D. E. Campbell. 2012. *American Grace: How Religion Divides and Unites Us.* New York: Simon and Schuster.

Raat, W. D. 1973. "Ideas and Society in Don Porfirio's Mexico." *The Americas* 30:32–53.

Reed, Howard S. 1954. "Revival of Islam in Secular Turkey." *Middle East Journal* 8:267–282.

Reich, G., and P. dos Santos. 2013. "The Rise (and Frequent Fall) of Evangelical Politicians: Organization, Theology, and Church Politics." *Latin American Politics and Society* 55 (4): 1–22.

Reveles Vázquez, F. 2002. "Luchas y acuerdos en el PAN: Las fracciones y la coalición dominante." In *Partido Acción Nacional: Los signos de la institucionalización*, edited by F. Reveles Vázquez, 111–164. Mexico City: Ediciones Gernika.

Robins, P. 1997. "Turkish Foreign Policy under Erbakan." *Survival* 39 (2): 82–100.

Rodríguez Lapuente, M. 1989. "El sinarquismo y Acción Nacional: Las afinidades conflictivas." *Foro Internacional* 29:440–458.

Roeder, R. 1973. *Hacia el México moderno: Porfirio Díaz*. Mexico City: Fondo de Cultura Económica.

Rojas, R. 2001. *La oposición parlamentaria al gobierno de Francisco I. Madero*. Mexico City: Centro de Investigación y Docencia Económica.

Román, J. 2000. "Oró el guanajuetense ante la imagen de la tilma de Juan Diego." *La Jornada*, December 2, p. 2.

Romero Silva, G. 1993. *Memorias del PAN*. Vol. 5, *1957–1959*. Mexico City: EPESSA.

Rosenblum, N. 2003. "Religious Parties, Religious Political Identity, and the Cold Shoulder of Liberal Democratic Thought." *Ethical Theory and Moral Practice* 6:23–53.

Ruiz, J. L. 2006. "Fox agradece oportunidad de server a México." *El Universal*, December 1. https://archivo.eluniversal.com.mx/nacion/146071.html.

Sakallioğlu, Ü. C. 1997. "The Anatomy of the Turkish Military's Political Autonomy." *Comparative Politics* 29:151–166.

Salih, M.A.M., and A. O. El-Tom. 2009. "Introduction." In *Interpreting Islamic Parties*, edited by M.A.M. Salih, 1–27. New York: Palgrave Macmillan.

Salt, J. 1995. "Nationalism and the Rise of Muslim Sentiment in Turkey." *Middle Eastern Studies* 31:13–27.

Saraçoğlu, C., and Ö. Demirkol. 2015. "Nationalism and Foreign Policy Discourse in Turkey under the AKP Rule: Geography, History and National Identity." *British Journal of Middle Eastern Studies* 42 (3): 301–319.

Sarfati, Y. 2017. "How Turkey's Slide to Authoritarianism Defies Modernization Theory." *Turkish Studies* 18 (3): 395–415.

Sarkissian, A. 2015. *The Varieties of Religious Repression: Why Governments Restrict Religion*. Oxford: Oxford University Press.

Sarkissian, A., and Ş. İ. Özler. 2013. "Democratization and the Politicization of Religious Civil Society in Turkey." *Democratization* 20 (6): 1014–1035.

Sartori, G. 1976. *Parties and Party Systems: A Framework for Analysis*. Vol. 1. Cambridge: Cambridge University Press.

Sayari, S. 2007. "Towards a New Turkish Party System?" *Turkish Studies* 8:197–210.

———. 2008. "Non-electoral Sources of Party System Change in Turkey." In *Essays in Honor of Ergun Özbudun*, edited by S. Yacıcı, K. Gözler, E. F. Keyman, E. Göztepe, and E. Özbudun, 399–417. Istanbul: Yetkin Yayınları.

———. 2010. "Political Violence and Terrorism in Turkey, 1976–80: A Retrospective Analysis." *Terrorism and Political Violence* 22:198–215.

Schedler, A. 2002. "Elections without Democracy: The Menu of Manipulation." *Journal of Democracy* 13 (2): 36–50.

Schmidt, S. 2009. "The Role of Religion in Politics: The Case of Shia Islamism in Iraq." *Nordic Journal of Religion and Society* 22 (2): 123–143.

Schwedler, J. 2006. *Faith in Moderation: Islamist Parties in Jordan and Yemen*. Cambridge: Cambridge University Press.

———. 2011. "Can Islamists Become Moderates? Rethinking the Inclusion-Moderation Hypothesis." *World Politics* 63:347–376.

Serrano Álvarez, P. 1992. *La batalla del espíritu: El movimiento sinarquista en el Bajío (1932–1951)*. Mexico City: Conaculta.

Sherwood, W. B. 1967. "The Rise of the Justice Party in Turkey." *World Politics* 20:54–65.

Shirk, D. A. 2000. "Mexico's Victory: Vicente Fox and the Rise of the PAN." *Journal of Democracy* 11 (4): 25–32.

———. 2005. *Mexico's New Politics: The PAN and Democratic Change*. Boulder, CO: Lynne Rienner.

Shirk, D., and J. Wallman. 2015. "Understanding Mexico's Drug Violence." *Journal of Conflict Resolution* 59 (8): 1348–1376.

Shugart, M. S. 2011. "Turkey's Electoral System and Its Effect on the Number and Size of Parties." *Fruits and Votes*, June 10. https://fruitsandvotes.wordpress.com/2011/06/10/turkeys-electoral-system-and-its-effect-on-the-number-and-size-of-parties/amp/.

Shukri, S.F.M., and I. Hossain, I. 2017. "Strategic Shifts in Discourse by the AKP in Turkey, 2002–2015." *Mediterranean Quarterly* 28 (3): 5–26.

Sigmund, P. E. 2003. "The Transformation of Christian Democratic Ideology: Transcending Left and Right, or Whatever Happened to the Third Way?" In *Christian Democracy in Latin America: Electoral Competition and Regime Conflicts*, edited by S. Mainwaring and T. R. Scully, 64–77. Stanford, CA: Stanford University Press.

Singerman, D. 2004. "The Networked World of Islamist Social Movements." In *Islamic Activist: A Social Movement Theory Approach*, edited by Q. Wiktorowicz, 143–162. Bloomington: Indiana University Press.

Smidt, C., L. A. Kellstedt, and J. L. Guth. 2017. "The Role of Religion in American Politics: Explanatory Theories and Associated Analytical and Measurement Issues." In *The Oxford Handbook of Religion and American Politics*, edited by C. Smidt, L. A. Kellstedt, and J. L. Guth, 3–42. Oxford: Oxford University Press.

Smith, A. E. 2016. "When Clergy Are Threatened: Catholic and Protestant Leaders and Political Activism in Brazil." *Politics and Religion* 9 (3): 431–455.

———. 2019a. *Religion and Brazilian Democracy: Mobilizing the People of God*. Cambridge: Cambridge University Press.

———. 2019b. "Religion, Politics, and the Secular State." In *The Routledge Handbook of Brazilian Politics*, edited by B. Ames, 87–102. New York: Routledge.

Smith, D. E. 1970. *Religion and Political Development*. Boston: Little, Brown.

Somer, M. 2011. "Does It Take Democrats to Democratize? Lessons from Islamic and Secular Elite Values in Turkey." *Comparative Political Studies* 44:511–545.

———. 2016. "Understanding Turkey's Democratic Breakdown: Old vs. New and Indigenous vs. Global Authoritarianism." *Southeast European and Black Sea Studies* 16 (4): 481–503.

Stark, R. 1999. "Secularization, RIP." *Sociology of Religion* 60 (3): 249–273.

Stepan, A. 2001. *Arguing Comparative Politics*. Oxford: Oxford University Press.

———. 2011. "The Multiple Secularisms of Modern Democratic and Non-democratic Regimes." In *Rethinking Secularism*, edited by C. Calhoun, M. Juergensmeyer, and J. VanAntwerpen, 114–144. Oxford: Oxford University Press.

Sullivan, D. J., and S. Abed-Kotob. 1999. *Islam in Contemporary Egypt: Civil Society vs. the State*. Boulder, CO: Lynne Rienner.

Sunar, I., and B. Toprak. 1983. "Islam in Politics: The Case of Turkey." *Government and Opposition* 18:421–441.

Super, J. C. 2000. "'Rerum Novarum' in Mexico and Quebec." *Revista de Historia de América* 126:63–84.

Szyliowicz, J. S. 1962. "The Political Dynamics of Rural Turkey." *Middle East Journal* 16:430–442.

Taagepera, R. 2007. *Predicting Party Sizes: The Logic of Simple Electoral Systems*. Oxford: Oxford University Press.

Taagepera, R., and M. S. Shugart. 1989. *Seats and Votes: The Effects and Determinants of Electoral Systems*. New Haven, CT: Yale University Press.

Tachau, F., and M. Heper. 1983. "The State, Politics, and the Military in Turkey." *Comparative Politics* 16:17–33.

Tamadonfar, M., and T. G. Jelen. 2013. "Quasi-establishment and Its Alternatives: Notes for a General Theory of Religious Identity and Religion/Regime Relations." In *Religion and Regimes: Support, Separation, and Opposition*, edited by M. Tamadonfar and T. Jelen, 241–252. Lanham, MD: Lexington.

Tangerman, M. 1995. *Mexico at the Crossroads: Politics, the Church, and the Poor*. New York: Orbis Books.

Taniyici, S. 2003. "Transformation of Political Islam in Turkey: Islamist Welfare Party's Pro-EU Turn." *Party Politics* 9:463–483.

Taracena, R. 2002. "Social Actors and Discourse on Abortion in the Mexican Press: The Paulina Case." *Reproductive Health Matters* 10 (19): 103–110.

Tarrow, S. 2010. "The Strategy of Paired Comparison: Toward a Theory of Practice." *Comparative Political Studies* 43:230–259.

Taş, H. 2015. "Turkey—from Tutelary to Delegative Democracy." *Third World Quarterly* 36 (4): 776–791.

———. 2018. "A History of Turkey's AKP-Gülen Conflict." *Mediterranean Politics* 23 (3): 395–402.

Taspinar, O. 2014. "The End of the Turkish Model." *Survival* 56 (2): 49–64.

Tepe, S. 2005. "Turkey's AKP: A Model 'Muslim-Democratic' Party?" *Journal of Democracy* 16 (3): 69–82.

———. 2008. *Beyond Sacred and Secular: Politics of Religion in Israel and Turkey*. Stanford, CA: Stanford University Press.

Thurber, C. 2014. "Militias as Sociopolitical Movements: Lessons from Iraq's Armed Shia Groups." *Small Wars and Insurgencies* 25 (5–6): 900–923.

Tibi, B. 2002. *The Challenge of Fundamentalism: Political Islam and the New World Disorder*. Berkeley: University of California Press.

———. 2008. "Islamist Parties: Why They Can't Be Democratic." *Journal of Democracy* 19:43–48.

Toft, M. D., D. Philpott, and T. S. Shah. 2011. *God's Century: Resurgent Religion and Global Politics*. New York: W. W. Norton.

Toprak, B. 1984. "Politicisation of Islam in a Secular State: The National Salvation Party in Turkey." In *From Nationalism to Revolutionary Islam*, edited by S. A. Arjomand, 115–132. New York: SUNY Press.

————. 2005. "Islam and Democracy in Turkey." *Turkish Studies* 6:167–186.

Trejo, G. 2009. "Religious Competition and Ethnic Mobilization in Latin America: Why the Catholic Church Promotes Indigenous Movements in Mexico." *American Political Science Review* 103:323–342.

Turner, F. C. 1967. "The Compatibility of Church and State in Mexico." *Journal of Inter-American Studies* 9:591–602.

Turunc, H. 2007. "Islamicist or Democratic? The AKP's Search for Identity in Turkish Politics." *Journal of Contemporary European Studies* 15:79–91.

Ulutas, U. 2010. "Religion and Secularism in Turkey: The Dilemma of the Directorate of Religious Affairs." *Middle Eastern Studies* 46:389–399.

Van Hecke, S., and E. Gerard. 2004. "European Christian Democracy in the 1990s: Towards a Framework for Analysis." In *Christian Democratic Parties in Europe since the End of the Cold War*, edited by S. Van Hecke and E. Gerard, 9–20. Leuven, Belgium: Leuven University Press.

Vives Segl, H. 2000. *Entre la fe y el poder: Una biografía de Jose Gonzalez Torres, 1919–1998*. Mexico City: EPESSA.

Wald, K. D., and A. Calhoun-Brown. 2014. *Religion and Politics in the United States*. New York: Rowman and Littlefield.

Warner, C. M. 2000. *Confessions of an Interest Group: The Catholic Church and Political Parties in Europe*. Princeton, NJ: Princeton University Press.

Weber, M. 1993. *The Sociology of Religion*. Translated by E. Fischoff. Boston: Beacon Press.

Wegner, E. 2011. *Islamist Opposition in Authoritarian Regimes: The Party of Justice and Development in Morocco*. Syracuse, NY: Syracuse University Press.

Weiker, W. F. 1963. *The Turkish Revolution, 1960–1961: Aspects of Military Politics*. Washington, DC: Brookings Institution.

White, J. B. 2002. *Islamist Mobilization in Turkey: A Study in Vernacular Politics*. Seattle: University of Washington Press.

White, P. 2000. *Primitive Rebels or Revolutionary Modernizers? The Kurdish National Movement in Turkey*. London: Zed Books.

Wickham, C. R. 2002. *Mobilizing Islam: Religion, Activism, and Political Change in Egypt*. New York: Columbia University Press.

————. 2015. *The Muslim Brotherhood: Evolution of an Islamist Movement*. Princeton, NJ: Princeton University Press.

Wiechers, L. L. 1988. "La secularización e integración del sinarquismo a la vida política." *Revista Mexicana de Sociologia* 50:201–216.

Wiktorowicz, Q. 2001. *The Management of Islamic Activism: Salafis, the Muslim Brotherhood, and State Power in Jordan*. New York: SUNY Press.

————, ed. 2004. *Islamic Activist: A Social Movement Theory Approach*. Bloomington: Indiana University Press.

Wilcox, C., and C. Robinson. 2018. *Onward Christian Soldiers? The Religious Right in American Politics*. New York: Routledge.

Wittenberg, J. 2006. *Crucibles of Political Loyalty: Church Institutions and Electoral Continuity in Hungary*. Cambridge: Cambridge University Press.

Wittgenstein, L. 1953. *Philosophical Investigations*. Translated by G.E.M. Anscombe, S. Hacker, and J. Schulte. Oxford, UK: Basil Blackwell.

World Bank. 2019. "GDP Per Capita (Constant 2010 US$)—Mexico, Turkey." https:// data.worldbank.org/indicator/NY.GDP.PCAP.KD?locations=MX-TR.

Wuhs, S. T. 2008. *Savage Democracy: Institutional Change and Party Development in Mexico*. University Park: Pennsylvania State University Press.

Yavuz, M. H. 1997. "Political Islam and the Welfare (Refah) Party in Turkey." *Comparative Politics* 30:63–82.

———. 2003. *Islamic Political Identity in Turkey*. Oxford: Oxford University Press.

———. 2006. *The Emergence of a New Turkey: Democracy and the AK Parti*. Salt Lake City: University of Utah Press.

———. 2009. *Secularism and Muslim Democracy in Turkey*. Cambridge: Cambridge University Press.

———. 2018. "A Framework for Understanding the Intra-Islamist Conflict between the AK Party and the Gülen Movement." *Politics, Religion and Ideology* 19 (1): 11–32.

Yavuz, M. H., and R. Koç. 2016. "The Turkish Coup Attempt: The Gülen Movement vs. the State." *Middle East Policy* 23 (4): 136–148.

Yeşil, B. 2018. "Authoritarian Turn or Continuity? Governance of Media through Capture and Discipline in the AKP Era." *South European Society and Politics* 23 (2): 239–257.

Yeşilada, B. A. 2002. "The Virtue Party." *Turkish Studies* 3:62–81.

Yıldız, A. 2003. "Politico-Religious Discourse of Political Islam in Turkey: The Parties of National Outlook." *Muslim World* 93:187–209.

Yilmaz, I. 2005. "State, Law, Civil Society and Islam in Contemporary Turkey." *Muslim World* 95:385–411.

Yilmaz, I., and G. Bashirov. 2018. "The AKP after 15 Years: Emergence of Erdoganism in Turkey." *Third World Quarterly* 39 (9): 1812–1830.

Yilmaz, K. 2009. "The Emergence and Rise of Conservative Elite in Turkey." *Insight Turkey* 11 (2): 113–136.

Yilmaz, M. E. 2012. "The Rise of Political Islam in Turkey: the Case of the Welfare Party." *Turkish Studies* 13 (3): 363–378.

Zaks, S. 2017. "Relationships among Rivals (RAR): A Framework for Analyzing Contending Hypotheses in Process Tracing." *Political Analysis* 25 (3): 344–362.

Zürcher, E. J. 2004. *Turkey: A Modern History*. London: I. B. Tauris.

Index

Luis Felipe Mantilla is an Associate Professor in the School of Interdisciplinary Global Studies at the University of South Florida.